CW00920761

THE TROLL INSIDE YOU

Before you start to read this book, take this moment to think about making a donation to punctum books, an independent non-profit press

@ https://punctumbooks.com/support

If you're reading the e-book, you can click on the image below to go directly to our donations site. Any amount, no matter the size, is appreciated and will help us to keep our ship of fools afloat. Contributions from dedicated readers will also help us to keep our commons open and to cultivate new work that can't find a welcoming port elsewhere. Our adventure is not possible without your support.
Vive la open-access.

Fig. 1. Hieronymus Bosch, *Ship of Fools* (1490–1500)

THE TROLL INSIDE YOU: PARANORMAL ACTIVITY IN THE MEDIEVAL NORTH. Copyright © 2017 by Ármann Jakobsson. This work carries a Creative Commons BY-NC-SA 4.0 International license, which means that you are free to copy and redistribute the material in any medium or format, and you may also remix, transform and build upon the material, as long as you clearly attribute the work to the authors (but not in a way that suggests the authors or punctum books endorses you and your work), you do not use this work for commercial gain in any form whatsoever, and that for any remixing and transformation, you distribute your rebuild under the same license. http://creativecommons.org/licenses/by-nc-sa/4.0/

First published in 2017 by punctum books, Earth, Milky Way.
https://punctumbooks.com

ISBN-13: 978-1-947447-00-4 (print)
ISBN-13: 978-1-947447-01-1 (ePDF)

LCCN: 2017945423
Library of Congress Cataloging Data is available from the Library of Congress

Book design: Vincent W.J. van Gerven Oei
Cover image: Lína Thoroddson

Ármann Jakobsson

THE TROLL INSIDE YOU

Paranormal Activity in the Medieval North

To Davíð Erlingsson,
unorthodox mentor

Table of Contents

Preface: Jitterbug

The present book may well spring from seeds planted in a postgraduate course offered at the University of Iceland on the subject of folktales, instructed by Davíð Erlingsson, some twenty years ago. The class consisted of the standard five or six students attending any postgraduate course at the university, all eager to learn more about trolls and other paranormal beings. There was though a collective tinge of disappointment building as the teacher seemed unable to get around to covering the advertised subject, rather relentlessly providing us with photocopies of various tables of contents and indices from nineteenth-century folktale collections and sometimes even of articles from the dominant Icelandic newspaper, *Morgunblaðið*, or foreign presses like *The Guardian Weekly.* When the week in which trolls were supposed to be discussed was upon us Davíð arrived with a photocopy from one of his favourite journals of a Nazi propaganda poster from World War II in which American culture was personified as a composite monster called "Jitterbug" that was set to destroy European culture.[1]

As the reader may well imagine, the students found Davíð's method of teaching them to think about Icelandic folktales baffling at first but the results have proven to be lasting: from that day onwards it was harder to take for granted the matter of classifying and categorising folktales, and at least one of this unorthodox instructor's students never forgot the lesson provided by the image of the

"Jitterbug" in lieu of more traditional imaginings of trolls. Thus it is that these now primitive photocopies have ex-cercised a profound effect on the present project: both in drawing attention to the actions through which categories and definitions arise, and in providing liberation from the preconceived notion that a troll is, like a dog or a cat, a well-defined and discrete zoological category.

This study is concerned with medieval Iceland, tradi-tionally believed to have been settled during the ninth cen-tury and formally Christianised around the year 1000.[2] The texts under analysis, the sagas, are late medieval sources, mostly from the fourteenth century although many of them contain storylines and themes that rely upon older narrative traditions.[3] The culture of medieval Iceland, dominantly Norwegian but also influenced by Celtic tradi-tions, was indeed Christian at this point but much involved with a pagan past and the transition from one belief sys-tem to another.[4]

Although this study is primarily concerned with writ-ten sources produced within one society during a couple of centuries, its focus is general rather than specific and is thus possibly of some interest to any scholar seeking an engagement with paranormal encounters from any time and place. While Iceland has never been a great power, culturally, politically or otherwise, it had during the Mid-dle Ages a literary culture which is remarkable in its scope for having developed within such a small society, the pres-ervation of which is no less astounding. Thus documents from Iceland form a significant, and perhaps to some ex-tent disproportionate, share of the preserved European documents from the Middle Ages.[5] Furthermore, they are of a varied nature, many of them dramatical histori-cal narratives which illuminate the human condition in general. Sagas are frequently compared to modern novels and their art is parallel to that of later fiction, and yet they were probably conceptualised as history, a narrative form that was flexible in medieval Iceland.[6] It is also the case that all study of a single individual, group, or culture may have implications for humanity in general, and this study is fashioned as a case study of general interest. I have thus tried to make it accessible not only to experts in Old Norse but also to whomever is interested in how paranormal encounters can be framed and indeed were framed in the culture of fourteenth-century Iceland.

It is a strange endeavour to attempt to write something intelligent in a language one does not possess. For practical reasons I tried to suppress my feelings of inadequacy while writing and even became accustomed to regard this book as a long poem, by which I mean that this is a book of ideas rather than an exhaustive catalogue of examples and matching interpretations. Instead of delineating every single paranormal encounter found in medieval Icelandic saga writing, the aim is to offer a path that might eventually lead to a better understanding of the subject, so it is to be hoped that readers will not miss their favourite scenes or characters too much but feel fortified enough to continue on their own neverending quest of textual interpretation. Readers who feel certain scholarly issues are ignored or not discussed thoroughly enough may also be advised to turn to the endnotes ("Textual Hauntings") for further enlightenment.

This is a study of a particular culture and particular late medieval narratives. Nevertheless the focus will not be on particularities but the general, in the belief that it is through the general application that the particular becomes interesting, even though the general is never interesting enough to particular humans unless it manifests itself in the particular.

Acknowledgments

I wrote this book in 2015 and 2016, after an involvement of almost eight years with the topic. My research was made possible through the generosity of two benefactors. One is The Icelandic Centre for Research's (Rannís) Icelandic Research fund, which generously funded the research project *Encounters with the Paranormal in Medieval Iceland* for three years (2012–14), and the other is the University of Iceland's research fund (Rannsóknasjóður), which supplemented the funding from Rannís with a smaller and yet substantial grant over five years. This book and much else would not have been possible without the assistance of these two bodies.

The book is the product of the aforementioned research project *Encounters with the Paranormal*, in which I collaborated with my colleagues and friends Ásdís Egilsdóttir, Torfi H. Tulinius, and Terry Gunnell at the University of Iceland, and Stephen Mitchell at Harvard University. Eight doctoral students participated in the project at some point or another: Andrew McGillivray, Christopher Crocker, Gunnvör Karlsdóttir, Miriam Mayburd, Kolfinna Jónatansdóttir, Arngrímur Vídalín, Anna Katharina Heiniger, and Marion Poilvez. Six MA-students wrote their theses within the parametres of the project: Timothy Bourns, Hildur Ýr Ísberg, Védís Ragnheiðardóttir, Ingibjörg Eyþórsdóttir, Steven Shema, and Zuzana Stankovitsová. Several other scholars and students were also involved at some stage. I also owe particular thanks to Daniel Sävborg and Karen Bek-Pedersen for prompting me to take a closer look at *Bergbúa þáttr*. Thanks are due to all those mentioned above who have in some way or other provided much aid to this book although I alone am responsible for its conception and eventual appearance.

My foremost co-worker in producing the actual tome was Christopher W.E. Crocker who, indispensably, has been the yin to my yang and the yang to my yin in the making of this book; I would also like to thank ace indexer Sarah B. Eriksen and the wonderful people at punctum books, mainly Eileen A. Joy and Vincent W.J. van Gerven Oei, for their warm welcome and vital assistance in improving the book. Furthermore I received significant help from Jacob A. Malone, Miriam Mayburd, Alec Shaw, and Sean B. Lawing. They all deserve my deepest thanks for their support.

Troll

GROUP OF MEN RIDING IN the west of Iceland along a mountain ridge look on as a troll, particularly "tröll eitt mikit" (a great troll), crosses their path.[7] This is an event thought worthy of mention in a narrative generally preoccupied with more prosaic concerns, Icelandic politics of the thirteenth century; thus, however, is it preserved for posterity. The riding party is headed by Ásbjörn Guðmundarson, the date of the sighting in the first months of the year 1244. The event is related in a single sentence with no further details but for a remark about the men's feelings, "varð þeim sumum ósvipt við, en Ásbjörn hrakti þá þar um" (some of them were startled, but Ásbjörn scolded them for it). However, the significance of this only just ephemeral yet palpably unresolved encounter may be realized when later during this same journey Ásbjörn drowns in a river, followed not long after by the death of the group's leader, the young magnate Tumi Sighvatsson.

In only a few sentences matters of life and death are related. The troll is ominous; it is also unknown. A simple binary graph could be used to explain the logic of this brief narrative of clear opposites. At one end: the known, the human, life, safety, civilization, and the audience itself, compelled to use Ásbjörn and his startled men as stand-ins. At the distant other end: the occult, the inhuman, death, danger, wilderness, and the extraneous other.[8] The troll has to represent all of those things. It is danger, death, and the vastness extending beyond the human grasp of the world. No small role has the troll. And yet it does nothing here on the ridge but circle the humans. Its power does not rely upon its specific actions. Its presence alone suffices.

The first thing readers of this book must do is refrain from imagining that they know precisely what a troll is. While in the nineteenth century Icelandic trolls were taxonomised, an endeavour worth returning to below, in a thirteenth-century narrative a troll has no such clear identity, not even within the human psyche. Trolls do not constitute a race or a species. The first step when considering the troll sighted on the ridge is to avoid the idea of a clearly demarcated group. Thirteenth- and fourteenth-century textual evidence from Iceland makes it clear that a witch is a troll but so also is a ghost or vampire, a demon, a possessed animal, and a mountain dweller. The evidence does not suggest that any one of these groups held primary claim on the term.[9] Thinking like a nineteenth-century scientist will not further one's understanding of the medieval troll. Furthermore, it might be useful to resist the glossarial impulse to treat medieval Icelandic words as concepts that are carefully defined as they are used.

Considering the location, a mountain ridge, where Ásbjörn and his men encounter the troll, it can easily be imagined to be a creature native to the mountains. This does not however preclude the troll from being also a figure that may reside much closer to home, such as a ghost or a witch, a demon or a possessed beast. Since no further statement is made about it, other than a vague reference to its enormity,[10] any vision we may conjure up may be more or less erroneous. Sober zoologists may gnash their teeth at this deplorable lack of classifiable characteristics.[11] And yet the audience knows all that it needs to know about the troll, which is its place in the binary outlined above.

Perhaps it is a modern rather than a medieval obsession to wish to understand everything. It might be superfluous to gnash teeth: the troll's very potency seems to stem from its occult state. Ásbjörn's men did not expect to understand the troll. They would probably not have asked themselves what it feels like to be a troll; the very idea being alien to them. How could these men understand a troll? They accept it as an other which they fear and they cannot imagine knowing it. Why is the troll not described? Possibly it is too distant, a black shape in the night. How then do they know it is a troll? One suspects their own feelings told them so. They are afraid, that is how they know.

The troll is danger; what is not dangerous and feared cannot be a troll. That much is evident in the men's startled reaction. The word "ósvipt" is well placed here, "svipr" denoting the human face, which each of the men loses with the onset of their dehumanising fear — they are defaced on the mountain ridge. Danger turns the world on its head. Like death it intrudes into the established order, snatches all imagined control from the humans who have set themselves up to be the protagonists of their own lives. Danger becomes an abyss, into which one can feel themselves helplessly falling. As an image of danger, the troll cannot be but terrible. Its very appearance is ominous. A troll may attack; there is no shortage of attacking trolls in medieval Icelandic literature. But the troll always attacks before it ever acts, its very appearance an attack on presumptions of order and of control.

In the story of Ásbjörn, the troll does next to nothing. It is sighted, nothing more; not described, never explained. The only thing we need to know is that it startles the men, momentarily unmasking their human faces. In the end, this troll-story is not about the troll but about the men who encounter it. Could that be the case with all troll-stories?

As we will come to see, it is no coincidence that ghosts, vampires, and zombies are also framed as trolls.[12] To living humans, the various guises of the undead serve as specific reminders of their own mortality. In this case the troll is an omen of both Ásbjörn's and his master Tumi's impending deaths. The omen hardly acts; its presence is enough to startle. The spectre of death is omnipresent in human existence as its denial, its end. The trauma of annhiliation tends to have many symbolic guises and the troll can represent it in several ways, both by predicting it and by becoming it, in the guise of an undead.

Some of the worst predators described in the Icelandic literature of the late Middle Ages are undead humans, and their occasional designation as trolls serves as a reminder of how the separation of the human and inhuman, or indeed otherness in general, may be vague. There is here an abundance of anthropomorphic otherness, including the undead, signifying the impossibility of total separation between us and them; what we are faced with instead is a shared uncanny relationship. While trolls are inhuman, they are essentially not absolutely separate or separable from humanity.[13] Uncanny otherness is perhaps the most potent of human threats, an attack on all notions of humanity and on order itself. Being both human and inhuman, the troll is chaos incarnate. Faced with such chaos, the strongest impulse may be to seek order, and imposing order has often been regarded as one of the primary duties of scholarship, intensely focused on the negation of its own futility.

The Truth Is Out There

THE PARANORMAL IN THE SAGAS can be regarded as a construction, both social as well as literary. It serves a narratological function, although narratives of the paranormal may still represent an actual belief system which existed outside of the texts. This belief system is certainly dominated in some way by Christianity, but parts of it may have pre-dated the advent of Christianity in the North only to then co-exist alongside the hegemonic Christian faith,[14] adapted to it to some degree though without becoming a part of its official ideology.

Despite pretence, the paranormal is primarily located within the human psyche. Thus, rather than venturing beyond the human mind, a more insightful exploration of the paranormal might begin by rather venturing towards and even into it. In such a venture one cannot dismiss the personal insights and experiences of simply being human. The premise of the humanities, which used to be taken for granted but has become more easily ignored in an age dominated by other disciplines, is that when it comes to the human, subjectivity is compulsory. The researcher can thus and perhaps must use their own insights and partly merge with their subject as they study the actions, experiences, and expressions of other humans. Some of the methods of the traditional humanities, literary analysis among them, predate the scientific revolution of the modern age, but when it comes to the human mind and its products, they still offer opportunities unparalleled by outside scrutiny.[15]

An acknowledgement of the fact that the paranormal is located within the human psyche is in this case coupled with another perhaps somewhat surprising premise: that all gods and monsters are essentially human. They are in various ways, and to various degrees, our doubles, and all texts about the paranormal are in some way also fundamentally concerned with humanity.[16] While the paranormal is always essentially occult and other, it often functions like a mirror to those who encounter it, a threatening and eerie path to some deeper understanding of the self. Since the term troll was used broadly in medieval Iceland and is one of the common terms used to describe a sorcerer or the undead, the troll may be regarded as a representative of the paranormal in general. The troll externalises danger and becomes in narrative that truth which is out there,[17] but in this study, the focus is no less directed towards the recesses of the mind, as we slowly approach the rationale of magic.[18]

The term *paranormal* is fitting precisely because to the average reader it will not suggest the Middle Ages, and thus it cannot be taken for granted, dismissed as a traditional or conventional term that can be safely deployed without intense scrutiny.[19] The word is also preferable to terms such as *supernatural,* more easily and frequently connected with the Middle Ages, because it does not immediately establish the notion that the unknown phenomenon encountered is somehow above or beyond the world of the humans who encounter it. Furthermore the stem *normal* in the former is preferable to the latter's *natural* since the focus here is fixed upon human experience, and on human society, rather than nature if it is envisioned, as it often is in the modern world, as all that is distinct from humanity. This term also draws attention to the idea of the norms of human existence. Thus using the term may assist us in the task of challenging the idea of the normal. In addition, working from the *normal* places more focus and primacy on the individual observer as a single living being; in contrast to the natural sciences, which, though founded on observation, are centred upon empiricism, which traditionally encourages the insignificance of the individuality of the observer.[20]

This study is thus focused primarily on paranormal encounters, not on the paranormal for its own sake, allowing for the moment for the existence of paranormal activity in the real world, but mainly exploring the experience of the humans who apparently encounter it. However, this is only one part of the focus. The other is on language; in this case on the semiotics of the paranormal. When the paranormal is encountered in a written text, it has not only been experienced but also framed within language. The language of the paranormal is essential when concentrating on the paranormal as it is related through written sources. This focus, on human experience and semiotics of the paranormal, will provide a method to study paranormal encounters outside of any cultural or geographic constraints. However, paranormal activity will also be considered within the framework of class, gender, and time, and there is an acceptance of the mutability of the paranormal and its relationship with chaos and control. Before venturing further into the medieval corpus, it is necessary to say a few words about those traditions which modern scholarship is based on but to which it is also, in a sense, opposed. A swift departure from the premises they offer is one of the foundations of this study.

Categories

THERE IS NO WORK OF greater importance for the reception of the medieval folk traditions of the North than the influential collection of Icelandic folktales, *Íslenzkar þjóðsögur og ævintýri*, compiled by Jón Árnason (1819–1888), Iceland's counterpart to the Brothers Grimm. Much like other folktale collections of that age, Jón Árnason's collection formed a central part of the romantic nationalist project of Iceland's intellectual elite taking place in the middle of the nineteenth century.[21] However, it is even more noteworthy for the fact that the taxonomy of the paranormal expressed in this and other folktale collections compiled during the nineteenth century has served as a framework for twentieth- and twenty-first-century scholarly thought concerning medieval and post-medieval paranormal activity in the North.

Jón's influential tome first appeared in Leipzig in 1862, was dedicated to no lesser an authority than Jakob Grimm ("hinum ágæta fræðimanna öldúngi ... höfundi alþýðlegrar sagnafræði"),[22] and was accompanied by an introduction written not by the collector himself but rather by the Icelandic scholar Guðbrandur Vigfússon, standing in for Jón who was far away in Iceland at the time.[23] The classifications employed in this volume were not entirely Jón Árnason's own either but were rather conceived of by German scholar Konrad Maurer who had recently published his own smaller collection, *Isländische Volkssagen der Gegenwart* (1860). They were indeed only slightly modified by Jón himself in his own work in close consultation with Maurer.[24]

The first three categories in the published collection are theological tales (*goðfræðissögur*, mostly tales of elves and trolls), ghost stories (*draugasögur*), and stories of witchcraft and magic (*galdrasögur*), and these categories have continued to dominate scholarly thought about such phenomena even to the present day. This classification or taxonomy is essentially a pragmatic one. Under the circumstances of publishing a book, it is of course necessary that the material be placed in some kind of order and for that a system is needed. However, such systems may sometimes acquire lives of their own, and inevitably the idea eventually began to materialise that otherwordly beings could, or perhaps even must be categorised discretely according to a sensible taxonomy such as that used to categorise the flora and fauna of the natural world; thus a folktale must either be a troll story, a ghost story, or a witchcraft story, but never all three at once.

This system of thought is partly inspired by the study of the natural world undertaken during the eighteenth and nineteenth centuries, and folklore taxonomists like Maurer and Jón Árnason were indeed following in the footsteps of their scientific counterparts, prominently the great Carl von Linné (Linnaeus) of Uppsala (1707–1778). The *Princeps botanicorum* and the Pliny of the North, hailed as a genius by such diverse figures as Rousseau, Goethe, and Strindberg, Linné constructed and expressed in his *Systema Naturæ* a system of binomial nomenclature applicable to all living things wherein each and every animal or plant belongs to precisely one species and one genus, a functional subsystem of the hierarchal biological classification system that also includes discrete categories of families, orders, classes, phyla, kingdoms, and domains.[25]

Pioneering scholars of folklore, including Maurer and his disciples in Iceland, subscribed to the same scientific paradigm as Linné and his "apostles," evident in that they too believed that classification was one of the central tasks of scholarship. Thus they invented a similar system for their own field, partly for pragmatic reasons but also trusting in the taxonomy's objective existence outside of the tables of contents accompanying their works.[26] The inevitable conclusion was that every paranormal being must also belong to a particular "species," and thus folklorists and their general audience became accustomed to regarding a ghost, a troll, and a sorcerer as three discrete categories of the paranormal, as attested in Jón Árnason's categorisation of *tröllasögur, draugasögur,* and *galdrasögur*.[27]

The taxonomy applied first by Maurer and then by Jón Árnason has provided a natural starting point for research of the Icelandic paranormal ever since 1862. Nevertheless, in the Icelandic texts of the twelfth, thirteenth, and fourteenth centuries, a ghost, a troll, and a sorcerer turn out, on closer inspection, to be not as clearly demarcated as this taxonomy suggests; indeed, as already observed, they may all be described using the term troll. Thus the study of the medieval troll must include ghosts and sorcerers as these figures feature even more commonly under the heading troll than those mountain-dwelling ogres who later usurped the term during the nineteenth century, after four centuries of slow but gradual semantic constriction.[28]

Of course post-medieval scholars did not instigate the semantic constriction of the term, but through the application of categories within the folktale collections they produced during this time, the constricted sense of the word troll became the scholarly analytic tool also used to discuss older texts. As a result the medieval vocabulary was subsequently eyed through the lens of nineteenth-century terminology and its later use. Thus modern scholars will sometimes ignore the older sense of the word troll, and when encountering the term might consequently neglect to examine carefully whether it might convey the older and wider significance of the word or the more recently constricted one. For example, when the Lutheran bishop Guðbrandur Þorláksson (c. 1541–1627) published his monumental book of hymns in 1589, wanting to eradicate "Þeir onytsamligu Kvedlingar / Trölla og Fornmanna Rymur" (the useless ditties, rhymes of trolls and the ancients),[29] he is probably not speaking of poetry about hairy and brutish ogres in the wilderness but rather of any poem with a heathen or paranormal theme.

One has to assume that scholars and scientists of the nineteenth century were well aware of the fact that there is a difference between a living organism that bears a physical existence and a paranormal being that does not. It also seems likely that they would have realised that it is not self evident that the methods used to taxonomise living organism should be used also to taxonomise non-existent creatures. And yet it seems that this distinction preyed rarely on their minds and pragmatism, rather than reason, appears to have often been a strict taskmaster. A scholar must always analyse data, and indeed categorisation was often the main tool of late nineteenth-century folklorists, attested also for example in the typology invented by Aarne and Thompson and by the later Thompson motif-index.[30]

Typology has scholarly repercussions that go beyond the actual act of categorisation: when a taxonomy has been created for the paranormal beings of the nineteenth century, it might seem logical to some to apply it also to those of previous centuries as well. Indeed, Guðbrandur Vigfússon began his introduction to the original printed version of *Íslenzkar þjóðsögur og ævintýri* with references to ghosts in the medieval *Eyrbyggja saga* and *Grettis saga,* and dreams and premonitions in *Njáls saga,* and thus surreptitiously invented a tradition that stressed a kind of continuity between the Middle Ages and the nineteenth century.[31]

Notions of a continuity of Northern folk traditions have managed to survive every attack to this day, and are revived in every generation, with subtle changes, without having ever really gone out of fashion.[32] Even though arguments can be made for such a continuity in certain cases, it may be jeopardous to make general assumptions from only limited or specific instances. Each case must instead be judged on its own merit. Another fallacy would be to assume that we always know what medieval concepts and terminology signify because we know what the same words were used to indicate during the nineteenth and twentieth centuries, without ever examining their actual usage in the medieval sources. A closer look at some of these words is merited, and will reveal that the hazards of assuming continuity on these grounds from present to past are all too real.

Unreal Fauna

TROLL IS NOT THE ONLY Old Norse word that seems
to have gone through a kind of semantic constriction during the late medieval and early modern pe-
riods. The Icelandic word for elves, *álfar* (sing. *álfr*), was
both used by Jón Árnason and his contemporaries and also
appears in numerous medieval sources, both poems and
sagas. Since many instances of the term's appearance are
brief and provide little information about what the word
might refer to, it has often been assumed that the medieval
elves are akin to the elves found in Jón Árnason's folktales,
the same elves even, and that is indeed how they have commonly been interpreted.

However, if scholars approach the Old Norse creatures
designated with this term without the prejudice that they
must share a species with post-medieval creatures of the
same name, it becomes more logical to interpret the evidence in such a way that the Old Norse *álfr* is a more unspecified term with a fairly broad significance, perhaps
indicating "any cultic paranormal being on a lower rung
than the actual Æsir, the high gods of Old Norse myth and
legend" (thus including the fertility gods termed Vanir but
also apparently covering a variety of other beings).[33] Thus
the Old Norse *álfr* is used to indicate not only a specific race
or species or even category of elves but rather any kind of
paranormal figure clearly superior to humans — somewhat similar to the way a modern anthropologist might
use the term "god" (or "deity") to mean "a god" rather than
"God." If we regard the term to be so broadly significant,
then it comes as no surprise that elves in the sagas some-

times seem to be minor deities or cultic figures and perhaps are only rarely a distinct race or species, and neither would it then come as a surprise that an elf could be also a human, a dwarf, or a troll.[34]

Old Norse terms describing the paranormal may thus, on closer examination, fail to correspond well to their later usage. For example, while the primary modern Icelandic term for ghost, *draugur* (plur. *draugar*), is well-attested in Old Norse texts (*draugr*), it is far from dominant in the Middle Ages, and in fact, some infamous undead of the Sagas of Icelanders (Víga-Hrappr of *Laxdœla saga*, Þórólfr twist-foot of *Eyrbyggja saga* and Glámr of *Grettis saga*, for example), are never referred to using this term in the respective sagas in which they appear.[35] Some such figures are, however, described as trolls, such as Sóti the viking in *Harðar saga ok Hólmverja*, who is said to have been "mikit tröll í lífinu, en hálfu meira, síðan hann var dauðr" (a great troll in his lifetime, but twice as much so once he was dead).[36] Although the Icelandic *draug(u)r* seems to have conveyed a similar significance during the Middle Ages as it has in post-medieval times, even that parallel remains ambiguous, in particular because this word, like many Old Icelandic words, appears also sometimes within a metaphorical setting in poetry.

To illustrate precisely how terminology from the Middle Ages is not as specific as scholars of the last two centuries have sometimes assumed an example from *Örvar-Odds saga* is informative. In this saga the eponymous hero's primary antagonist, the master criminal Ögmundr Eyþjófsbani who haunts Oddr throughout the saga as if committed to the idea that there can be only one,[37] is at one point said to be "it mesta tröll ok úvættr, er skapaz hefir í norðrhálfu heimsins" (the greatest troll and ogre that has emerged in the northern hemisphere).[38] He studies witchcraft and illusions from an early age. It is also said that the Permians "blótuðu … hann ok tryldu hann svá, at hann var engum mennzkum manni líkr" (worshipped him and trolled him so that he became unlike any human being), and men believe that he should "eigi síðr kallaz andi en maðr" (rather be called a spirit than a human).[39] The implication here is that in the beginning Ögmundr was human, but underwent some kind of ritual or at least procedure, referred to as trolling ("trylla") but never more clearly explained, that seems to have shifted him from one state of being to another.[40] There is no mention of him dying in the process, but some such transformation seems nevertheless to have taken place since the saga indicates that he cannot be considered a human any longer, and also that he cannot die. Ögmundr himself later admits that he has become inhuman, "nú em ek eigi síðr andi en maðr" (now I am no less a spirit than a man), and also states "ek væra dauðr ef ek hefði øðli til þess" (I would be dead if it were in my nature).[41]

Ögmundr is said to be "svartr ok blár" (black and blue), a description used of many Icelandic ghosts, but he is never directly described using the words scholars commonly associate with ghosts in the sagas, although there is mention of "jotnar," "fjandr," and "troll" (giants, devils, and trolls) in the different versions of this saga.[42] Even though Ögmundr is referred to as a spirit ("andi") but not a ghost,[43] there is strong evidence which suggests he should be counted amongst the undead. Something of a medieval Frankenstein creature, having been re-animated like a revenant, it is stated that Ögmundr can no longer die — perhaps precisely because he can no longer be counted among the living.[44] It is left up to the audience of *Örvar-Odds saga* to choose how they would like to refer to Ögmundr: as a devil, demon, troll, spirit, or ghost or perhaps all of the above in chorus. Providing evidence of the common indeterminacy of medieval terminology, this example also demonstrates that, when it comes to the paranormal, the more difficult it becomes to classify or name a monster, the greater is the power that it might wield.[45]

It was only during the eighteenth century that scholars began to interpret the paranormal figures of the Middle

Ages as constituting particular races, corresponding to non Indo-European neighbours of the Germanic people of the North, such as the Sami. The practice can be found, for example, in J.F. Neikter's *De gente antiqua Troll* (published in 1793–1799) wherein the author firmly categorises trolls as an "old race."[46] Since then modern scholars have continued to deal with medieval terms such as *álfr* and *troll* as indicative of members of particular races or species, equivalent to words like horse, Caucasian, or Swede.[47] However, such taxonomic practice is a largely a post-medieval invention, analogous to the way scientists have categorised the natural kingdom, even though medieval paranormal beings were not conceived of by people who used anything resembling modern zoological classification systems to comprehend this aspect of their reality.[48] Thus imagining these terms to be indicative of particular species or races of otherwordly creatures is a post-enlightenment notion. Terms such as *troll* and *álfr* were indeed far more widely encompassing during the Middle Ages, denoting, in the case of *troll*, every kind of malevolent paranormal creature originating with magic as well as those who practice it, and, in the case of *álfr*, every kind of being, human or otherwise, believed to have suprahuman powers and thus worthy of a cult.

Nevertheless, notions of taxonomy did exist during the Middle Ages and medieval Icelandic sources yield some valiant medieval attempts to taxonomise otherworldly beings. One such attempt can be found in *Bárðar saga Snæfellsáss* wherein the narrator tries to explain the protagonist's nature by tracing his genealogy to good-looking and large giants (*risar*) who mated with smaller but shifty and vicious trolls, but finally opting for his fosterage with unspecified mountain-dwellers (*bergbúar*) as the main causal explanation for Bárðr's displacement from the human world to the otherworld of the mountains. However, at least according to the surviving textual evidence, the author of this saga was alone in his particular taxonomical project which is not even entirely consistent within this single text.[49]

By and large, the medieval terminology, when explored with intentions of specificity, tends to obfuscate more than enlighten: a dwarf may well be an elf (as seen in such dwarf names as Álfr and Gandalfr), a dwarf may be referred to as a troll or at least act like one,[50] and the same figure may be characterised as a troll, a giant (*jǫtunn or risi*), and even a man in the same source,[51] leaving the task of specification and categorisation to modern scholars with only their nineteenth-century equipment in hand.[52] Consequently, these paranormal beings remain steadfast in their refusal to submit to the precise categorisations anachronistically applied by nineteenth- and twentieth-century scholars. Perhaps the enterprise was doomed from the beginning for the very reason that the essential nature of the occult is to remain beyond utter comprehension, its power wholly reliant upon the doubt and uncertainty that it arouses in those whose experience or encounter it, and subsequently in the stories such experiences or encounters inspire.

Cave

DOUBT AND UNCERTAINTY ARE CENTRAL to the late fourteenth-century *Bergbúa þáttr,* a brief and little-known medieval prose narrative, which tells of a man called Þórðr who lives in the Westfjords of Iceland,[53] and who is introduced as a prosperous man in the prime of his life ("á góðum aldri"). The narrative concerns a single episode from his life, taking place during the winter when Þórðr travels to church with one of his servants in tow. The journey is a long one, and while the two are on the road a snowstorm breaks out. Þórðr acknowledges that they are lost, and since he does not want to journey into the dark in this weather they seek shelter immediately under a steep cliff where they unexpectedly find a cave previously unknown to them. Þórðr prudently and conspicuously uses his staff to mark a cross at the mouth of the cave, and they rest close to the entrance, not wanting to venture further inside.

Given these details it is perhaps not all together surprising when, during the first third of the night, the men hear something ("nökkut") moving inside the cave. This terrifies the unnamed servant, who attempts to flee, but Þórðr stops him by instructing him to sit still and tells him to pray, remarking that if men run out into the night their eyes may deceive them, a statement not clarified further. The two make the sign of the cross together and pray to God for mercy when they hear awe-inspiring noises coming from within the cave. Looking into the darkness they see two large lights almost like two full moons and suspect that these eyes must belong to a creature of some enormity. They next hear a mighty voice reciting with a great din a poem of twelve stanzas, more or less in the skaldic metre although the last line of each stanza, eerily and uncharacteristically, is repeated. This happens three times during the night and while the poem is recited (taking up more than half of the narrative),[54] they see the big moving lights but otherwise see nothing.

After the third recitation of the poem, the eldritch presence seems to retreat deeper into the cave and soon Þórðr and his servant see the light of the day and hurry out from the cave. When Þórðr exits, he places his foot on the cross he had previously made at the entrance to the cave. The pair go and find the church they were heading towards but discover that they are too late for the service. On the way home, they reach the place where they thought that they had spent the night but find no cave there and feel this to be extraordinary. The two return home and Þórðr remembers the poem, but the servant does not recall a single word. The next year Þórðr moves his farm closer to the church, but the servant dies. Þórðr himself has a long life and does not experience any queer things, and the narrator wraps up this story by informing us that this event was an extraordinary thing.

The timing and the setting of this encounter both seem to be highly significant. In fact the tale does not take place at any certain time in history although the casual mention of Þórðr's journey to a church service indicates that Iceland has been Christian for some time when the events takes place. This is unusual; the Christianization of Iceland around the turn of the first millennium may be one of the main reasons why the late tenth and early eleventh centuries attracted overwhelming attention from twelfth- and thirteenth-century historiographers, who on the other hand seem to have largely neglected the events and history of the late eleventh and the twelfth centuries, if the surviving saga literature provides any indication. The apparent obsession with this particular period in history might indicate that Christianization was regarded as a significant break from the past in the history of Iceland, more decisive, for example, than the death of the Icelandic commonwealth in the late thirteenth century. The preoccupation with the shift from pagan religions to Christianity is significant, as paranormal activity tends to be closely identified with the pagan past in the thirteenth- and fourteenth-century historiography of Iceland.[55]

The focus in this study is on narratives which take place in Iceland, where there is greater intimacy between the events they describe and their implied audience.[56] In spite of much scholarly debate over the last two centuries, there is still no consensus opinion concerning the precise origins of the Sagas of Icelanders as a literary genre. For the last few decades, there has been general scholarly agreement that in their present written form, the sagas are texts from the thirteenth and fourteenth centuries although their manuscript preservation does not preclude the idea that some might be even younger.[57] It still seems somewhat unsatisfactory, however, to regard the final compositions as strictly works of art by individual creative authors and dismissing the traditions behind them altogether. A saga in its finished form may be a late medieval work of art, and yet large chunks of its material are probably traditional. Nevertheless the sagas are much too far removed from the pre-Christian past to be regarded as undiluted or credible sources from or about that era. Identifying a motif in a Christian text as genuinely pre-Christian will never be easy when the sources are so overwhelmingly late and perhaps irreversibly diluted.[58] The chronological aspect of the paranormal will be returned to later in this study (see "Time the Devourer" below).

The only temporal marker in the tale described above, the mention that Þórðr is on his way to attend "tíðir" (canonical hours) during the "hátíðir" (holidays, meaning Christmas, Easter or possibly Pentecost),[59] is also crucial in that, importantly, during the whole encounter his mind must be clearly focused on the spiritual life. The sign of the cross he makes at the mouth of the cave is a clear statement of this fact.[60] In the constant struggle between good and evil, Þórðr has confirmed his place within the Christian camp and is thus perhaps better suited for the ordeal that awaits him than is his hapless servant.[61] It cannot be entirely overlooked, however, that at the same time Þórðr also gives the seemingly un-Christian creature in the cave its due in memorising its poem, perhaps concurrently ensuring his own survival.

The weather and the landscape serve a vital function in many a paranormal encounter, and *Bergbúa þáttr* provides a good example of this. The encounter comes about on the very account of the sudden onset of snow where, in the far North, the weather and the cave-dweller may well serve as a Scylla and Charybdis to the vulnerable human traveler. Furthermore, its setting is within stone, in the cave which serves as an entrance to the otherworld and which appears and then disappears according to an unknown set of rules.[62] That stones, carved by nature into various shapes that may sometimes resemble anthropomorphic beings to the human eye, can acquire a mystical quality, possibly precisely on account of their quiet immobility, is well known to us even in this civilized age of human conquest.[63] Caves are also traditional settings for liminal encounters in medieval Iceland, perhaps naturally so given the island's abundantly rocky landscape where the human so often encounters and is so often dwarfed by stone.[64]

The mysterious cave, their lithic refuge, is imposed on Þórðr and his servant by harsh necessity and the two are clearly reluctant to venture further into its unknown depths than necessary. For someone who denies the existence of the paranormal, such reluctance makes little sense, since other humans are the only dangerous animals inhabiting Iceland that could take up residence in a cave like this. Rationalist modern people are not likely to regard stones as intentionally dangerous in themselves, but it is abundantly clear from the narrative that they, and the narrator as well, have been trained to expect the worst from any cave encountered in the wild. In Iceland, perhaps excepting for their own kind, land and sea are the fiercest natural predators of humans, and their uncompromising nature naturally contributes to the claustrophobic and paranoid atmosphere pervading the small portion of the land defined as normal, human, and civilised.

Petrified

T IS ONLY NATURAL THAT the two humans upon whom *Bergbúa þáttr* is focused carry their own expectations of the ensuing encounter with them into their temporary rocky haven, and, perhaps unsurprisingly, they are in some way realised. The unknown something encountered in the cave remains an unknown something throughout and even beyond the tale. In many paranormal encounters the audience is tempted to focus on the unknown element, as if their attention is drawn there by a clever illusionist, and to forget the humans who experience the paranormal and subsequently frame their experience in language. In *Bergbúa þáttr*, it is the experience of the individuals that is emphasized above explicating the nature of the chthonic monster that they encounter. A monster narrative it remains and yet its primary focus seems to be the human thoughts and emotions awakened by this monster's appearance, or at least its presence, which are externalised in the narrative.[65]

The two humans involved are clearly established as binary opposites. There is the protagonist and hero Þórðr, the one who lives, and the anonymous servant who is fated to die. The servant fears and even attempts to flee from the paranormal while Þórðr remains calm and composed throughout, possibly even unaffected by his dark and cavernous surroundings. The petrified servant is also unable to remember even a single line from the paranormal poem whereas Þórðr remembers the whole thing and in doing so somehow seems to ensure his own survival.

In the poem itself it is actually stated, as clearly as is possible in this opaque poetic form, that the listeners' survival may depend on their remembering it and perhaps this is why it is repeated three times. Paranormal beings may not, however, always be so accommodating and may generally tend towards repetition, somewhat in accordance with Freud's theory of the death drive.[66] This may be a sign of the essentially thanatic nature of monsters and perhaps fear itself, that thanatic impulse which dominates the servant while Þórðr maintains his self-control, possibly his own erotic life force, that instinct for survival which helps people to embrace and enjoy life instead of stagnating in the overwhelming fear of death.

Constantly throughout the narrative we are told what Þórðr and the servant *hear, see,* and *remember*. We are also told of acts or rituals that are somehow essential to their survival, though in ways never clearly explained in the narrative. It seems that these two humans represent the audience and the choices each of its members faces: to be, like the nameless servant, a fairly average and anonymous human who fears the unknown and loses his head in crisis situations, or to be righteous or even heroic like Þórðr, the good Christian who is resourceful, remains calm and gains strength from the rituals of Christianity and, presumably and ultimately, from his imperturbable faith.[67]

Apart from its large and luminous eyes, the creature in the cave never reveals itself and remains mostly unidentified and likely unidentifiable. The two glowing eyes are the only identifiable feature of this metonymic monster, a creature whose physical form is never fully revealed but rather represented only by a terrible part of what must be an even more unimaginably terrible whole. Like a Lovecraftian monster or the eponymous enemy in *The Lord of the Rings,* this creature could never be more terrible if it ever revealed its whole self and thus it does not. Like all danger it is at its most potent lurking in the darkness, watching rather than attacking, preying from a distance and leaving fear to do its work from within.[68]

The skaldic poetry that the two men hear recited throughout the night indicates that this creature should be considered a "bjargálfr" but the word *álfr* (elf) should not lead us, for example, to imagine the fair and angelic beings of Tolkien's Middle-earth; the word conveys, as mentioned above, a broad significance and may include any superhuman figure, mostly benevolent and yet still dangerous, that has to be venerated or at least placated by humans, perhaps through cultic practices.[69] Thus the "bjargálfr" may save us, since it is in its power to do so, but may also become destructive, as this narrative seems to strongly suggest.

The role of the poem within the narrative is ambiguous and not surprisingly so since it is clearly a nebulous ode. Its pagan nature is evident in the abundant heathen kennings used with references to heathen gods like Þórr and Óðinn (Þundr) and giants such as Surtr, Hrungnir, Hrímnir, and Aurnir. Thus the "bjargálfr" in the cave is situated within a heathen parallel universe,[70] and its presumably superhuman powers belong to a past which is evil, savage, and, most importantly, has refused to go away as the past is supposed to do. It uncannily remains in the present but is nevertheless slowly disappearing into the cavernous depths, shadowed from the light of Christianity. The poem's reference to the eruption and the apocalyptic imagery is hardly interesting as evidence that Icelanders knew of volcanic eruptions — a fairly self-evident fact — but due to the atmosphere of threat and doom that such events inevitably signify.

When Þórðr and the servant, the latter only temporarily, have escaped the doom that had been glaring at them through the darkness, the terrible luminous eyes, they speak of the whole experience as "undr" (a wonder), a statement that defies simple classification. A wonder can be either good or evil, Christian or pagan, miraculous or magical. Its occult nature is fundamental to the continued existence of the wondrous; the wondrous is an impossible riddle, it is everything which cannot be explained and must retain its enigmatic state.

As it turns out the servant is under a curse — the audience will have suspected this from the outset since in this sort of narrative the bell must be tolling for someone. His death has been more or less predicted in the impenetrable skaldic verse, and thus his worst fears, which seemed so silly only moments ago, are in fact realised. Following his moment of fear already exiled from life itself, as the terrified must always be, he is now permanently exiled. The tragedy of this lies in the fact that his is the same fear familiar to every mortal human, presumably including everyone in the medieval audience of the tale, fear of the sudden displacement from life to death, which is beyond all imagining, despite any of the epistemological systems that have been invented to rationalise and reduce it. The servant has no name of his own precisely because he is only all of us, as we really are: timid, vulnerable, and easily disposable humans.

In stories, however, we are allowed to choose another role and a more heroic ending. In the end, the narrative of this paranormal encounter focuses on the survivor, Þórðr, who escapes doom. The audience is thus offered the opportunity to identify with this heroic man, rather than the everyman who accompanied him, and to survive along with him; indeed its members are encouraged to do so, evident in the particular focus on his survival provided at the end of the story, a survival in this case based on Þórðr's resourcefulnes and his Christian faith in the transcendence and the immortality of the soul. The survivor is indeed the most important person in any disaster narrative as only the survivors are able to relate their accounts of the event.[71] Identifying with the survivor provides a sense of relief so enormous that it can only be acquired through a close brush with death. As everyone who wants to will know, though, Þórðr's release is only temporary and any

eventual or eternal salvation must remain strictly a matter
of faith.

Troll Space

HE SHIFT AWAY FROM THE traditional scholarly tendency to accept the externalisation of danger in encounters with paranormal beings, such as the hidden cave monster in the story of Þórðr and the servant, is a direct consequence of accepting the unreality of the paranormal. But if paranormal beings are not real, then why should a scholar's attention be directed towards them and not towards the humans who experience these phenomena?

And yet, by not treating paranormal figures as a part of the natural fauna of the world and thus transferring our focus from the external to the internal, the unreal paradoxically becomes real again. Instead of unreal paranormal apparitions external to humanity and reality, our subject becomes certain internal experiences that must be considered to be real in the minds of both the witnesses and, presumably, also the narrators of the accounts through which they are related. Internalised thus, each troll becomes a perichoretic part of the human consciousness, immanent in humanity but somehow retaining an aspect of its inhuman identity.[72] The troll, so categorically alien, is then seen as an essential part of us: residing within us, like a menacing double or an uncanny ancestral core.[73]

An interpretation of *Bergbúa þáttr* focusing primarily on its metonymic troll, revealed to witnesses who dare not seek to envision its whole but only regard its enormous eyes and hear the din of its voice, can easily be imagined. In such an interpretation, troll space would be located outside of the human mind, somewhere within the landscape or geography of the natural world. Conversely, our approach is to locate this space within the human consciousness as an expanse of danger and trauma; an existential crisis that can be externalised through the appearance of monsters but is essentially a wholly internal one at its core. *Bergbúa þáttr* is then not a story about an anonymous cave-dwelling beast, though it might feature one, but rather about two humans and their experiences. Troll space exists within each of these humans, and indeed also variably within each member of the narrative's audience. Likewise, the story about Ásbjörn and his men's ephemeral encounter with a troll along a mountain ridge concerns not so much this nebulous other but rather Ásbjörn and his entourage. The troll to whom they bear witness, whatever its origins might be, is an enemy situated within their own psyches.

Troll space is a psychological rather than a geographical entity,[74] and the study of trolls certainly does not entail leaving humanity behind. The quest for troll space is unusual in that it is apparent from the beginning that its boundaries must remain essentially elusive. The assumption here is that troll space is real, but that it is anything but independent of human consciousness. Man and troll are inextricably intertwined. Like the holy trinity, they are the same and yet also manage to remain different entities altogether.

The recognition that troll narratives are existential narratives will lead, however, only to a brief eureka moment since, on closer inspection, all narratives are, albeit with varying subtlety, existential in that their primary function is formative. As Davíð Erlingsson has phrased it, narratives "make men," and, in fact, an awareness of this general and metaphorical aspect of narrative has always been fundamental to the structuralist study of literature.[75] However, the existential approach may have a particularly transformative effect on the exploration of troll narratives within the field of Old Norse studies, a field in which scholars have tended to focus upon and highlight the specific with the consequence that the general is often dismissed as trivial or superfluous.[76] Thus the idea that troll narratives are primarily concerned with the human condition need not be a dramatic discovery, and yet it introduces an important critical stance which will be further utilised in the remainder of this study and is thus what political strategists might refer to as a potential "game changer."[77]

In the study of the sagas, it is their apparent realism that has most often been highlighted.[78] While it is true that the sagas are realistic especially in their fairly direct relevance to the realities of their medieval audience, the trope of realism comes with two inherent dangers: one is the constant use of the term realism as defined according to modern scientific notions of reality, and the other is a negation of the symbolic value of the fantastic which may misinform saga interpretation.[79]

The misleading nature of just such an approach can be demonstrated through a brief analysis of *Fóstbrœðra saga*, a biography of the two early eleventh-century blood-brothers and poets Þorgeirr and Þormóðr. The modern reader's instinct may be to treat these figures as actual flesh and blood humans from the distant past. This approach, however, leaves the two men and their story strangely elusive, Þorgeirr in particular being a rather unconvincing realistic character, with whom the audience — a fourteenth-century audience as well as a modern one — might have a hard time empathising. Exaggerated in his warlike demeanor, he spurns women, rarely laughs, and is at one point in the saga described as "óblíðr hversdagslega við alþýðu" (usually unfriendly to everybody).[80] In one instance Þorgeirr even decapitates a stooping man for no better reason than that his stance offered too good a chance for such a blow to let it pass.[81] His blood-brother Þormóðr, who is his opposite in being an ardent womaniser, also seems a softer and kinder protagonist altogether. And yet he decides to dedicate his whole life, after Þorgeirr's death, to seeking vengeance for his unsympathetic fosterbrother, which thus changes the saga into a revenge narrative. A realistic interpretation of this saga can only leave the reader strangely unfulfilled. It might thus be far more fruitful to approach the pair as spiritual ancestors of Dr Jekyll and Mr Hyde, in that the contrasting characters of the two men might make sense only if the audience thinks of them as one composite personality the extremities of which are externalised in two distinct characters. On this symbolic level the story works whereas it might seem somewhat bizarre as a realistic narrative.

Narrative realism is thus founded not on a correspondence between the narrative and reality as defined in a world dominated by scientific and technical truths but on an uneasy contract between a text and its audience wherein the audience chooses to accept the reality of a narrative that they still know has been constructed. Such a contract seems to have been in place between the Sagas of Icelanders and their original audience, one guaranteeing a reality to which both were a party. This reality would not have excluded paranormal entities, and yet, however real such beings were perceived to be, their value to the audience, indeed the value of any constructed history of the past, would still have been largely symbolic. The story, true or false, believable or not, is always told to "make a man."

Coda: In Which the Audience Is Unexpectedly Addressed

Reader, you will now have noticed the word "audience" cropping up repeatedly. In literary criticism, focused on the text, on language, the audience is essentially elusive, outside the text, even though the text is always, no less essentially, infused by an awareness of its audience, its very *raison d'être*. Thus the audience is a somewhat spectral part of any narrative, even though certainly a more tangible biological entity than the text itself — as you will know by pinching yourself as you read this — and yet textual interpretation can only confront it as a wraith, as the expectation of reception. Still, just as the spectator of the paranormal is the protagonist of this book, the audience is also "the secret hero of these poems," the very reason for any narrative of a paranormal encounter — the secret residence of all ghouls. The audience will be present in all which follows, often invisible, and yet central to all happenings.

Trollspeak

KEEPING IN MIND THE EFFECT of the locutions of the unknown on its audience, the parlance of the trolls seems to demand further attention. Even though the din of the skaldic *drápa* recited in *Bergbúa þáttr* produces a powerful effect, paranormal others do not speak only in obscure, skaldic verse.[82] In some narratives, trolls are more clearly intelligible, and their speech relegates human witnesses to the uneasy role of interpreters.

The events of Ch. 52 of *Óláfs saga Tryggvasonar,* a hagiographical kings' saga composed in Iceland c. 1200 by an otherwise unknown Þingeyrar monk named Oddr Snorrason,[83] take place shortly before the death of the heroic and chivalric King Óláfr Tryggvason around the turn of the first millennium. Here the king is sailing north to Hálogaland,[84] anchors his ship when night falls, and asks his men to remain on the ship until the next morning. However, two of the king's men awaken during the night and leave the ship to go on a private excursion. Soon they come upon a mountain with a cave and notice that "váru trǫll mǫrg við eld" (many trolls were at the fire).[85] These trolls are conversing about the great missionary king and his antagonism to their lot, and their trollspeak will be quoted here in its entirety:

They heard that one of them spoke and said — they identified him as the leader of the trolls:

"You will know that King Óláfr has come to our regions and will tomorrow go ashore and attack our homes and drive us away."

Then a second troll answers: "That is not a good prognosis since I will tell you that we met once. I was living in Gaulardalur in the south close to Earl Hákon my friend and this was a bad change when this one replaced him as the earl and I had many good dealings. And once when the king's men had a game close to my abode I found their noise unpleasant, and I did not like them, and I entered the game with them so that I was invisible to them, and I left them so that one had a broken hand. The next day I broke the foot of another and I thought the prognosis was excellent. And on the third day I entered the game and wanted to attack one of them. And when I grasped one, that man grasped my thighs and I felt his touch burned me and I wanted to escape but I could not and I realised then that this was the king. And wherever he touched me I burned and I have never been as miserable and finally I went down under and then I left and came here to the north."

Then a second demon spoke: "I came to where the king was feasting and wanted to betray him with a drink and took the guise of a fair woman and stood with a horn near the trapeze-shaped table and well adorned. And during the evening when the king saw me he stretched out his hand to take the horn and then I felt sure of success. But when he took the horn he struck my head with it with such strength that I thought it would break and I had to use the lower passage and this is what I got from our meeting."

And then a third troll spoke: "I will tell you how I fared. I came to the room where the king lay and the bishop in another bed and I took the guise of a fair woman. The king said: 'You, woman! Come and scratch my leg.' And I did that and scratched his leg and made him itch all the more. Then the king fell asleep and I loomed over him and wanted to kill him. But in that moment the bishop struck me between the shoulders with a book and I was so injured that every bone broke and I had to take the lower passage. But the bishop woke the king and asked to see the foot and plague had entered it and the bishop cut out the spot and it became whole again. This is the mark he left me with."

And having heard this, they returned to the ships.

But the morning after they told the king and the bishop what they had seen and heard and they recognised about this. But the king asked that they would not do this again and said it was very dangerous to go there. And then they walked up and cast holy water and chanted and destroyed all monsters there. And after that the king went to Þrándheimr with great prestige.[86]

The laconic tone and lack of wonder demonstrated by the human protagonists is at first striking.[87] The two humans who witness the talk of the trolls are almost invisible in this narrative, but since the king has already specified the danger of and warned against their straying from the ship, their thrill during this session of eavesdropping is palpable even if the author felt it superfluous to depict or to mention it explicitly.[88]

The focus here is on the trolls' discourse, opening up a set of questions commonly raised in light of many monster narratives throughout the ages, since such monsters are frequently not content to merely grunt or roar but are able to strike up a curiously intelligent conversation in an intelligible language. This fact alone compels the audience to consider the partial humanity of the trolls and to wonder whether or not the sophisticated and structured way in which they emote their concerns about the king might negate their bestiality. Or should we perhaps regard the human witnesses as translators and interpreters? One may note the uneasy application of categories upon these ogres, variously referred to as trolls, demons, or all monsters — the trollish, demonic, and monstrous seeming to belong together in one broad category.[89] Possibly this unease reflects the confusion of the witnesses who, like Ásbjörn and his men on the mountain ridge, cannot fully understand what they see and hear but know that they are in the presence of some kind of paranormal peril.

The evident fact that here man and troll share a language immediately makes the encounter more intimate. The moment the alien speaks intelligibly it is displaced from one category of the monstrous to another, no less monstrous but now uncannily so in its intimate otherness. The troll remains alien and yet becomes familiar, and the marriage of its familiarity and strangeness makes it eerie and uncanny, frightening in ways different from those monstrous others that are wholly unfamiliar and seem to be utterly alien. This kindred dynamic shared between protagonists and monsters is indeed an essential theme of medieval Icelandic monstrosity.[90]

In this way the near-invisible human witnesses again draw our attention. How can the experience described be separated from its retelling; is it even possible to separate the two in any narrative of otherworldly experience? We have no direct access to the paranormal encounters of the Middle Ages, indeed from any age, as such, only textual attempts to put inexplicable experiences into words and thus, to some degree, make sense out of nonsense. The sense, as well as a part of the experience, rests though not in the supposed lived experience but in the minds of other humans. When discussing the experience, an effort must thus be made to discuss the possible paradigms for its conceptualisation. Paranormal experiences thus become inseparable from language since language cannot but define and shape the experiences it is used to describe.[91]

In this case, the paranormal experience is the discourse: long speeches by trolls expressing their vulnerability when faced by the powerful king, and in which everything is perverted and topsy-turvy as we are forced to momentarily adopt the point of view of the enemy. In this inversion, the humans hiding in their very midst may seem uncomfortably akin to the troll attempting and failing to hide amongst the royal court. The spies, our representatives in the narrative, have now descended unnoticed into an inverted otherworld, experientally if not spatially, into a world where troll is the norm, perhaps unsettling the known cosmology.

With no description of the physical appearance of the trolls, the focus here is indeed on their behaviour, mostly as described by the trolls themselves. These creatures are characterised neither by the nature of their speech nor their appearance but by their self-proclaimed unusual and seemingly magical powers. The "second troll" reveals its ability to become invisible to the king's men although the king himself seems fully aware of its presence, possibly through his own transcendental powers.[92] Then a "second demon" describes its own ability to metamorphose into a beautiful woman, once again failing to fool the perceptive king who turns out to be a most able defender against such dark arts. The fourth speaker, the so-called "third troll," claims to possess the same powers, the only difference being that it was a bishop and not the king who once saw through its disguise as a beautiful woman. All three speakers reveal that their magic skills are used to maim, poision, and make people itch in order to infuse their legs with the plague.[93] Their arts are very dark indeed although they ultimately turn out to be no match for humanity's and civilization's able defender King Óláfr and God's agent, the bishop.

After suffering defeat all three villains end up having to escape through "the lower passage,"[94] indicating that these are creatures of the infernal regions, the netherworlds occupied by the devil himself and all his demons. Their accounts also reveal that such beings are most successfully foiled by the holy book or by persons who possess an aura of the sacral, such as the holy king himself or the bishop. In the end, they are driven away by holy water and chanting, and thus their opposition to the sacred is drawn in no uncertain contours.[95]

This is far from the only paranormal visitation described in this particular narrative; the king himself faces a multitude of other hostile visitors throughout the saga, including assassins, who turn out to be witches, demons or even heathen gods.[96] The message conveyed throughout the narrative is that the paranormal walks among us, or at least it did so at the dawn of the last millennium, in the period during which the North was Christianized. It sometimes becomes hard to draw a clear line between the normal and the paranormal in this transcendental history; we are in a world replete with demons, witches, and trolls — the various heathen spirits of *Óláfs saga* seem as ubiquitous as the aliens in *Men in Black,* many of which may remain undiscovered — who in spite of their paranormal powers are as much a part of the reality the saga describes as are the king himself and his men.[97]

In Oddr's *Óláfs saga,* the binary opposition between the sacred and the profane, the Christian and the pagan, God and the devil, that provides the interpretative framework for such paranormal encounters. However, while God is plain, unified, and intact, no such simplicity characterises his enemies. God and his saint-like king oppose a plethora of monsters with different names and different guises.[98] And, on occasion, we are presented with their strangely familiar and yet macabre discourse which reveals, whether we want to hear it or not, that far from being utterly alien there is an essential familiarity, even intimacy between man and troll.

Witchcraft Epistemology

OCUSING ON THE TROLLS' USE of language quickly leads us away from the trolls themselves and back again to the humans attempting to define the paranormal: from their trollspeak to our own.[99] An investigation of the occult essentially becomes a journey into the human mind which entails a displacement from the artistic illusion of diversity: instead of trying to understand many species of paranormal others, the mysterious phenomena are taking place within the minds of only a single Linnéan species. Although distinction may prove a useful analytic tool in any cultural analysis of the paranormal, exploring the parallel functions of apparently diverse paranormal beings may be equally illuminating.

In various handbooks on supernatural beings from all over the world, a shrewdness of articles are accounted for on each supposed species of beings, if not all with their own identity card, at least with their own lexical entry. In reference works in which cultural variety is a primary concern, a zombie, a vampire, and an Icelandic *draugr* each must have their own entry. Although the geographical and chronological separation of various kinds of paranormal others is a worthy subject for investigation, these creatures, however, also share important common features and, more importantly, common functions within the narratives in which they appear. The same applies to the various types of *moras, succubi,* and old hags that magicians send to bother and even kill others, often in their sleep.[100] Many types of imaginary beings have been so identified and categorised, and, of course, it is a significant cultural historical fact that zombies come from Haiti and vampires from Eastern Europe.

However, when individual human experience is contemplated it might be even more fruitful to refrain from distinguishing and to rather consider the similar function of these diverse paranormal beings, keeping also in mind that unlike living creatures who may exist in the same way whether we refer to them as cats, dogs, seals, or walruses, these non-existent creatures do not exist independently of human thought and consequently of human vocabulary, terminology, and taxonomy. A living creature may not rely upon a name or a word to ensure its existence, but there is no paranormal being which "exists" independent of the vocabulary used to describe it. Rather than flesh, blood, and bone the paranormal is indeed wrought in thought, imagination, and in words.

But what is the nature of the efficacy of the words used to account for the paranormal? Though some of these will be examined below, it must be stressed that this vocabulary is not at all technical in its nature. One cannot assume that a single word always conveys the same specific significance or even that the same being is always referred to using the same word. While scholars often thrive on clarity and definitions, the medieval vocabulary of the paranormal tends to be a muddle and this is consciously reflected in some of the language usage of this book. Accordingly I have not hesitated thus far to call the same creature a ghost, a vampire, or a zombie, not because they are all apt words, but rather to create an estrangement effect as a reminder to the reader that we have entered an area without discrete and unwavering definitions, taking seriously and demonstrating the idea that Enlightenment-style taxonomy is not helpful in understanding medieval, occult phenomena. Thus all confusion of terminology is deliberate and serves as a reminder that we are moving away from technical language.[101]

As we have already seen, the vocabulary of paranormal otherness is far from unified or simple in thirteenth-
and fourteenth-century Iceland. No word was commonly
used denote "the paranormal" as such, which may betray
conceptions of any kind of strict binary between it and
the "normal." There is, however, an abundance of terms
used to describe magic, and a large portion of that which
is paranormal originates in the practice of magic and sorcery. Occult beings (trolls, giants, dwarves, elves, and *dísir*) tend to be associated with witchcraft. If we look first at
English — the language of this book — the terms "magic,"
"witchcraft," "sorcery," and "shamanism" all cover similar
ground, though perhaps carrying different connotations.
The term "shamanism" was popularised by Mircea Eliade
some decades ago,[102] and as a Tungusic word with currency in ancient Siberia has served well those scholars who
suspect that there is a connection between Old Norse *seiðr*
and the rituals of shamanism, although its use as a generic
term for all witchcraft can be called into question given
what is known of its specific origins.[103] With their Greco-
Roman roots, the terms "magic" and "sorcery" tend to
carry negative connotations, having long been used pejo-
ratively by Christian authorities, whereas "witchcraft" is a
Germanic word, albeit one no less negative in the connotations it bears.[104] None of these words are exact parallels for
the terms describing the harnessing of the paranormal in
the sagas, such as "fjǫlkynngi," "forneskja," "galdrar," and
"trollskapr," all of which also bear connotations worthy of
deeper exploration.

While the story of the creature in the cave described in
Bergbúa þáttr takes place some time after the conversion
of the North, the story of the two disobedient courtiers
found in *Óláfs saga* centres directly upon it. King Óláfr was
perhaps the leading figure in the conversion myths of Iceland, though several Icelanders also played their own significant parts, including Snorri goði, who will merit more
attention below. Following the conversion of Iceland, this

important magnate from the West of the island calls on the aid of an old crony called Þrándr stígandi, described thus: "Þrándr var manna mestr ok sterkastr ok manna fóthvatastr; hann hafði verit fyrr með Snorra goða ok var kallaðr eigi einhamr, meðan hann var heiðinn, en þá tók af flestum trollskap, er skírðir váru" (Þrándr was a big man and strong and swift on foot; he had been with Snorri goði previously and was said to be not of one body when he was heathen, but trollishness faded from most when baptised).[105] The phrase "eigi einhamr" is a well-known element in the vocabulary of sorcery in the sagas; witches were believed to shift shape ("fara hamfǫrum") when they performed their magic,[106] and such metamorphosis is mentioned, for example, in a graphic account of Óðinn's shamanism in *Heimskringla* (see "The Witchfather," below).[107] That his transmogrificative ability is connected with Þrándr's pagan faith is evident from the narrative, as is the fact that such is implicitly counted as "trollskapr," a word sometimes used as a synonym for both "fjǫlkynngi" and "fítonsandi,"[108] and in other cases clearly refers to magical powers, often possessed by paranormal beings and ogres ("óvættir").[109] Sorcery and shapeshifting are commonly regarded as trollish behaviour in their very nature,[110] and in this account from *Eyrbyggja saga,* it is suggested that such rituals were commonplace in pre-Christian times. Baptism more or less, if not altogether, terminates such trollishness, firmly relegating it to the past. Þrándr used to be "eigi einhamr" but his "trollskapr" seems to have evanesced along with the heathen religion, having no place in a new Christian world.

This chronological aspect of magic and the paranormal is even more evident in the term "forneskja," which could be glossed as "ancient." The word is used in the sagas as a synonym for each of "galdrar," "fjǫlkynngi," "kynngikraptar," "hindurvitni," and "heiðni"[111] to denote superstition, as well as all and sundry magical and paranormal behaviour,[112] and as a chronological term for the ancient pagan past and the customs that belonged to that past.[113] In another episode found in *Eyrbyggja saga,* also situated soon after the Christianization of Iceland, the word clearly suggests both the powers of magic and the belief that they essentially belong to the past. When Þóroddr of Fróðá and his band of sea-dead men visit their previous abode at yuletide, when the wonders of Fróðá are beginning, the people at the farmstead are pleased rather than frightened: "Menn fǫgnuðu vel Þóroddi, því at þetta þótti góðr fyrirburðr, því at þá hǫfðu menn þat fyrir satt, at þá væri mǫnnum vel fagnat at Ránar, ef sædauðir menn vitjuðu erfis síns; en þá var enn lítt af numin forneskjan, þó at menn væri skírðir ok kristnir at kalla" (People welcomed Þóroddr since this was seen as a good omen because men held the belief that people were made welcome at Rán if the sea-dead attended their own wake; but then the ancient lore had not been exorcised even though people were baptisted and Christian in name).[114] It is acknowledged here that the Christianization of the land is not accompanied by the sudden demise of all heathen customs, beliefs, and superstitions. On the other hand, it is accentuated that these beliefs are "forneskja," that they belong to the past and do not have a bright future. The fact that "forneskja" and Christianity are opposites is also made very evident here, that although pagan beliefs and superstitions survive alongside Christianity their proper place is in the past, with the ancients.

The words "galdrar" and "fjǫlkynngi" are also terms commonly used to describe magic in the sagas. Of these, "galdrar" seems more neutral,[115] originating in ritualistic acts themselves and, specifically, in the noise emitted during their performance.[116] This is attested, for example, in the phrase "galdra þú mér gal" appearing in the poem *Grógaldr* (The Chant of Gróa (?))[117] and also in the behaviour of the witches Kotkell and Gríma, described in *Laxdœla saga* (see further "Immigrant Song," below), who raise a platform and, apparently, stand upon it chanting: "þat váru galdrar" (it was magic).[118] That "galdrar" involve noise is also evident in poetic kennings in which the word is used along with a single weapon (as a *pars pro toto*) or weapons in general, in the same way that other words indicating noises such as "dynr" are used. Thus *dynr sverða, gnýr geira, gnýr stála, skjalda glymr, vápna galdr,* and *galdr hjǫrva* are six battle kennings in which weapons and noise go together.[119] A metonymical shift can thus be noted, wherein the noise apparently accompanying acts of witchcraft ended up denoting the craft itself. In the sagas, the term "galdrar" is often used alongside "forneskja" and "fjǫlkynngi,"[120] and, occasionally, with "gørningar," a less common word that mostly seems to relate to man's interference with the forces of nature.[121]

Some less common words that may accompany "fjǫlkynngi" include "atkvæði," another word signifying speech or chanting that seems to originate in the ritual of magic, and "kuklaraskapr."[122] While "fjǫlkynngi" (vast-knowledge) does not itself appear in *Eyrbyggja saga,* the wise Geirríðr — who will be discussed at greater lenth below ("Popular") — is reported to be "margkunnig" (multi-knowledged),[123] which obviously conveys similar connotations and runs to the heart of the semantics of the term itself, referring not to ancient knowledge but to great knowledge, wisdom, and learning that mostly characterises witches, trolls, and berserks but which remains far beyond the capabilities of the average man.[124] Such knowledge is clearly coveted and can be both taught and learned,[125] but it does not often appear without mention of its nefarious essence, evident in parallel constructions such as "illska (badness) ok fjǫlkynngi," "eitur (malice) ok fjǫlkynngi," and "grimmd (cruelty) ok fjǫlkynngi."[126] The term is pagan as well, indeed used to depict both Norse and Roman paganism,[127] and the pagan god Óðinn's "fjǫlkynngi" is clearly expressed in *Heimskringla* (see "The Witchfather," below).[128] These examples demonstrate that the knowledge in question is indeed magical knowledge, with the word "fjǫlkynngi" in particular having become a generic word for magic at some point, although it seems to have been accompanied by a variety of synonyms, many of which seek to create distance while paradoxically bringing the reader closer to understanding.[129]

The further one delves into medieval vocabulary, in stark contrast to modern scientific terminology, the more clearly its unspecific nature emerges.[130] As one stands baffled, it is, however, possible to find incertitude pleasingly apt, an element of mystery befitting the subject. Thus we may approach an understanding of medieval attitudes towards paranormal activity by noting that the vocabulary of magic leaves us mostly with insinuations and vague implications, perhaps on purpose, as it is the nature of the occult to resist utter identification, arriving surreptitiously, catching us unaware.

Causality

THE NARRATIVES EXAMINED THUS FAR are dramatic in nature, showing rather than telling, their purposes expressed through acts rather than sober attempts to define images of the universe — as is the art of the saga. Ideas of causality are adumbrated but rarely elaborated upon or explained. The reasons for this become manifest when specific episodes in which attempts are made to talk about the paranormal and even to define it are closely examined. Immediately contradictions begin to emerge, binaries between rationalism and superstition cannot be sustained and reality becomes slippery. Language, man's tool for imposing order, becomes rather an implement of chaos.

In the preceding chapters the focus has been placed upon descriptions of paranormal encounters and the experiences of the humans who sit facing the trolls. However, the actual experiences described are inseparable from the causal explanations attached to each encounter. Tagging along with experience are matters of identification, classification, and rationalisation. The human is Cartesian in that he exists since he thinks. Words may not always come easy and yet they will arrive in the end and wrap up the experience, taking not only care of but also exercising some sort of control over it. As unknown as the occult may be, it never arrives or departs without an implied causality, even if it is never completely summarized or explained.

In medieval Iceland, the identification of the occult was an endeavour fraught with contradiction, and this may be best illustrated with a case study of three paranormal encounters involving the same historical figure whose own relationship with the paranormal was essentially incongruous. This man was by his very social standing a liminal figure, in one famous incident even straddling divergent tectonic plates, but, perhaps more meaningfully to the medieval audience, historically situated on the crest between two religions: organised Christianity and the nebulous heathen customs that preceded its arrival, himself presumably a former pagan official who had quickly adapted to the new Christian ways. The three paranormal encounters involving this figure are indicative of the essential contradictions that the causal explanations of occult phenomena entail: everything is explained and identified, yet things remain also crucially unexplainable and only nominally identified.

Rationalism in the Lava Field

THE MEDIEVAL CAUSAL MODELS EMPLOYED to make
sense of the paranormal can indeed be located within a single person who in turn may be considered
a Christian rationalist, a believer in demonic phenomena
or even a ruthless pragmatist that makes use of the paranormal as it suits his grander purposes. Such a man is the
noble Icelander from the conversion period who has already been mentioned above, albeit perfunctorily, Snorri
Þorgrímsson (963–1031), usually referred to as Snorri goði
and a contemporary of King Óláfr Tryggvason.[131] Snorri's
relationship with the paranormal is interestingly but un-
settlingly diverse and yet perhaps typical for his own time.
It is perhaps no less typical than how our own century has
dealt with our ancestor's belief in trolls, a topic that is difficult to ignore when discussing definitions of the paranormal.

As previously mentioned, the Christianization of Iceland around the turn of the millennium was regarded as
a seminal event in the sagas from the thirteenth and fourteenth centuries. From the thirteenth century onwards,
the narrative tradition concerning the Christianization-
parliament of the year 1000 includes a particular riposte
issued by Snorri, one of the leading magnates on the Christian side of the conflict.[132] The legend has it that in the middle of the parliamentary debate at Þingvellir a man comes
running in and announces a volcanic eruption at Ǫlfus,
likely to overrun the estate of Þóroddr goði, another recent
convert among the magnates. Reasoning the coincidence of
the eruption, the pagans at parliament remark that it is not

surprising that that the gods have grown angry given some of the remarks made during the debate. To this, Snorri goði retorts: "Um hvat reiddusk guðin þá er hér brann hraunit er nú stǫndu vér á?" (What then angered the gods when the lava burned that we are standing on now?).[133]

Snorri manages to silence the heathens with this powerful comeback,[134] so powerful that it is still reported in the textbooks used by Icelandic schoolchildren today.[135] The cultural significance of his one-liner has been considerable during the twentieth and twenty-first centuries, as it evidently was also during the fourteenth century.[136] However, the joke was never explicitly interpreted in the medieval sources, the author's of which, as a rule, are content to narrate without providing overt, critical commentary. The only thing certain about Snorri's apparently rhetorical question is that it is far less innocent than it might seem, but all else is left open to interpretation, including to what extent Snorri understands the origins of lava and of igneous rock.

Later interpreters though were not slow to recognise in Snorri a kindred spirit, a kind of medieval Icelandic Richard Dawkins even, the rational man who undermines superstition with clever mockery. During the twentieth century, scholars and pundits such as the Rev. Gunnar Benediktsson (1892–1981) regarded Snorri's remark as a prime example of "Icelandic thought," characterised by stoicism and earthbound rationalism,[137] and geologist Þorleifur Einarsson (1931–1999) referred to it as "the first geological commentary."[138] The Snorri that appears in this anecdote held strong appeal for nineteenth- and twentieth-century rationalists, their own epistemological reasoning firmly grounded in the scientific thought of the technological revolution.[139] The wise man who calmly asks what could have angered the gods when the lava on Þingvellir originated is eagerly interpreted as a man of (scientific) reason and logic, with reason even occasionally defined as a particularly Icelandic attribute.

The contradiction, however, between scientific thought and the fact that Snorri was in fact speaking as a member of one religious camp on the precipice of war with another faction, siding with the Christian God against the ancient pagan gods, did not seem too worrying for the "rationalist" interpretation of Snorri's geological gag. This same contradiction was indeed also present in the life of most of Iceland's intellectual elite during the twentieth century, most of whom were professed Christians who nevertheless believed in science and whose rationalism was wedded to their nationalistic ideals. During the twentieth century a belief in a God who had only created lava indirectly seemed most natural and rational and thus Snorri's faith was easily moulded to fit such a model. His Christianity could be regarded as genuinely devout but it must nevertheless be reasonable from the point of view of modern science, much like that of the faithful Icelandic scholars of the twentieth century. These scholars were nominally Christian but did not care much for the paranormal and tended to believe in the sagas, albeit somewhat selectively, as factual historical sources, applauding their realism and rationality while dismissing and ignoring the abundance of paranormal elements described within them. Accepting Christ but disliking much of the paraphernalia of religion, in particular Catholic miracles and saints, many twentieth-century scholars of Old Norse history and writing believed that they were men of enlightenment and reason with a deeper understanding of the laws of nature than their ancestors, with Snorri the medieval rationalist standing out as a notable exception.[140]

This particular disassociation was noted by the scholar Jón Helgason (1899–1986) who, when discussing *Egils saga*, noted that that, "Þegar fram liðu stundir þótti ekki lengur tilhlýðilegt að trúa á seið, en um leið og menn gáfust upp á því var meginstoðinni kippt undan skilningi á flani Egils til útlanda. [...] Það er hæpið að trúa því að ef galdur er tekinn úr galdrasögu, verði afgangurinn sönn saga" (In the fullness of time a belief in magic became unbecoming but when that was abandoned the foundation for understanding Egill's wanderings abroad was gone ... It seems strange to believe that if magic is taken out of a magical tale what will remain is a true story).[141] This acerbic comment is well known and yet it remains a common trope to refer primarily to the sagas as "realistic narratives," if not necessarily true in every detail. The emphasis on their supposed realism, defined very much in relation to modern perceptions of what is or what only can be real, has subsequently often lead scholars to ignore the paranormal elements frequently described in the sagas.[142] Thus the paranormal becomes an elephant in the room, obvious to all and yet generally ignored.

Returning to Snorri, if he had truly embraced Christianity in the year 1000, he had far from dispensed entirely with the paranormal, adopting instead somewhat of a new framework of causality, with God, the father and son, positioned as the creator of all things and the saviour of mankind. Indeed the natural phenomena to which Þingvellir owes its existence would within this framework be identified as miraculous, a part of the larger miracle of nature that forms a part of the fundamental miraculousness of creation itself.[143]

What Snorri actually means with his retort nevertheless remains opaque. Though he seems to be poking fun at how the heathens use the phenomena of volcanic eruptions selectively to argue their own case, the notion of the wrath of the gods is unlikely to have been wholly alien or objectionable to him, given that he not only grew up in pre-Christian Iceland but had even served as a goði, a religious office of vague contours in pre-Christian Icelandic society.

Indeed one must wonder what accepting the supremacy of Christ actually meant to a person born into and raised in the pagan world. As shown above, in Oddr's Óláfs saga, the victory of Christ does not cause the utter disappearance or erasure of the other gods. Instead they continue to wander the earth opposing him, much like magicians and trolls, superseded but not entirely displaced by Christ.[144] Thus interpretations of Snorri's remark other than considering it to be a breezy dismissal of the credulous belief in the anger of the gods may be possible. One possibility may be that those present at the Christianization-parliament generally accepted the pre-settlement age of the lava at Þingvellir, its very age making it unlikely that the anger of the gods spurred by human activity is necessarily the only causal explanation for the appearance of lava. The local movement for Christianity being new, Snorri may also be pointing out that, as the lava predates the coming of Christianity to Iceland, the anger of the gods who made it must have been caused by something other than Christ or the adoption of this new faith.

One must also not overlook the practical function of the riposte is to not offer an answer to the question posed but simply to kick the ball into the other court again and to get the heathens entangled in complicated and unconvincing arguments about only tenuously related events. For Snorri's purposes, silencing his opponents, or drawing them into an unrelated argument is enough to ensure his own victory. He may not have been an Enlightenment rationalist, but the Snorri described in this anecdote was indubitably a clever pragmatist and a skilled debater.

Zombies in the Crack

W ITH RESPECT TO THE PREVALENT myth of Snorri goði as a man of reason and even a medieval post-Enlightenment thinker, another famous verbal sally attributed to him might raise certain problems. In *Brennu-Njáls saga*, Snorri becomes secretly embroiled in the battle of the alþingi in 1012, on the side of Ásgrímr Elliða-Grímsson, Gizurr the White, and other magnates determined to gain compensation for the arsonous attack at Bergþórshváll.[145] Snorri attempts to keep the group's primary opponent Flosi and his men from the stronghold at Almannagjá, where they could easily defend themselves from attack. When Flosi and his men arrive in flight, Snorri stands in the way and asks Flosi who is chasing after him. Flosi angrily replies: "Ekki spyrr þú þessa af því, at þú vitir þat eigi. En hvárt veldr þú því, er vér megum eigi sækja til vígis í Almannagjá?" (You do not ask this because you do not know it already, but is it you who is denying us the keep of Almannagjá?). To which Snorri replies: "Eigi veld ek því ... en hitt er satt, at ek veit, hverir valda, ok mun ek segja þér, ef þú vilt, at þeir valda því Þorvaldr kroppin-skeggi ok Kolr" (I am not the cause of this ... but it is true that I know who is the cause of it and I will tell if you want that this is caused by Þorvaldr Croppedbeard and Kolr). The narrator of the saga then identifies these two gentlemen: "Þeir váru þá báðir dauðir ok höfðu verit hin mestu illmenni í liði Flosa" (They were then both dead and had been the most evil men on Flosi's side).[146]

As is often the case in the Sagas of the Icelanders, this "explanation" of the rejoinder fails to explain much to a modern audience.[147] Why does Snorri attribute actions in the battle that are so clearly his to dead men? As Matthías Þórðarson has noted, the identity of the two apparently undead retainers seems to have become blurred in the transmission from the original riposte to the surviving written saga texts.[148] These two men are thus in all probability not two recently dead criminals from Flosi's gang, but were originally two notorious historical figures mentioned in Ari's *Íslendingabók:* Þórðr kroppinskeggi, whose grandson was called Þorvaldr and seems to have inherited both his grandfather's cut of beard and his nefarious nature,[149] and his slain slave Kolr. While Þorvaldr the grandson was guilty of fratricide, his grandfather Þórir had murdered a slave in Bláskógar, in the land that later became the hallowed ground of parliament,[150] and this infamous deed had consequences of great magnitude since it lead to the land becoming available for the general public. The slaying of Kolr thus eventually became a murderous precondition for the sacred role of Þingvellir as the central parliament of Iceland.[151]

In this heated exchange Snorri thus seems to be effectively evoking two renowned ghosts of Þingvellir to explain why Flosi and his men are kept from the sanctuary of the keep.[152] As Matthías Þórðarson has also remarked, it is far from certain why Snorri replies in such a fashion, but he suggests that Snorri's intention is to disassociate himself from direct involvement in the conflict by attributing Flosi's inability to enter this space to the local bogeymen. It is also possible to focus on the potential irony of the answer, and Matthías indeed argues that Snorri would have also wanted Flosi to understand that he and his men are indeed the real cause. Thus Snorri may also be teasing Flosi and goading him to enter upon a learned debate about paranormal activity, which is bound to be fruitless since presumably neither Flosi nor anyone else present can fully explain the nature of ghosts any more than they can explain the origins of lava.[153] In each instance, Snorri is thus taking full advantage of the nervous uncertainty that ordinary humans experience when faced with the unexplained and possibly unexplainable.[154]

The Snorri that emerges from the exchange of words documented in *Brennu-Njáls saga* is not Snorri the great sceptic and rationalist who refers to the laws of nature as we too understand them to silence his opponents, but Snorri the ghostmonger, certainly rational enough in his own way but not shying away from using otherworldly explanations to make his point. While it could be argued that Snorri's words are coldly ironic and that in no way do they reveal his own belief in ghosts — his very use of irony might even be said to demonstrate his own irreverence for the superstitious fears of others — it is nevertheless evident that he finds ghosts useful on occasion to explain his actions and the nature of the world around him.[155] If we can speak of Snorri's particular brand of rationalism, it is one saturated in cynicism.

In fact, it is impossible to know whether the "real" Snorri goði actually believed in ghosts or not or even if it was assumed to be the case in thirteenth-century historical traditions.[156] However, in some way he clearly occasionally used them in causal explanations to win arguments. And, in fact, this joke serves much the same function as did his quip about the lava at Þingvellir: it misdirects and silences his opponents. For this same purpose, Snorri uses ghosts just as well as geology, and by no means does he consequently take the side of science and rationality against the occult and the unexplained.

In evoking undead villains like Þorvaldr and Kolr, Snorri acknowledges a — if not his own — belief in magic. Such legendary trolls as the aforementioned Ögmundr Eyþjófsbani, sorcerer, zombie, and malignant spirit, are magical to the core, with Ögmundr in particular having undergone a magic ritual that "trolls" him and renders him undead. In the theory of miracles, magic is their antithesis, and during the Middle Ages there seems to have been a strong link between magic and all paranormal activity not associated with Christ and his saints.[157] Can magic then explain the zombies at Þingvellir, if not the lava? They are certainly not miraculous.

What angered the gods when the lava at Þingvellir emerged? Why are there zombies in the crack of this hallowed place a decade later? The thirteenth- and fourteenth-century Icelandic authors to whom the sagas are anonymously attributed seem, like Snorri, keen to leave such questions unanswered, having imagined their ancestors sitting firmly on the fence of causality when explaining the paranormal.

Goði as Exorcist

ROM *KRISTNI SAGA* TO *BRENNU-NJÁLS saga*, Snorri goði is easily recognised for his wit and irony as well as his ability to emerge victorious from a verbal exchange by sometimes invoking and sometimes questioning the paranormal. From a modern viewpoint, however, Snorri appears to be somewhat inconsistent in his attitudes towards the paranormal and thus not well suited to the role cast for him by many twentieth-century scholars. In *Eyrbyggja saga*, Snorri again appears within a narrative centred on the paranormal, this time called in as a chieftain who takes full part in fighting the occult forces that haunt the farmstead Fróðá and threaten his region on the Snæfellsnes Peninsula shortly after Christianity has been officially adopted in Iceland.

In this narrative, Snorri does not seem to take the "Fróðá wonders" lightly at all; this time there is no debate that needs to be won and no ironical comments are reported. On the contrary, Snorri contributes his sage advice to an exorcism performed at Fróðá to turn out the demons. Snorri advises both the burning of the bed linens of the late Þórgunna, who was perhaps the cause of all the wonders at Fróðá, and the conducting of a paranormal trial strongly resembling an actual parliament, a sort of exorcism-by-law, the judgement of which the surprisingly law abiding ogres eventually respect. Snorri also provides a priest to perform an exorcism by holy water after all of the demons have apparently left.[158] Thus Snorri's eclectic range of remedies spans the oddly secular to the orthodox, perhaps regarded as complementary rather than rival modes of defense against the dark arts. Here the hegemonic faith and the superstitious stand together in the fight against dark forces, as they so often do, as both the traditional rules of the commonwealth and the new religion work in concert to expel the undead.

Medieval authors may have believed that Snorri goði understood the geological origins of lava but he also seems to believe in ghosts firmly enough to know of the various rituals used to expel them. It is also worth noting that to Christians a belief in the wrath of heathen gods may render one worthy of scorn but that does not mean that Christians did not have their own occult forces to contend with, employing their own tools such as holy water and chanting of the kind which King Óláfr used against the trolls of Hálogaland. Similar methods are employed in the exorcism at Fróðá. In both instances, magic is very real and powerful even if Christianity proves more powerful still and eventually triumphs.

In light of this synthesis of the pagan and Christian it is perhaps interesting to note that Snorri is often referred to with reference to his status as a goði, often glossed simply as "chieftain" or "magnate." The word may also suggest that before Christianity, Icelandic magnates, or at least those serving as goðar, served some kind of important religious function.[159] As implied in several saga narratives,[160] the regional magnates are clearly expected to cleanse their regions of such evil spirits, so presumably that was one of the things expected of a goði, and thus of Snorri, whom we then have to regard as more of a professional exorcist than an amateur enthusiast. Considering this role, Snorri's ironic comment about volcanic fire during the conversion-parliament may not be as modern or rationalistic as its interpretation by contemporary scientists suggests, and a professional exorcist may indeed prove to be a poor example of an exponent of rational scientific thought around the turn of the first millennium.

The audience of *Eyrbyggja saga* may learn what brought an end to the wonders of Fróðá but from the saga they never learn their exact cause or their certain nature. The events are hardly miraculous, and the defensive presence of the exorcist rather suggests they are magical and demonic, as one would expect of hauntings of the undead. And yet these ghosts are strangely passive and neutral, perhaps more wondrous than evil.[161] What Snorri actually thinks of them is never revealed either but only are his remedies explained. Neither does Snorri attempt to speculate about the causes of the alleged zombies at Þingvellir in *Brennu-Njáls saga*, nor, indeed, about the origins of the lava at that hallowed place in *Kristni saga*. Snorri only poses questions, wisely keeping his own counsel, and so too do the sagas' authors. But how could such wonders ever really be defined? Are they miracles or magic or are they wonders precisely because they ultimately defy any clear explanation?

As demonstrated above, the troll is frequently found in darkness, its shadowed appearance fraught with ambiguity. It speaks, has its own point of view, and is intimately alien. However, as the undead are by no means the least significant trolls, the troll might also be intimately human, like us, and yet utterly alien. All these apparent contradictions make difficult demands on any attempt to explain them clearly and when it comes to causal explanations, we enter — or perhaps cannot escape — the same nebulous arena. Illustrious historical figures like Snorri goði often appear in many different sources,[162] reacting in different ways when encountering the paranormal. Sometimes seemingly reasoning like a modern rationalist, Snorri also introduces ghosts to a debate where they had not been present before, and to him exorcism is a serious endeavour. Twentieth-century scholars may have desperately wanted Snorri to think like a modern rational man, but the utter rationalism of medieval saga heroes remains in fact a fairly

irrational scholarly myth, one that would likely be unrec-
ognisable to the sagas' medieval audience.

Troll on Your Doorstep

THE ICELANDIC AUDIENCE OF THE late Middle Ages would inevitably encounter trolls in the highlands; Iceland is assuredly mountainous. However, doorsteps to the paranormal may also be found closer to home, evident, for example, in a troll-story concerning the Icelandic ghost Hrappr who, following a well-known behavioural pattern of zombies, stays within the vicinity of his home, his continued presence tied to material goods left behind, a common trope in ghost stories. The troll is indeed not only at home in the distant wilderness, but is ubiquitous, attached to humans like death is to life. Together forever we go.

Even *Laxdœla saga,* a saga primarily concerned with kings and courts, romance and love, manners and customs, riches and wealth, has its monsters lurking in the shadows. One such monster, Víga-Hrappr Sumarliðason roams around Hrappsstaðir after his death, leading to the desertion of the farm as the undead "deyddi flest hjón sín í aptrgǫngunni" (killed most of his servants in his haunting).[163] When still living Hrappr had told his wife that he wished to be thus buried in the kitchen doorway: "ok skal mik niðr setja standanda þar í durunum; má ek þá enn vendiligar sjá yfir hýbýli mín" (and I am to be interred standing there in the doorway; then I can better watch my house).[164] For Hrappr the doorway clearly serves as a liminal space, his aim perversely not to travel to other worlds but rather to refuse to leave this one, his static ambition strongly connected to an unnatural bond with his house, material goods, and home turf. Hrappr becomes an undead through narrow-minded selfish avarice, his refusal to take leave of his worldly possessions. His savage lust for dead things recalls the legendary Fáfnir who infamously turned himself into a serpent in order to guard his treasure on Gnitaheiði: dragon and undead equally reluctant to leave their worldly possessions behind.[165] The similarities between dragon and undead may be no accident, indeed both are humans fallen into monstrosity, but for the moment it suffices to focus on the latter and some of its characteristic actions.

It is indeed gold and treasure that as often as not keeps spectral watchmen in this world they are supposed to leave; perhaps as an integral and most potent aspect of the ill fate that legends often attach to treasures and great wealth, more powerful even than death itself.[166] In Hrappr's case it is no great hoard that he guards, but rather his land that he refuses to let go of, and which presumably has "sentimental value" to him and only him. This is though the very land on which the regional magnate Óláfr the Peacock later builds the farmstead at Hjarðarholt, where his son Kjartan, the most heroic and courteous figure of *Laxdœla saga*, grows up, excelling in everything but is perhaps still not able to escape Hrappr's ancient devilry in the end.[167]

When the magnate takes over at Hjarðarholt the ghost seems finally to have been overcome, but the audience of *Laxdœla saga* may wonder whether the curse has been lifted completely,[168] since powerful ghosts like Hrappr may not be so easily cleansed.[169] Óláfr's distinguished father, Hǫskuldr Dala-Kollsson, had previously buried Hrappr and moved his corpse to a remote area following which "nemask af heldr aptrgǫngur Hrapps" (Hrappr's hauntings somewhat decreased). However, Hrappr's son "tók ærsl" (became crazy) after living for a short time at Hrappsstaðir, and though the craze goes unexplained, there may be an implication that it was caused by his zombie-father's ghostly visitations.[170]

When much later Óláfr decides to raise his farmstead at Hjarðarholt, precisely where Hrappsstaðir used to be, the land is easy to acquire because of its resident ghost. Soon the place becomes haunted again, evident when one of Óláfr's servants does not want to go alone into the byre since Hrappr stands "í fjósdurunum og vildi falma til mín" (in its doorway, trying to claw at me), as befits a vicious vampire. Ólafr resorts to seeking out Hrappr's cairn, finds out that his corpse is still not rotten, it is *ófúinn*, and burns the undead cadaver, finally obliterating him from the story (or does he?).[171] As his father Hǫskuldr had before him, Óláfr the magnate takes on the role — one of many burdens of greatness — of one tasked with mundifying the land of the kind of evil that Hrappr had embodied.

It is no wonder that ghosts are hard to expel. It is indeed their very nature to refuse to leave this world when their time has come: the most unwanted guest imaginable.[172] Obviously their undead existence is a kind of selfishness, since every human is allotted only a limited time in which to live and has to accept its limits, however painful their annihilation might be. In *Hervarar saga ok Heiðreks* the eponymous Hervǫr tells her father Angantýr: "samir eigi draugum / dýr vápn fela [bera]" (it does not befit ghosts / to carry a fine weapon).[173] The ghost has broken the laws of time and space, which also happen to be economic laws, namely having to do with inheritance, since the dead ought to leave possessions and land behind for their ancestors, but fiercely refuse to do so. In this, one can see a congruity between the relationship ghosts share with the living and that which older generations share with youth, the latter characterised by the older generation's reluctance to allow youth to assume control, bringing to mind issues that generations of humans have had to face with the inevitability of aging.[174]

Many ghost stories found in the medieval Icelandic sagas concern either vampires or spectral watchmen like Hrappr. The vampire troll, a potentiality which exists in all undead, merits further discussion but first it may be useful to examine the watchers, ghosts who remain undead in order to watch over and protect the assets they refuse to relinquish wholly. Usually dominating only a small area that they have made their own, these fiends can still be very aggressive, albeit less infectious than those parasitic vampires, incubi, or mares whose main objective for walking the earth seems to be to attack the living, drive them out of their wits, and infect them with vampirism. The latter being an excellent metaphor for the viruses unknown to medieval man or those diseases, known if still remaining nameless for centuries, which may cause the disintegration of the human body from within.[175]

In such medieval Icelandic narratives, the watcher is often found in his mound, guarding a great treasure he cannot leave or allow the living to enjoy. This kind of greed is a *raison d'être* for every spectral enemy: they will not give up their territory or property and refuse to let the living take their place. This selfish denial of the natural order is characteristic of the undead troll, its negation of the laws of nature the very attribute which makes it demonic, along with the magic powers it possesses to wreck, maim, and murder.

The mound may be protected by witchcraft or fire, and entering it, even being in its proximity, can be extremely hazardous. These watchers normally do not harass the living outside of the mound and its vicinity, preferring to remain defensively huddled until the tranquility of their grave is disturbed by some heroic figure that has made a sacred vow, seeking to gain honour from the courageous act no less than enjoying the treasures to be recovered from inside the mound. Inside, the ghost in the mound will defend his turf zealously, even killing those who approach before they enter with the gust and stink that wafts in its vacinity. The lethal odour which characterizes the watcher is a characteristic feature of the demonic other, an unmistakeable mark of hell or the netherworlds, clearly indicating to the audience that such occult enemies might originate from there. The infamous Glámr, for example, who eventually became Grettir the strong's enduring nemesis is said to be "gustillr" (foul of breath) just before meeting his end as a human, his essentially demonic nature revealing itself at the precipice.

In mound-breaking narratives, undead warriors discovered inside their mounds may also be a horrible sight to behold. They attack and fight the hero and even curse him before typically succumbing to his greater physical prowess or the paranormal aid he receives from certain holy helpers. There are some methods to permanently expel such figures; one is to cut off the creature's head and to place it near its derrière. The affiliation shared between hell and the buttocks, the rear end often considered to be the demonic "other face" of anthropomorphic others, is, along with the terrible stench that is also often associated with the aforementioned lower passage (see "Trollspeak"), one of the most enduring metaphors for the demonic.[176]

The use of the word troll in referring to these ghostly figures reveals the same thing as the stench so often mentioned in mound-breaking narratives, which is that an ordinary person cannot have an afterlife without demonic forces at play, and in the troll, ghosts and magic are united. Behind the ghost, devilry must be at work and the terrible stench betrays clearly its machinations, telling a story that language alone is unable to relate.

Never Forget

BEFORE BURNING VÍGA-HRAPPR'S BODY AND, as far as that is possible, terminating his hauntings, Óláfr the Peacock had met the zombie in the doorway of his own byre. Óláfr had then launched a spear at Víga-Hrappr and tried to grapple with him, demonstrating through his actions that a true magnate fears nothing. As noted above, nefarious spirits are closely allied with fear and are thus partially incapacitated by a simple show of courage. Óláfr is fully awake during this encounter but much later he experiences a mostly unrelated paranormal encounter during a bout of sleep, shortly after having had the eighteen-year-old ox Harri butchered. The ox had had remarkable talents and these may have been no accident, since after the animal's death Óláfr dreams of a large and angry woman appearing before him. She tells him that he has ensanguined her son and that she will react in kind, choosing his favourite son in returning the favour. When Óláfr awakens, he feels that he still briefly sees the woman, and he "þótti mikils um vert drauminn ok segir vinum sínum ok varð ekki ráðinn svá at honum líki. Þeir þóttu honum bezt um tala er þat mæltu at þat væri draumskrǫk er fyrir hann hafði borit" (was impressed by the dream and tells his friends and none could decipher it to his liking. He liked those best who said it was a false dream that he had experienced).[177] Denial is always an attractive solution to any problem, but it may prove futile in this case.

Paranormal encounters in dreams and sleep are a subject in their own right and, as my aim here is not to map all paranormal motifs found in medieval Icelandic texts, the generally liminal nature of sleep will only be noted here and not analysed further.[178] However, the dream woman's emphasis on reciprocity is worth pondering since this is an attribute common to paranormal encounters described in the sagas and one of those features that indeed posit paranormal figures as human doubles. The troll you meet in a cave or in your slumber will indeed act as a mirror, whether it is successfully trying to magnify your fears or simply coldly informing you that unyielding relentless payment is due for all of the mischief one commits in life. The troll is relentless. It never forgets or forgives, calculating your crimes with mathematical precision and, then, callously collecting any outstanding debts. Óláfr the Peacock, as sage as he is benevolent, knows this already — what else do we dream than that which we already know? — but the unnamed woman hammers the message home that there will be blood. It is a mathematical certainty.[179]

Long before the age of unsmiling functionaries gathering their strength from relentless computers who tend to "say no" at the most importune and punishing moments,[180] the same hardcore ruthlessness was embodied in paranormal others. They often also, however, brought the same unimaginative, mathematical precision to the aid of those fortunate humans who had somehow managed to acquire a store of good karma.[181] The well-known folktale AT 156, famous in the Aulus Gellius's version *Androcles and the Lion*, highlights the commonly benevolent aspect of this unflinching law. As the apparition of the late or possibly undead legendary heroine Guðrún Gjúkadóttir, visiting the teenager Jóreiðr in her dreams in *Sturlunga saga*, remarks, she is a friend to her friends.[182] Similarly, many indigenous Icelandic romances contain narratives in which the hero acquires a paranormal helper through a good deed.[183] In sagas taking place in Iceland, however, this phenomenon is rare,[184] the humans here having rather to soldier on as the otherworld offers mostly hostility and danger. As Þórðr's fate in *Bergbúa þáttr* indicates, however, survival in the face of the paranormal is possible, both through strength of mind and strength of rituals, and, possibly, through some kind of truce with the paranormal threat, which in his case involved memorising and disseminating its verse.

Whether benevolent or hostile, these occult forces are mostly characterised by elephantine memory and a blind adherence to the laws of reciprocity. They are blind and deaf to excuses as well; no extenuating circumstances are possible. The audience knows, and sees the injustice in this. Óláfr, for example, had meant no harm in slaughtering his ox, and the entitled magnate whose life has been characterised by wealth and success can hardly believe he has been singled out to be damned for it, eagerly seeking denial from every quarter. Yet the paranormal has already reared its ugly head as an unforgiving and unflinching *memento mori*. Blood has been spilled and the dream woman will extract her own pound of flesh, caring naught for the quality of mercy.

The dream woman inside Óláfr the Peacock's subconsciousness who refuses to forgive or forget is perhaps so relentless precisely because she is inside his head, a creature born of his unresolved guilt.[185] In this instance, not uniquely, the human mind is far more merciless to its own possessor than any alien creature ever could be.

Whether this lack of forgiveness, presented more as an irrefutable natural law than an act of will, is seen as pagan or un-Christian is not clearly specified in the text. Such dream women stand outside of the official religion, still not official in Iceland when the encounter is purported to have taken place (close to 970), but the half-Irish and widely travelled Óláfr would certainly have been exposed to it. Throughout the story Óláfr never expresses any doubts about the powers of the dark forces he encounters but, as already evident in his struggle with the ghost Hrappr and in more examples that follow below, he actively opposes them on numerous occasions, fulfilling his role at the apex of the civilised world.

The mnemonic function of the paranormal other may be linked to its seemingly fundamental identification with the past, a thread which will be pursued at greater length below. Another fundamental thread evident here is the emphasis on the callow of this scene. The dream-woman's "son," the butchered ox, represents youth, as does also the son of the magnate the dream woman intends to collect in compensation for her own loss. The vulnerability of confident, unsuspecting youth, carefree and liberated from the timidity of the old, is indeed an important theme in some of the most memorable paranormal encounters found in the sagas.

The Confidence of Youth

THROUGH A DREAM, ÓLÁFR THE Peacock's night visitor claims from him flesh and blood, not to be extracted from his own body but rather figured as the loss of his young son Kjartan. The theme of threatened youngsters is a common international trope, with royal and noble children at particular risk due to their special status.[186] The fourteenth-century versions of the aforementioned *Óláfs saga Tryggvasonar* (see "Trollspeak") contain, for example, a brief tale in which the spilled blood of youth is the main theme.[187] Set during the turbulent Christianisation of Iceland, the main protagonists of this tale are Síðu-Hallr, then living at Hof (Temple) in Álptafjǫrðr, who was enlisted as the lawspeaker of the Christians during the same parliamentary assembly at which Snorri goði managed to become famous for his wit, and his son Þiðrandi who is an ideal youth, said to be "manna vænstr ok efniligastr" (a handsome and promising man) and "inn vinsælasti hvar sem hann kom, því at hann var inn mesti atgervimaðr, lítillátr ok blíðr við hvert barn" (very popular wherever he came on account of his accomplishments, modest and kind towards every human being).[188] Everyone admires Þiðrandi and that fact alone seems to seal his fate, as it makes him the perfect ritual sacrifice to those dark pagan forces wanting a final emolument from their human friends who have begun to abandon them.

Þiðrandi's good manners are indeed the direct cause of his downfall. Someone (or something) knocks on the doors at Hof during the night following a splendid party. Hallr instructs that no one answer the door, but Þiðrandi, a virtuous and well governed youth though he is, still carries within him some seeds of teenage rebellion, and jumps up from his bed, remarking that it is shameful to ignore guests who may be in need, and, clearly not necessarily expecting friends only, goes out into the night with his sword raised. There he is attacked by nine sword-carrying women dressed in black, though nine women in white are also said to be close by. These women are later said to be "dísir" and "fylgjur" by a neighbouring prophet, figures previously worshipped by the family who have taken it upon themselves to murder Þiðrandi as a final sacrifice, presumably to make up for all the lost future ritual offerings that they feel cheated out of by the Temple-family's conversion to Christianity.

As already mentioned, medieval words used to describe the paranormal do not necessarily refer to specific or discrete kinds of beings and "dísir" (presumably related to Lat. *deus, dīs* in the gen. and abl. plur.) is another fairly broad term, possibly denoting any kind of female power(s) deemed worthy of a cult,[189] while "fylgjur" may more specifically refer to the relationship that certain paranormal beings share with human individuals or families. The Þiðrandi-narrative somewhat uniquely depicts the "fylgjur" as "konur" whereas in other sagas, their shape is either not specified or they take the shape of different kinds of animals.[190] There is no contradiction, though, if instead of regarding "fylgjur" as only particular kinds of paranormal figures, the word is considered to refer to their function, their intrinsic entanglement with a certain person or family, in this case the family of Síðu-Hallr. And, while some readers might inevitably think of Valkyries when visualising these lethal women, there is no explicit mention of such figures, and if the impulse to taxonomise is controlled, there is no need to bring them into the picture, except to acknowledge that armed and dangerous women on horseback appear in various contexts in medieval Norse literature.

The narrative implies that the "fylgjur" claim Þiðrandi precisely because he is an accomplished and chivalric youth, buoyant, handsome, and polite. He is the very essence of modernity as it was imagined by the saga authors of the mid- to late-thirteenth century, much influenced by romance literature, regarding the commonwealth as old and stagnant and the king and his court as the epitome of the modern world.[191] Þiðrandi is a perfect knight, a young man excelling in looks and manners who, even more importantly, is already widely travelled and popular wherever he goes. He embodies modernity, which must be hateful to the heathen spirits originating and stagnating in the past. It must also be acknowledged, though, that there may also be an element of desire in the fear and loathing such spirits exhibit, particularly in this case given that it is precisely Þiðrandi they want as a final offering in the termination of the family relationship. Hallr's last unwilling sacrifice is a proper sacrifice in that he gives up precisely the son whose future was brightest and most befitting the new age. There can be no doubt that the loss, and the sacrifice, is greater still because of Þiðrandi's youth. Youth is the greatest of all assets, the greatest power, the most precious, fragile, and fleeting thing anyone can possess.

Being the son of a magnate, born of privilege, and well on the path to success, Þiðrandi is hardly unimportant or anonymous. These particular attributes make him a particularly alluring and sweet sacrificial lamb. However, youth as a more general attribute, possessed at some point by more or less everyone, may be, for the dark forces he encounters, Þiðrandi's most desirable quality, and consequently the ultimate source of his vulnerability. Healthy, invincible, strong, and fearless youths, idealised in myths of dragonslayers such as Sigurðr who knew no fear,[192] may not only attract healthy or reverential attention but also its opposite: jealousy, envy, and undesirable obsession. Just as the fire escape that ensures your route to safety and thus enhances your security can also be a way for intruders to reach your third floor apartment, thus posing also a security risk, the attractive person cannot control whom or what kind of attention they might attract. The greatest asset and strength of the flawless can paradoxically prove to be a hidden flaw and also their greatest weakness. Beauty is triumphant and yet vulnerable.

Although it may also be a social accident, the first victim of any troll haunting is indeed often a youth.[193] As anyone who has read an Icelandic ghost story will tell you, young shepherds are particularly vulnerable to zombie attacks. Snorri goði's old adversary and occasional ally, Þórólfr twistfoot's first human victim upon his return from death is a "smalamaðr" (shepherd), first pursued by the troll and then found blue and dead in the vicinity of his presumed killer's grave with every bone in his body broken. Following the oxen who had become "trollriða" (trollridden) and the birds who fall dead to the ground in the vicinity of the grave, the youth who minds the sheep seems a natural subsequent prey of the vampire.[194] Usually anonymous in these narratives, the audience is not particularly invited to empathise with the shepherd. His is a menial task reserved for the unskilled, and he is thus by necessity beneath the imagined audience, as are the anonymous people of the sagas more generally: farmhands, maids, and messengers.[195]

The Sagas of Icelanders are not fairytales and, as a rule, underprivileged youths never turn into princes unless their blood demands it to be so. Their vulnerability may still be no accident. The Icelandic zombie may not have a particular lust for young blood and yet this paranormal danger seeks out the boys who mind the sheep, alone in the night, their callow youth possibly making them particularly easy prey.[196]

Coda: The Katanes Beast

The haunting of youths may prove an epidemic phenomenon and not just in medieval narratives. Echoing the old sagas and early folktales of Iceland, an egregious paranormal encounter took place much later in Katanes in Iceland during the summer of 1874, the very summer a king visited Iceland for the first time and brought its people a new constitution. There is a big pond on Katanes and suddenly an animal or monster is sighted there, mainly by youths. This animal was the size of a big dog but the tales of youths, stigmatised as mischievous and rebellious on account of their age, are easily ignored and disbelieved. The next summer, however, more people began to see the animal which by now had grown, and in 1876, the older generation begin to bear witness to the animal as well, now as big as a bull of three winters, its mouth enormous, its claws dangerous.

The shepherds, presumably the same teenage lads who originally saw the monster, refuse to tend their sheep at night and in the end Hilmar Finsen himself, the governor of Iceland, is called in to help. After more attacks, a man with a gun is hired and anticipation is rife, but promptly punctured by an anticlimax, as the strange beast now vanishes, never to be seen again in Katanes or anywhere else. The strange case comes to a close with a somewhat mundane legal proceeding concerning the rifleman's fee, proving that neighbourly rivalries over small amounts of cash may be just as potent and enduring a force in the world as its terrible ogres. The beast itself was never seen again.

With growing frenzy in the region, the tales of the beast suddenly shifted from the margins of society to the centre, in fact it is soon all but forgotten that they even originated in the accounts of the youths. But one wonders if the shepherds of Iceland were, near the cusp of the country's leap into the modern world, finally taking their revenge on the zombies of Iceland by making the last prominent troll appear and then disappear for all time. Monsters swallow teenagers, but perhaps teenagers also regurgitate monsters. One may wonder to what extent all disturbances in the force may be intertwined with the socially disruptive youngsters who tend to be the first suspects, victims, and witnesses when strange beasts begin to rear their ugly heads.

Not only do the origins of these beasts remain uncertain, their eventual fate is also tenebrous. However, the disappearance of such beasts may bring no true relief: their powers residing in their uncertain nature and their disappearance meaning only that they remain forever unexplained, leaving behind a far more potent mystery, and the lingering possibility of a perhaps unexpected and devastating return.

Popular

THE VULNERABILITY OF YOUTH, THE perversity of magic and its strong connection to erotic desire are all played out in a narrative found in *Eyrbyggja saga*,[197] a saga — as mentioned above — much concerned with the advent of Christianity and the heathen past with its sorcerous "forneskja" and its rituals, both open and clandestine. Indeed the clash between public and respectable ancient lore and clandestine nefarious magic lies at the heart of an episode found in the early part in the saga (chs. 15 to 20). On the one hand there is Geirríðr in Mávahlíð, daughter of Þórólfr twistfoot, later a notorious vampire,[198] mother of the quiet and placid Þórarinn, and sister of the popular chieftain Arnkell, who is upon introduction said to be "margkunnig" (wise in lore).[199] On the other hand is her neighbour, a widow called Katla, beautiful but unpopular, at least according to the saga, and her son Oddr is described as loud and talkative, a troublemaker and a slanderer.

The ancient wisdom is there to be harnessed, but it takes a youth to upset it. Conflict arises between these two women when Gunnlaugr Þorbjarnarson, the nephew of Snorri goði, begins to pay frequent visits to Geirríðr. This young man is "námgjarn" (eager to study) and in fact studies magic under Geirríðr.[200] Katla is not pleased and once, when Gunnlaugr pays her a visit on his way to Mávahlíð, she remarks that more women may know a thing or two than Geirríðr. Katla insists that Gunnlaugr stay the night, but he continually refuses. Then, one evening, Geirríðr asks Gunnlaugr to stay with her, and seems to sense mares in the air ("margir eru marlíðendur"), cryptically adding that fair is foul and foul is fair.[201] She also remarks that Gunnlaugr does not seem very lucky at this moment. Such a portent is rarely innocent or proven unfounded in the sagas, and indeed, later that night, Gunnlaugr is found witless and bloody, his flesh torn from his bones. Katla and Oddr are quick to point the finger at Geirríðr and call her a succuba. Gunnlaugr's foolish father then accuses Geirríðr of being a "kveldriða" (night hag) and is aided in seeking legal redress by the ubiquitous Snorri goði. However, Arnkell and other chieftains are allowed to and do swear an oath on Geirríðr's behalf.

After a brief respite, the strife between Þorbjǫrn and Geirríðr's son Þórarinn escalates and ultimately results in battle. Oddr Kǫtluson cannot be hurt since his mother has made him an impregnable tunic, a token that Katla's boast that she too knows a thing or two was not an idle one. Geirríðr has also played her part in the conflict, inciting Þórarinn by calling his placid disposition unmanly.[202] When Oddr begins to brag about having hewn off the hand of Þórarinn's wife,[203] after previously claiming that Þórarinn had done it himself by accident, Geirríðr seizes her chance and informs Þórarinn and Arnkell, guiding their wrath towards Oddr and Katla.[204]

The two magnates seek Oddr at Katla's abode, but she hides her son from them using illusions.[205] It is not until Geirríðr herself joins in the search that Oddr is found. When Katla sees her rival, she remarks that now "Geirríðr trollit" ("Geirríðr the troll") has arrived, knowing illusions will no longer suffice, rather labelling her rival a "troll" and making full use of the fear and loathing connected to the word. Geirríðr arrives in her black cloak, walks straight towards Katla and pulls a sealskin bag that she has fortuitously brought with her over her rival's head, thus implying that there is a risk of Katla using her eyes to perform evil magic.[206]

Oddr is now found and promptly hanged, one male youth slain in compensation for another. Katla herself is stoned to death, but before her execution, she proudly admits to having caused Gunnlaugr's injuries. Furthermore she curses Arnkell for having remarked to Oddr, when the latter was about to swing from the gallows, that he had an evil mother. She claims that Arnkell will indeed get worse from his father than Oddr from her, which indeed comes to pass much later in the saga. Thus the episode carries heavy repercussions in the greater scheme of the saga. The primary protagonists in the drama of Gunnlaugr's studies of the occult are, however, never mentioned again. The audience is not even told whether or not Gunnlaugr survived the ordeal,[207] Geirríðr vanishes from the story, and the wicked Katla, unlike some other demonic figures of *Eyrbyggja saga*, remains dead.

In this episode, good and bad lore are presented as fundamental opposites, with Geirríðr's wisdom, on the one hand, pitted against Katla's witchcraft on the other. The primordial character of these actors is somewhat suggested by their symbolic names, Katla's bringing to mind a magician's cauldron and Geirríðr's name indicating that she is indeed a "rider," a transubstantiate being that may also be called a "fylgja," "hamhleypa" or be grouped with "marlíðendr," "kveldriður," "myrkriður" and "túnriður": hags, shapeshifters or peripatetic minds of sorcerers and witches.[208] Their affinity with ghosts and the undead is unequivocal, and the attack on Gunnlaugr smacks of the actions of vampires and succubi. In spite of her suggestive name, though, it is not Geirríðr who acts the vampire but rather Katla who may, like a modern TV villain, even have committed the crime with the primary intention of framing her rival.

The method by which Geirríðr is vindicated is also highly relevant to the dichotomy the two women seem to represent. It is revealed early on that Katla is unpopular ("eigi við alþýðuskap"). On the other hand, it soon becomes evident that Geirríðr is very popular among those who count. Twelve men of good standing swear that she is innocent of the crime she is accused of, and thus the case against her is abruptly quashed.[209] This was a well-known method to dispel witchcraft accusations for centuries, meaning that unpopular people were more likely to be accused of sorcery and, consequently, convicted and executed for the crime.

The nature of one's relationship with the netherworld may thus descend into a popularity contest in which one is judged according to their relationship with the upper class. A woman with important family connections knows and makes use of "ancient lore" whereas the woman with no such connections, who is also possibly foreign, is a sorceress, a practicioneer of rather "dark arts." A witch with important relatives may emerge unscathed from serious charges, even if opposed by the wily Snorri goði, whereas the witch with no noteworthy family hardly merits a trial at all, and is, as it were, already condemned by her own unpopularity. Witchcraft, like so much else, ends up being a question of upbringing.

Cultural Hegemony

T FIRST GLANCE, THERE MAY seem to be an eerie randomness about the fate of the two competing witches, but on closer inspection the outcome of their conflict is the inevitable result of a social system that is piercingly consistent. Magic and the lower class function in close harmony whereas even magnates and priests are allowed to possess a respectable talent for seeing into the future without any of the accompanying social stigma. The lack of trappings contributes to their respectability. A sinister witch, like Svanr, who appears in *Njáls saga,* may wave the hide of a goat to cause a cloud of fog,[210] but the famous Gestr Oddleifsson has premonitions instead, and, in the same way modern day scientists interpret the evidence before them, he is able to soberly decipher dreams without being specific about any involvement of the unearthly: he simply possesses the skill of knowing the future.

Unlike Geirríðr, who in spite of her excellent family connections is still vulnerable to accusations of witchcraft, Gestr Oddleifsson is simply, without qualification or mention of magic rituals, "inn spaki," a wise man, "spekingr at viti, framsýnn um marga hluti" (a sage who could foretell many things). Owing to the lack of dramatic performance of his talents, intertwined with his social connections, Gestr is never portrayed as one flirting with the occult or in a sinister light. His skills are never explained, but there is clearly nothing dark about them.[211] Gestr is a good Christian following the conversion and is on good terms with all magnates. Hence his gifts are beneficial to society at large, and he is, in fact, the very last person who might get branded a troll, despite even his exceedingly special talents.

The good of society is the ultimate yardstick. An elderly wise man that has premonitions has nothing in common with a witch who during the night preys on noble youths. The dichotomy between the real and unreal is important to modern scholars, but in the texts themselves the binary between benevolent and hostile is more plainly fundamental. Gestr's gifts are never used against others; that is why they cannot have anything to do with magic. When it comes to Geirríðr, the issue is for society to determine if her knowledge of ancient lore is harmful or not; if it is neither hostile nor anti-social then it cannot be magic.

The same applies to the eponymous hero of *Njáls saga* who is presented more or less as the Gestr Oddleifsson of Southern Iceland. Njáll of Bergþórshváll is characterised not only by his foresight and gift for premonitions but also by his good will ("heilráðr ok góðgjarn"), alluded to on more than one occasion in the saga.[212] Even though, unlike Gestr, Njáll has certain adversaries who call his powers into question, he is never accused of witchcraft or sorcery. However, his manliness is notably challenged repeatedly in the saga, which may owe something to the well-known connection between magic and the feminine, discussed at greater length below. The people who do this are presented as vile and detestable and are indeed scorned by all the magnates appearing in the saga, who as a rule are all noble and benevolent. There is certainly a fantastical element in *Njáls saga*, manifested not so much in the many occult occurrences described in the narrative, but rather in Njáll's invincibility. Throughout the story, he is revered by society at large and by all of the respectable members of the community. Even though his sons take an active part in many disputes and brawls, Njáll himself remains above all violence, and before the tragic slaying of his foster-son Hǫskuldr, an attack on Bergþórshváll itself is never even a possibility. Even when tragedy does strike, it is not directed at Njáll himself, and he is indeed offered immunity from it.

This most famous of sagas seems to turn saga-logic — including the place of magic — on its head,[213] not least in the portrayal of its eponymous hero. Small, beardless, and feminine, of relatively insignificant birth,[214] lacking a *goðorð*, advisor to a hero constantly under attack, and father to sons involved in several killings, Njáll remains unassailable through it all and enjoys the universal adoration of all of the respectable men of the community. Apparently the reason for this is his immense legal acumen and his benevolence. But to what extent does this reflect actual social practice? Is this the real life or is this just fantasy? How can we believe in the impregnable status of this palpable outsider?

What the saga narrative demonstrates here is the importance of cultural hegemony. Njáll has power, the power of *Grágás*,[215] and that means that he is a public intellectual rather than a magician. His social standing is far too superior — in the social hierarchy presented in the saga he is equal to such notables as Skapti the lawspeaker and the noble Christian magnate Síðu-Hallr — and that means that nothing he does could possibly be interpreted as magic, accompanied with its nefarious connotations. Sorcery simply does not happen at the summit of social distinction where Njáll safely resides.

Immigrant Song

DESPITE THESE ESTEEMED AND NOBLE men, it must be said that the witch Katla from *Eyrbyggja saga* is not the only unpopular occult practitioner found in the sagas. In *Laxdœla saga*, for example, Óláfr the Peacock and other shining representatives of civilization and of light also have to contend with an immigrant family from the Hebrides comprised of Kotkell, Gríma, and their two sons, Hallbjǫrn slíkisteinsauga and Stígandi. Few words are minced in their introduction in Ch. 35 of the saga: "Ǫll váru þau mjǫk fjǫlkunnig ok inir mestu seiðmenn" (they were all very sorcerous and the greatest shamans).[216] Consequently, their region is "ekki vinsæl" (not popular), a prime example of Old Icelandic understatement. They find a protector though in the equally unpopular Hallsteinn goði who uses them as any unscrupulous magnate might use the scum of the earth, as thugs to make miserable the lives of those who stand in his way.

One of their victims is Ingunn, mother-in-law of Guðrún Ósvífrsdóttir, whose son Þórðr refuses to suffer in silence and seeks out Kotkell and his wife, threatening them with lawsuits. Their answer is witching: "Síðan lét Kotkell gera seiðhjall mikinn; þau fœrðusk þar á upp ǫll; þau kváðu þar harðsnúin frœði; þat váru galdrar. Því næst laust á hríð mikilli" (Then Kotkell had a platform of sorcery erected where they all posted themselves. They recited ponderous lore there, which were charms. Then a storm broke out).[217] This paranormal tempest descends upon the seafaring Þórðr and his companions at the worst possible time, and in spite of Þórðr's fortitude in the face of the turbulent waves, they all drown.

The patronage of Hallsteinn momentarily saves his Hebridean henchmen from execution, but they are expelled from the county to seek abode with Þorleikr, Óláfr the Peacock's brother. This arrogant and foolish magnate takes them in and another, new region now becomes tainted by their magic and unpopularity. Þorleikr soon falls into temptation in employing Kotkell and his rabble to wreak revenge on his own adversary Hrútr. They again conjure up a "seiðr" which is not described in explicit detail, although there are suggestions of noise emitted in the words "seiðlæti" (magic racket), which may sound to the innocents like something of a siren song ("fǫgur kveðandi," fair chanting).[218]

With their sorcery they manage to kill yet another impetuous youth, twelve-year-old Kári, the son of Hrútr, who becomes restless and must venture outside in spite of his father's warnings. This time, however, no mercy is shown to the malefactors. The aged Hrútr, now grieving for his dead son, seeks out Óláfr the Peacock, renowned disciplinarian, ghostbuster, and man of action, and the latter characteristically wastes little time. The witches attempt to flee, but Kotkell and Gríma are soon caught and stoned to death, their grave thenceforth known as Skrattavarði (demons' cairn). Hallbjǫrn is forcefully drowned, but not before he is able to curse Þorleikr. He also later appears after his death, following the natural progression from witch (troll) into undead (troll). Stígandi evades capture for a while but he, too, is later caught with the help of a female shepherd. He is then pelted to death, but not before he lays waste a beautiful grassy spot on the hillside with his evil eye.

The wickedness of these aliens is unmitigated. Even though they are not specifically referred to as trolls, indeed the word hardly appears in Laxdœla saga,[219] the swift justice meted out to them by Óláfr clearly marks them as otherworldly beings whose persecution requires no trial, and they are expectedly and promptly exterminated like common vermin. There is no doubt that their treatment is partly explained by their status as immigrants. Arriving from the Hebrides, Kotkell and his kin lack any family connections of note in Iceland. However, their cruel fate can only partially be explained by xenophobia. Óláfr himself claims descent from Irish kings, proud of being an "ambáttarsonr" (son of a slave) when he woos and wins his wife Þorgerðr Egilsdóttir.[220] But assuredly the audience of this saga is not encouraged to draw any parallel between his noble Irish blood and the Hebridean trailer trash he is now forced to cleanse Iceland of in order to fulfill his duty as a magnate. Óláfr's foreign lineage serves as a mark of his distinction whereas they remain the lowest of the low, people with no genealogy worthy of mention.

The notorious fiend Glámr is similarly alien hailing from Sweden, which, though some have thought so, may not be all that revealing about general attitudes towards Swedes in medieval Iceland.[221] It assuredly means though that he, too, is an individual without any lineage or possessions in Iceland, in short a person of little repute whose eventual demonic fate may be a natural consequence of his inherent outsider status, as the alien to Iceland inevitably becomes an alien of Iceland.

Oedipal Conflict

THE AFOREMENTIONED FEUD BETWEEN THE two aged witches in *Eyrbyggja saga* cannot be considered only a class conflict, but must also be regarded as a family affair; indeed, how often are the two not intertwined? The conflict begins and ends in desire. The sorceresses' apprentice is at the heart of the conflict between the two mature ladies, Geirríðr and Katla, and yet he acts out a strangely passive role. The attractive and vulnerable youngster Gunnlaugr is a mere object that the two wise women desire, as becomes evident in the exchange when he stops over at Katla's place on his way to Geirríðr's. She asks whether he is going to Mávahlíð to "klappa um kerlingarnárann" (stroke the biddy's groin), revealing that whether or not Gunnlaugr is actually providing Geirríðr with sexual favours in exchange for her teachings, Katla attributes Geirríðr's interest in him to lust, revealing also that she is herself similarly inclined. He retorts that Katla is no younger than Geirríðr; this is indeed a conflict of age and gender as well, where the old women possess knowledge and power and the young man is the object of desire, not merely as a desirable male youth but also as an eager student of magic.

The carnal aspect of the master and student relationship is a well-known trope even in our age, usually with an older man and a younger woman filling these roles, respectively. In *Eyrbyggja saga*, the situation is, however, reversed. It is here the women who possess the desired knowledge and the young man his youth and sex appeal.[222] But he is reluctant to accommodate the women, not only repeatedly

refusing to spend the night in Katla's home, but his undoing is his subsequent refusal, possibly provoked by an unease originating in Katla's insinuations, to spend the night
at Mávahlíð when Geirríðr invites him to stay there.

When attacked and "ridden," Gunnlaugr is no longer
merely an object but has become prey; he is victimized
and thus exemplifies the vulnerability of youth. Somewhat paradoxically, as the desired male, he also retains all
of the power, including the power to refuse both women
his nightly favours and to choose his own instructor in the
occult. Also, somewhat in the typical fashion of teenagers,
both Old Norse and modern, he demonstrates no fear of either woman, perhaps unwisely and to his own peril.[223]

Gunnlaugr is more than just a conquest, though, being
also a potential heir to both women. Both desire him as a
pupil, as a surrogate son to the two older women who, inci-
dentally, are each introduced along with their own biological sons in ch. 15 of *Eyrbyggja saga*. If we were to regard this
symbolic episode as a "family drama," it concerns maternal as well as prurient longings, although Gunnlaugr's biological mother does not appear in this episode even though
she, Þuríðr at Fróðá who is later indirectly responsible for
the Fróðá wonders and thus paved the way for Snorri goði
to act as an exorcist, is one of the central figures of the subsequent narrative.[224]

Considering the reputation that seems to follow those
who practice *seiðr,* which will be returned to below,[225] and
the close connection shared between magic and the female
gender, Gunnlaugr's interest in the occult, in queer practices, may seem slightly subversive. The eponymous Bósi
of *Bósa saga* indeed rejected magical instruction from his
nanny Busla stating that he would rather progress in the
world through his "karlmennska" (manliness),[226] which
would have apparently been undermined by his studying
magic. Why, then, would a young man from a good family
wish to learn witchcraft? Gunnlaugr may not necessarily
long for a career in sorcery, though he does demonstrate a

desire for theurgic knowledge. His motives are left unexplained, his eagerness to learn unexplored.

This dramatisation of the witch as mother highlights the witch's uncanny nature: something "familiar and old-established in the mind and which has become alienated from it."[227] On the one hand, as mother, she represents the pinnacle of familiarity, as what could possibly be more familiar than the source from which we all emerged? On the other, as witch, she epitomizes the improper and the occult.[228] The word "forneskja," already encountered above, encapsulates a similar uncanny binary: the past should be familiar, more so than the future, since it has already happened and is known, whereas the future always remains unknown (hence our eagerness to know it). And yet, the past remains uncanny, as it is in the very passing of the past that the doom of the future lay, that same judgment which makes dead people frightening, especially the ghosts of those we thought we knew, of whom we have several examples in *Eyrbyggja saga* — Geirríðr's zombie father being but one. Death is uncanny but so are fathers and mothers in that they symbolize the past and birth, and at the same time they symbolize progress and eventually death.[229]

The two wise women appearing in this episode represent the uncanny face of the mother, her intimate alterity, the mother as a representative of ancient lore, of danger, of death. And yet Geirríðr and Katla present two vastly different faces of death. Geirríðr's name suggests a Valkyrie, a noble creature who serves the gods and brings dead men to Valhǫll. And still, even noble death on the battle-field is frightening in its unfamiliarity to the living — skaldic poetry about death in battle on the whole being less preoccupied with the joyous afterlife in Valhǫll than carcasses, corpses, and, especially, the scavengers that feast on the lifeless bodies left behind on the battlefield.[230] Katla is less ambivalent and more frightening. She represents the mother as a forbidden figure of lust, she who invites the youngster to her bed, but whose flirtations mask a grave

THE TROLL INSIDE YOU

danger, as what she really wishes to do is to ride him until death is upon him. This siren is also a vampire, a mare.

It is difficult to ignore the idea that the ambiguity of the witch mother in the sagas echoes the giant mothers found in *Snorra-Edda.* The giant is generally also an uncanny figure, both antagonist and ancestor to the gods. Even counted amongst the Æsir are several giant women, such as Skaði and Gerðr. According to *Snorra-Edda,* the high god Óðinn's mother was indeed a giant, Bestla Bǫlþornsdóttir.[231] He is not said to have studied magic with her, but may have had a surrogate mother as a teacher of ancient knowledge in the sibyl (perhaps also a giantess) who is the narrator of *Vǫluspá.*[232] There are Odinic echoes in Gunnlaugr's quest for sorcerous knowledge, gained from something like a giant mother in the neighbourhood, and it may be his undoing that there happen to be two such figures in the vicinity, one good and one bad. Together they form something of a unit not unlike the figure of the Old Norse giant, compelling in its contradictions: old, powerful, helpful, dangerous, wise, wild, ambiguous, and ultimately uncanny.

When the giant mother is divided into two representatives in the flesh, one is good and the other bad. But if Geirríðr and Katla are two faces of the same figure, is the symbolic figure that they each represent, the witch mother, is she good or bad? Perhaps not so easily understood, she is uncanny, and it is notoriously difficult to state anything about the uncanny, otherwise it would not be so. If Gunnlaugr had not failed, had not been ridden, his story might have become one to be imitated: how to succeed in witchcraft without nearly dying. It is indeed possible that with Gunnlaugr's downfall, *Eyrbyggja saga*'s shadow protagonist Snorri goði lost a significant competitor, one whose studies in the occult could have made him a powerful adversary.

The Witchfather

GUNNLAUGR'S ODINIC QUEST MAY SEEM less of an anomaly in that tracing any journey through the realm of Old Icelandic witches and trolls might inevitably lead us to Óðinn, high god and necromancer, especially evident when exploring the matter of magic and gender. In *Heimskringla*, Óðinn's sorcerous abilities are described in no uncertain terms:

> Óðinn kunni þá íþrótt, svá at mestr máttr fylgði, ok framði sjálfr, er seiðr heitir, en af því mátti hann vita ørlǫg manna ok óorðna hluti, svá ok at gera mǫnnum bana eða óhamingju eða vanheilendi, svá ok at taka frá mǫnnum vit eða afl ok gefa ǫðrum. En þessi fjǫlkynngi, er framið er, fylgir svá mikil ergi, at eigi þótti karlmǫnnum skammlaust við at fara, ok var gyðjunum kennd sú íþrótt.

> (Óðinn knew the most potent art and practised it himself, that which is called sorcery, and that is how he knew men's fates and things not yet passed, and to cause death or unhappiness or illness to others, or take their senses and powers from them and give to others. But this magic, in its execution, is so queer that men could not practice it without dishonour and so the goddesses were taught this art.)[233]

More famous as the patriarch of the gods, the Alfǫðr in *Snorra-Edda*,[234] Óðinn is here depicted as a powerful witch whose arts are both dark and disturbing. They are, indeed, too queer for other men to imitate without risking dishonour, a strange paradox when considering just how can the actions of the patriarch be androgynous? How can imitating the actions of the highest-ranking male power in the world render one queer?

Óðinn, as he is described in *Heimskringla,* is a cunning Asian monarch arriving in the North during the migration period. Along with his fellow Asians, he is successful in duping the innocent Scandinavians into venerating him as a god.[235] In addition to his knowledge of *seiðr,* he is a shapeshifter who can be in two places at once.[236] Even though Óðinn was in all likelihood a genuine pre-Christian Germanic and Northern deity, there are hardly any authentic records of him from that period. He did, however, retain a significant cultural presence in the post-pagan North as a haunting diabolical spectre that could variously be interpreted as a demon, a zombie or a witch,[237] or, somewhat paradoxically in *Snorra-Edda,* as a representative of fallible humanity encapsulated in the narratives of the Æsir facing off against the invincible, infernal, sylvan, oriental, fiendish rancor of the giants and their various nefarious allies.[238]

Whether regarded within the parameters of euhemerism or not, Óðinn is a paradoxically human deity.[239] In the sagas he is sometimes occult and untrustworthy, but in *Snorra-Edda* he is the protagonist of the narrative with whom the human audience is encouraged to empathise. In *Heimskringla* he is both alien and intimate, an Asian immigrant to the North but also the ancestor of the Norse kings. This is a paradox perhaps shared by all ancestors whose blood flows through us but who nevertheless belong to a distant, nebulous, and somewhat intimidating past — to the ages to whom all of the dead belong, to paraphrase Lincoln's grieving Secretary of War, Edwin Stanton, at his president's deathbed.

It is in this context that the witch king of the North is presented in thirteenth-century royal biographies, as humanity's ancestor, and in the everlasting war with giants and trolls depicted in the *Snorra-Edda* and alluded to in Eddic poetry, he has become the representative of frail humanity, commonplace rather than elevated, the normal and familiar rather than the other. In *Heimskringla*, he recognisably remains the same figure presented in the *Edda*, but in addition he is also a deviant and hostile force, a potent necromancer who will rob people of their wits and health and well-being. Ambivalence is drawn to its limits in the figure of Óðinn the witch, so deviant that his arts would cost anyone — excepting him alone — their manliness, and yet he is at the same time the all-father, the patriarch of the gods and the Norse kings, the apex of respectability. Violating not only the imagined binary between good and evil, he also risks traversing back and forth between male and female bodies, losing none of his potency or even his godly virtue in the process. This may be regarded as the prerogative of the god: the labyrinthine apparatus of dead ends that make human life exist within clearly demarcated boundaries can be safely ignored by him — or her or they since a god is unfettered even of the strictures of gender.

Óðinn the patriarch can give himself leave to be a witch and as queer as he wants. He is male and yet he can also become female without losing any of his masculine potency. Those abominable acts that mark Kotkell or Gríma and their kin as anti-social and demonic outlaws who unambiguously deserve death, and make the death sentence that Gísli Súrsson passes and executes upon Þorgrímr Nose in *Gísla saga*, whose trollish and queer sorcerous acts are the nascence of the hero's misfortune,[240] unquestionably just, can be performed with impunity by Óðinn. The *ergi* encapsulated in his sorcerous rituals, sadly but perhaps crucially never described in explicit detail in the sources, would taint all others but Óðinn himself remains safe from any associated stigma. He is a god and cannot be stigmatized and is alone in being safe from the vagaries of respect. [241]

Even though never stated directly in *Brennu-Njáls saga*, the prophetic Njáll whose lack of facial hair allows his enemies to refer to him as a woman, is, on the other hand, perhaps not entirely immune from the stigma of androgyny. As previously mentioned, his paranormal powers are benevolent, unlike Óðinn's necromancy, which is specifically hostile towards some. It could be inferred, though, that queer practices may be somehow involved here since Njáll is repeatedly branded as unmanly in the saga, mainly with reference to his lack of facial hair. If androgyny is a sign of the witch, then Njáll, son of one of the few named female settlers and possibly an Irish immigrant,[242] must awaken some suspicion. And yet he is a patriarch like Óðinn, also almost superhuman in that his advice helps his clients emerge unscathed from every trial, and his prophetic powers, so closely connected to the institutions of society and the order they represent, cannot possibly be identified as witchcraft. Although the modest hero of the saga,[243] Njáll may still be regarded as a liminal figure straddling the boundary separating the normal and the paranormal, where the distinction between male and female is blurred.

In this way we can regard Njáll as an Odinic figure, although no direct references to Óðinn are made in *Njáls saga* (his only mention in the whole narrative is in Hjalti Skeggjason's infamous ditty from the Christianization conflict in which he calls Óðinn a bitch, a "grey," making full use of the deity's feminine aura),[244] and indeed Njáll's fierce adherence to the Christian faith is reiterated on several occasions in the saga.[245] But would it really be necessary to mention Óðinn, god and bitch, explicitly in a saga in which the protagonist is both patriarch and benevolent magician? When confronting this aspect of the saga its audience would inevitably ask the same kind of question the audience of *Heimskringla* might ask when the latter is confronted with Óðinn's witchcraft: can our hero really get away with this queer relationship with the occult, here manifested in his naked chin? Odinic or not, Njáll has clearly usurped the god of poetry's position atop the Mount Olympus of the North, and his supremacy remains unchallenged throughout the saga, though he does finally sacrifice his life for an even greater existence in the next world, professing his enduring faith in the Christian God all the while.[246]

Like Óðinn, Njáll is undeniably sly, and any cunning magnate will inevitably bring to mind the god of wisdom, poetry, and ravens, as similarly exemplified in a famous scene found in *Sturlu saga.* Here, as late as the year 1181 with Iceland supposedly a Christian land now for generations, an angry priest's wife named Þorbjǫrg endeavours to symbolically castrate and demonise the chieftain Sturla Þórðarson by coming at him with a knife, attempting to gouge out one of his eyes and thus marking him for all to see as Odinic.[247] With this act she would also be marking him semi-pagan, sorcerous, and queer, as his missing eye would be a symbol not only of slyness and wisdom but also of magic and deviance. The wife of a Christian priest must be taken seriously when she attacks a magnate with a knife, although Sturla cleverly manages to deflect the attack. She is here not simply making the statement that Sturla is too sly for his own good. Indeed, a truly noble and Christian magnate could never be compared to Óðinn unless he himself has something of the night about him. Þorbjǫrg's knife graphically relates its own story, whether the audience trusts its account or otherwise: the story of Sturla Þórðarson, patriarch of the Sturlung family, but to some also a witch, a hostile deviant with paranormal powers.

For a good Christian, Óðinn's demonic presence cannot be reduced to mere slyness. Albeit a crafty illusionist and a treacherous foreign king, Óðinn was always more than that: the troll of trolls, a demon, an undead, and a witch, his practices queer and his powers utterly alien.

Don't Feed the Trolls

N FACING ÞORBJǪRG'S ATTACK ON his eye Sturla is thus
aligned with several other figures found in Icelandic
saga writing facing attempted or actual social exile
and demonisation. Þorbjǫrg mostly allows her knife to do
the talking for her and though she does invoke Óðinn, she
never directly calls Sturla a troll or accuses him of *ergi*.
Such accusations are not necessary. Óðinn is a witch and
that means that he is a troll and that his actions include
ergi. The intimacy of this vocabulary is exemplified in *Gísla
saga*, wherein the necromancer Þorgrímr Nose (see "The
Witchfather") is said to perform his *seiðr* ritual with "ergi"
which is later also referred to in the saga as "trollskapr."[248]
The trollish and the queer are inseparable, just as witches
and vampires are, intertwined in a demonic mass of en-
mity. Which means, of course, that when referring to
someone as a troll, one is not just kidding but making uncompromising ontological statements.[249] In effect Þorbjǫrg
is suggesting through her actions that Sturla, like Örvar-
Oddr's aforementioned nemesis Ögmundr (see "Unreal
Fauna"), may be more spirit than man, a genuine troll that
haunts the human like a demonic shadow.

To those of the enlightened nineteenth century, with
science slowly becoming the dominating thought paradigm, it was the animal that so easily became the shadow of
humanity, its pursuing demon. "I am not an animal! I am a
human being," cried John Merrick to his persecutors in David Lynch's *The Elephant Man* (1980). In the medieval sagas,
dominated by Christianity, the natural pursuing demon is
the troll, humanity's nebulous double and antagonist. In

the sagas, in lieu of the beasts of the animal kingdom, the primary metaphor for bestiality is precisely the troll, and a saga hero may be accused of being one by frightened members of the public. This is perhaps most famously done to Grettir, the protagonist of *Grettis saga*, whose tale is characterised by the ambiguity of his place in the universe.[250] Trollhunter, vampire slayer, and ghostbuster, Grettir is frequently confused for the very trolls against whom he defends humanity, possibly unfairly tainted by the association, possibly on account of his dubious status as an outlawed man of noble blood.[251]

Both the professional trollhunter and the outlaw are essentially liminal figures and Grettir complicates the matter with his generally unruly behaviour and by frequently acting out the part of a trickster of uncertain allegiance. After his great swimming feat in Norway, for example, Grettir looks enormous in the darkness, "sem troll væri" (like it was a troll), thus leading to his tragic accidental brawl with the sons of Þórir of Garðr. Some time later a woman he carries over Eyjardalsá in Bárðardalr is similarly uncertain whether she has been transported by "maðr eða troll" (a man or a troll).[252] This ambiguity haunts Grettir, a human with special abilities in a community replete with hostile and dangerous trolls. His real business in Bárðardalr is to fight the zombies of the valley,[253] but despite their reliance upon his special skills the civilized world is frequently unsettled by his strength. Their fear is not unreasonable, though, as the story of Glámr in the same saga provides an example of how those brought into a community to fight the ogres that threaten it may easily metamorphose into far more dangerous monsters themselves.[254]

Given the broad significance of the term troll, it is impossible to know whether or not the woman that Grettir helps across the river is worried about him being a witch, an undead or a different kind of troll. Such a consideration may not be that relevant, indeed she probably does not really care about unearthing his true nature. She likely cares only about herself and her own safety in the presence of a troll whose demonic magic might put her at great risk.

One of Grettir's primary antagonists, Þórir of Garðr, had earlier in the saga remarked that Grettir is not only strong but "fjǫlkunnigr" (sorcerous), which to him means that "hér er við troll að eiga, en ekki við menn" (we are dealing with trolls here rather than humans).[255] Perhaps those of a sore loser, his comments serve to stigmatise and demonise his opponent and deny him his humanity, but Þórir is perhaps also bewildered by Grettir's accomplishments and in genuine terror of this strange adversary.

Grettir is not the only such figure in the sagas thus demonised for political gain. The same might be also said of Skarphéðinn Njálsson of *Njáls saga* who, once while partaking in the civilized business of parliament, goes to plead with various magnates of Iceland and is taunted by all of them. The first, Skapti Þóroddsson, describes him as "mikill maðr ok fǫlleitr, ógæfusamligr, harðligr ok trollsligr" (a large man and pale, unfortunate looking, harsh and trollish), and not only does Skapti refuse to come to the aid of Skarpheðinn and his brothers, he also pretends not to recognise Skarphéðinn, and he insinuates, albeit without trying to actually gouge his eye out with a knife, that Skarphéðinn is a demon, perhaps not Óðinn but perhaps something not too far off.[256]

Thus, in spite of Njáll's fundamental association with law and order, even his sons may occasionally appear demonic to other Icelanders, reminding us of the caprices of fortune. When someone is branded a troll, accusations of *ergi* may not trail far behind. Indeed a major theme in *Njáls saga* is how gender is used in certain power struggles,[257] including, perhaps more covertly, the dangerous relationship between gender and magic.

Coprophagy in the Fields

NJÁLL'S MISSING BEARD WHICH MAKES his gender ambiguous becomes a significant issue when the feud between his wife Bergþóra and Hallgerðr of Hlíðarendi has escalated to the extent that the latter has commissioned verses in which Njáll is referred to as "karl inn skegglausi" (the beardless codger). In these same incendiary verses his sons are called "taðskegglingar" (dung-beardlings), insinuating that their beards are makeshift, that underneath it all they are as beardless as their queer father and that he has made them cover their chins with faeces, as he has cleverly used natural fertilizer on his own fields, to help them each sport their own beards. These insinuations lead to multiple killings. The notion of Njáll having lost his beard through the queer practices of witch-craft is bad enough, his sons' wearing faeces to make up for it exponentially worse.[258] Not only because faeces are disgusting, but because the insinuation is also a demonic one.

As mentioned above ("Trollspeak"), the human rear end and its products frequently signify the demonic to the degree that a bottom can hardly be innocent; folktales and literature from many cultures provide a myriad of examples of this connection. The disgust associated with excrement is perhaps sufficiently universal to preclude a detailed discussion of the subject here;[259] all that is necessary is to note briefly the extent to which the human body frames our ideas of the universe,[260] also apparent in the relationship between the anus, including its occasional stench and its products, with the netherworld. With this in mind, however, we can focus on the demonic aspect of the *Njáls saga*'s

THE TROLL INSIDE YOU

dung affront. Just as Þorbjǫrg's attack on Sturla is not only meant to make him lose the function of one of his eyes but is also intended to mark him as a demon, Hallgerðr's nefarious, tacit suggestion of coprophagy is intended to stigmatise Skarpheðinn and his brothers permanently as odorous trolls. This is not the only or final attempt described in *Njáls saga* that others make to brand Skarpheðinn as a demonic other, and it is to this cosmological insult, no less than the affront against their manhood, both inextrably linked to the suggestion of necromancy, that the brothers are compelled to react with force. Their supposed dung-beards are deemed not only indicative of the brothers' queerness and the femininity they purportedly mask but also their practice of witchcraft with which *ergi* is as intertwined as it is with a lack of manliness.

Consuming faeces is not only inadvisable for health reasons, indeed that may have been the least of people's concerns in medieval Iceland, it is also a means of turning the human body and, as it is the microcosm of the world, the universe itself along with it on its head, causing confusion between what is up and down, and, given the supposed directions of the hinterlands, the holy and the unholy. When faeces covers the mouth, face and rear have been symbolically interchanged, and the humans who have brought about this change imitate the behaviour of trolls and demons whose chthonic nature makes them naturally prefer the infernal. Indeed, the troll's anus may become its most familiar face in a troll narrative.

In *Vatnsdœla saga,* for example, we are introduced to yet another foul immigrant, although her alien origins are unspecified; she may or may not be Hebridean. The woman, Ljót, is another witch-mother, particularly of the benevolent magnate Ingimundr's future assassin Hrolleifr, and, like Katla, she is introduced as an unpopular woman: "lítt var hon lofuð at skaplyndi, ok ein var hon sér í lýzku, ok var þat líkligt, því at hon var fám góðum mǫnnum lík" (Her temperament received scant praise and she was singular among humans and this was only to be expected as she was unlike any good men).[261] Again unpopularity is here a sure sign of the witch. The saga's audience is thus clearly expected to respect popular wisdom and despise the extraordinary and unaccepted alien.

Apart from once presenting her son with an impregnable tunic and having been rumoured to have performed a pagan magic ritual referred to as "blót," Ljót makes her mark near the end of the saga, when after her son has killed his aged benefactor Ingimundr in a dastardly manner, Ingimundr's sons seek their revenge. When they have arrived to kill Hrolleifr, they see a strange sight:

> Ok er þeir bræðr kvámu at, mælti Hǫgni: „Hvat fjanda fer hér at oss, er ek veit eigi, hvat er?"
>
> Þorsteinn svarar: „Þar fer Ljót kerling, ok hefir breytiliga um búizk."
>
> Hon hafði rekit fǫtin fram yfir hǫfuð sér ok fór ǫfug ok rétti hǫfuðit aptr milli fótanna. Ófagrligt var hennar augnabragð, hversu hon gat þeim trollsliga skotit.

> (And when the brothers arrived, Hogni asked: "Which demon comes here at us, that I cannot recognise?"
>
> Þorsteinn replies: "This is the crone Ljót, and has transformed her appearance."
>
> She had pulled the clothes over her head and proceeded backwards and had the head between her legs. Her glance was far from pretty, how she could gaze at them trollishly.)

Ljót's queer, topsy-turvy stance, her head positioned between her legs and her clothes pulled over her head, presumably leaving her naked in the nether regions, is rather fitting given common association between infernal beings and the lower regions of the human body, with anus replacing the human face.[262] As in the aforementioned passage from *Óláfs saga* ("Trollspeak"), this association with the human rear end signifies the infernal nature of the troll.

The powers of this witch-demon are not taken lightly in the saga, although they are ultimately conquered by Ingimundr's sons' good fortune. She in fact tells them that if they had not seen her, she had intended to "snúa þar um landslagi ǫllu" (transform the whole landscape) and craze them in the manner of Óðinn so that they would run with the wild beasts. But as she has been spotted, she dies "í móð sínum ok trǫlldómi" (in her transmogrified trollish state), which might indicate that her sorcery, having failed to hit its mark, was ultimately turned against her in the end.

The use of the word *móðr* here is in some respect typical for the ways in which the Old Icelandic textual sources treat the topic of shapeshifting. While a variety of glosses for the word can be found in modern dictionaries,[263] it is not easy to say precisely what it signifies, no more perhaps than its English variant "mood." Something is happening with the mind or the soul, a kind of movement, but what exactly is it? Content with suggesting to their audience that some kind of magical transformation that pertains to the essence of the individual is taking place, there is no precise description of the process; there never is, and that may even be the point. The audience can only guess and be disgusted, and know that the violence of this procedure is such that Ljót herself is killed, presumably by her own inverted magic gone wrong.

The depiction of Óðinn found in *Heimskringla* only alluded to queer magic. *Vatnsdœla saga*'s depiction of the aged witch Ljót, her naked posterior meeting her face in some kind of demonic ritual, her trollish glances serving as virtual laser beams that can demolish the entire landscape, may well constitute an attempt to portray queer magic rituals in practice. Her contorted stance, reinforced by her threat to turn the land all awry, demonstrates not only the power of her magic but also its eventual aim. In this grotesque scene, the troll is inversion itself. It is not only evil but also queer, and the queer stance that Ljót must assume to practice these dark arts exemplifies the threat of chaos encapsulated in the actions of the troll. The troll here emerges as the ultimate destroyer whose actions instigate such chaos that nothing can emerge unscathed.[264]

Please! Let Me In!

JÓT'S NEFARIOUS AMBITION WAS TO attack not only its inhabitants but also the very earth itself and to deplete it of its bounties. Such depletion is often the primary purpose of parasitic monsters such as incubi, succubi, hags, moras, and vampires, and such parasitic motives can also be conceptualised as fundamentally trollish.[265] Though some undead remain in the confines of their mounds, dangerous only within their own limited territory, other trolls are essentially vampires, meaning that they actively seek to infect others with their own trollish nature. A prime example of the workings of such ghostly infections or vampirism can be found in *Eyrbyggja saga* in the hauntings of infamous undead Þórólfr twistfoot, protagonist of what must be considered one of the most extensive medieval Icelandic ghost stories.

In life, and particularly in his old age, Þórólfr had been a man full of frustration and hate, which he directed at the young and vivacious and his own son in particular. After his undeath his hatred is transformed and multiplied into an undead's animosity towards all living things. Many of the undead described in the sagas were unpopular and marginal during their human lives, their undead atrocities natural continuations of the misery they had experienced in life and thus perhaps partly an indictment on the shortcomings of human societies and their inability to embrace all of their members equally.[266] If not evidently frustrated and malicious, they are still unpopular for some unstated reason, like Garðarr (or Garði), for example, the foreman of Þorsteinn Eiríksson's farmstead in Lýsufjǫrðr (Amerag dla) in Greenland, first to die in the so called Lýsufjǫrður-wonders and thus the cause of all the ensuing haunting.[267] Most of the legendary ghosts of medieval Iceland started out as shunned, anti-social, troublesome, and gloomy people, all with an air of misery hovering over them and later to metamorphose into infectious paranormal other-ness.[268] In fact one of the undead of Fróðá, which Snorri goði had to exorcise and expel with his mock trial, was in life a practising witch: the line between ghostly visitations and witchcraft is always a thin one. And if the social stand-ing of the future undead does not indicate clearly enough their potential for pestilential vampirism, there are always various clues in the event of death itself: the corpse often appearing strangely upright, its eyes to be avoided at all costs.[269]

Along with the later Fróðá wonders, Þórólfr twistfoot's hauntings are a prime example of a ghost epidemic with an emphasis on its infectious threat.[270] When Þórólfr begins to roam no-one is safe in the open air after sunset, with cattle becoming *trollriða* (trollridden), the parasite famil-iarly conceived as a rider, riding its victim into a craze. The aim of the parasitic undead, the vampire, seems to be to "troll" or craze people, to infect and thus recruit them to join their own zombie cohort. Þórólfr soon begins gather-ing followers, the first of which is a shepherd, chosen — as mentioned above — as is the lot of such youngsters more on account of his vulnerability than his potential for evil. He is once found *kolblár* (blue as coal) and is soon seen in the company of Þórólfr, filling the role of monster as well as that of victim.[271]

This dual role of victim and troll taken on by what were originally ordinary humans such as the hapless shepherd is a particularly haunting aspect of vampirism: the fragile innocents also risk infection of trollishness. Even young-sters and children can preternaturally graduate to an af-terlife as frightening ghouls before ever getting the chance to reach their full human potential. The fourteenth-centu-

ry sagas of Guðmundr Arason contain a haunting narrative about an infant who becomes a ghoul: the horror story
of Selkolla.[272] A maiden child is born at a small farm and a
man and a woman are asked to carry it to the local church
for baptism. But, overcome by lust, they stop at a stone
called Miklisteinn to copulate (possibly their only chance
of such release in a society which expected everyone apart
from the ruling class to be more or less celibate) and while
they are at it, something seems to come over the infant.
When they return to it, it looks "blue, dead and terrible"
so they abandon it, but on their way back home they hear
a terrible cry and the infant now seems alive but so monstrous that they dare not approach it. The innocent infant
betrayed by adults now becomes an ogre threatening the
whole region, reminding us that ghost and horror stories
are nourished by unhappiness and crime. It becomes the
role of the bishop, as exorcist, to drive away this ogre that
walks in broad daylight, sometimes looking like a beautiful
woman but sometimes with the head of a seal, and in the
former guise seduces respectable husbands by taking on
the appearance of their wives. In this narrative, it is hard
not to discern the guilt of the whole of society that in the
end takes on the form of this demon, and we are also re-
minded that the most terrifying ghoul may originate in a
harmless infant.

In the case of the hauntings of Þórólfr, his whole cohort,
victims and monsters, all hail back to the original monster whom the vampire hunters must eventually confront.
When Þórólfr is dug up much later, he is described as "enn
ófúinn ok inn trollsligsti at sjá; hann var blár sem hel ok
digr sem naut" (still not rotten and trollish to behold; he
was blue as Hell and big as a bull).[273] There is in this case
no mention of a foul odour or stench, but most of the other
common motifs are present. The corpse has not yet begun
to rot, being neither dead nor alive, and yet it is hideous to
look upon.[274]

The trollish corpse of the vampire connects the undead with witches, giants, ogres, possessed animals, and heathen gods.[275] Þórólfr is also as blue as Hell, like Grettir's nemesis Glámr whose body is also discovered "blár sem hel, en digr sem naut" (blue as Hell, but big as a bull).[276] The colour blue is redolent of the netherworld and its queen Hel, which in Christian times must have somehow become conflated with the Christian Hell.[277] It is in this instance a demonic colour, reminding the audience of the essentially alien nature of the undead, familiar though Þórólfr may have been in life. The undead represent hell on earth and are as demonic as other trolls in spite of their human origins, their intimacy, which may in fact seem to make them all the more frightening.

Hiring a vampire slayer to deal with the undead may also lead to infection, as is the case in *Grettis saga*.[278] At one point in the saga Þórhallr of Forsæludalr hires a particularly fearless shepherd to deal with an ogre that has been bothering him. This vampire slayer is the infamous Glámr, complete with gusty stench. Though still human he is also already somewhat demonic upon his arrival, but after having fought the ogre to the death, Glámr becomes an even greater threat than the monster he had expelled. Þórhallr then must hire another ghostbuster, the foreign Þorgautr, whom Glámr promptly kills but fails to infect with his inherited trollish nature. Finally, one more expert trollfighter is called in, Grettir the strong.[279] He alone can destroy the ghost but also must pay a price — the eyes of Glámr following him wherever he goes, his nightmares becoming the last vestige of the ghostly infection making its way through Forsæludalr.

This tale of trollish vampirism drives home the commonly uncanny nature of the undead. Formerly human, the ghost is our double, and its own foul fate must be regarded as a threat to us as well. The ridings of the witch and the crazing of the troll both tap strongly into the fear of death that vitalizes ghost stories, while also gaining

some strength from fears of actual kinds of bodily infections, recognisable but seemingly not well understood at
the time. The agency of the undead is inexplicable apart
from the fact that they are after us and want to make us
like them. This is partially a metaphor for the inevitability
of death, although here undeath takes the place of death,
the latter a phenomenon which utterly resists all representation. The spectral vampire goes beyond physical death, is
its negation as it presumably robs its victims of their human souls and denies them the eternal life that is the hope
of all mankind. This salvation is never certain, though, and
narratives of the parasitic undead tap into those feelings
of doubt and uncertainty. The vampire thus functions as a
figure of that abyss of nothingness that we fully expect in
spite of all our hopes.

The Fragile State of Humanity

AMONG THE FAMOUS UNDEAD OF the Sagas of Icelanders is Sóti the Viking whom Hǫrðr Grímkelsson encounters in Götland, when enlisted to break the Viking's mound. Sóti is said to have been "mikit tröll í lífinu, en hálfu meira, síðan hann var dauðr" (a great troll in life but even more since he was dead).[280] The word troll, as usual, is not defined explicitly here but witchcraft is seemingly implied. In life Sóti was clearly a hostile user of magic and in death he is an undead, a zombie, a greater evil still. Like Þórólfr twistfoot, but presumably unlike the shepherd he had attacked and the others in his entourage, Sóti does not become a troll in death but is already trollish while he lived. His metamorphosis from witch to undead is thus one of degree rather than nature as he remains a troll throughout the transformation. The same applies to the aforementioned Víga-Hrappr of Laxárdalr (see "Troll on Your Doorstep") who is said to be difficult in life but even harder to deal with in death.[281] The undead are often more potent in death than in life, and it must be stressed that their powers are entirely malicious and can only be used to kill, maim, and destroy.[282]

As revealed in the aforementioned story of Örvar-Oddr's nemesis Ögmundr Eyþjófsbani, who was "trolled" by the Permians, one's trollishness may be a dynamic state. This is particularly evident in the use of the verb *trylla* (*tryllask, trylldr*), suggesting — to borrow a phrasing from Simone de Beauvoir — that one is not born, but rather becomes, a troll,[283] often in un/death but sometimes while still living, presumably through the use of magic.[284] When "trolled" the human transforms and is no longer the same recognisable being they had been before. In some cases a metamorphosis into a bestial form signifies the transformation from human to troll.[285] In other cases, a more subtle transmogrification is implied, the troll is "eigi einhamr" (not of one body),[286] which may indicate a similar state of witchcraft as that depicted in the following description of Óðinn's sorcery:

> Óðinn skipti hǫmum. Lá þá búkrinn sem sofinn eða dauðr, en hann var þá fugl eða dýr, fiskr eða ormr, ok fór á einni svipstund á fjarlæg lǫnd at sínum ørendum eða annarra manna.

> (Óðinn could switch shapes. Then the body lay as sleeping or dead, but he was then bird or beast, fish or worm, and could in one moment go to remote countries to do his business or that of others.)[287]

In spite of this description, there is often considerable ambiguity about what shape-shifting actually entails. Indeed, the word *hamr,* like the aforementioned *móðr,* has an ambiguous sense in the Old Norse texts, and there is also comparable ambiguity about the concept of *fylgjur,* those paranormal beings who have an undefined, possibly even parasitic rather than symbiotic, relationship with their human counterparts, and whether or not bestiality is a necessary part of that particular metamorphosis.[288]

The state of being or becoming "trolled" is symptomatic of the uncanny nature of the troll. Much like a human transformed into a dragon — such as the evil Fáfnir[289] — zombies were all once humans, fairly normal or particularly evil, and witches still remain so, though partly transformed by magic into something non-human. Thus it could be argued that the troll always retains a past that links it to normality. Even Þórólfr twistfoot was not always a twistfoot, and thus there is in the very concept of the troll an element of

corruption. Much like the death the undead simultane-
ously negate and confirm, the troll, having been at some
point "trolled," is a somewhat devestating reminder of the
fragile state of humanity, originally created in god's own
image. Humans cannot deny the troll as an image of their
own possible future, and so the troll, the very antithesis of
humanity, is still an essential part of humanity.

Its dynamic state is essential to the troll — as integral
as are magic and malevolence. Witches, ghouls, possessed
animals, even nebulous mountain-dwelling ogres, are neither discrete species of the otherwordly nor even are they
firmly separable from humanity. They are, in a sense, all
or any of us, which means, of course, that we are also, in
a sense, them. These two states of being, human and troll,
are separated only by magic and the passage of time, the
former a somewhat obvious but the latter a no less essential element in the cultural myth of the troll.

Time the Devourer

N VAMPIRE STORIES AND POSSIBLY other witchcraft narratives, a fear of ghosts always seems to be inter-twined with a fear of the past, encapsulated in the word "forneskja," at once referring to magic and suggesting also that the very past itself is inherently magical and demonic. If the past is terrible in its very nature, time itself becomes an enemy and our own ancestors, those of previous generations to whom the present owes everything but who are no longer present and whose demise and absence is hateful to us in that it signifies our own eventual absence, become actors in legion with the terrible past. This may be the reason why Norse myths sometimes present giants such as Óðinn's mother as the primordial ancestors of the world, an outlawed species of outdated humans.[290]

In this giant myth of the outlawed ancestor turned enemy, there are echoes of the Greek myth of Kronos, the god who devoured his own children because he feared that one of them would supplant him. In the end he regurgitated them all and thus provided them each with a second birth, becoming in a sense their mother as well as their father, while his youngest son Zeus became his eventual heir. This myth is a metaphor of birth and death, inverted so that Kronos's devouring of his children results in a second birth. The Kronos myth, like the Oedipal myth, is concerned with generation gaps, the emphasis though placed not on the father's vulnerability but rather on parental aggression. This may be a more logical perspective in that throughout the course of history parents have been much more likely to kill their children than are children to kill their parents.[291]

The myth of Kronos was influential during the Middle Ages. It had its counterpart in the Bible, in the tale of Abraham and Isaac and the narrowly avoided sacrifice on Mount Moriah. In Iceland, the Kronos myth is related in a truncated form in the fourteenth-century manuscript *Hauksbók*, wherein Saturn is said to kill and eat all of his children except for Jupiter, who then expels him.[292] An indigenous version of the myth is found also in *Ynglinga saga* wherein the saturnine King Aun sacrifices all of his sons to Óðinn so that he can carry on living himself. He continues sacrificing his sons even when bedridden from old age until at last the Swedes stop him and save his youngest son Egill, who eventually becomes his father's heir and ancestor to the kings of Norway.[293]

In the Middle Ages, the name Kronos had become assimilated with the Greek word for time, *chronos.* Thus the Kronos story was interpreted as a myth concerning the onward march of time.[294] Originally the god Kronos was an old and little-known divinity, whose character is distinguished by internal contradiction and ambivalence in the surviving Greek sources. On the one hand he was a benevolent god of agriculture, on the other he was a dethroned, exiled, and solitary god dwelling at the uttermost end of the land and sea, ruler of the nether gods. He was father of both gods and men, but also the devourer of children and the castrator of Uranus, and he was himself subsequently castrated by his own son Zeus. Only later was the figure of Kronos merged with Saturn, the Roman god of field and crops, who seems to have originally been a force of good but who during the Middle Ages had acquired most of Kronos's negative attributes. Saturn was commonly associated with Melancholy during the Middle Ages, his colour supposedly dark and black, his nature cold and dry. He was also supposed to be the god and planet of the old, as well as of cruelty and avarice.[295] Such notions are echoed in Icelandic sources, including *Alfræði íslenzk,* in which it is stated that those born in the hour of Saturn are dry and cold, evil and untruthful, secretive, and volatile; furthermore, they tend to become old.[296] The prevailing wisdom of European learned sources was that Saturn's children were the unhappiest of mortals, and in the systematised ages of man, Saturn was allotted the final and saddest phase, old age, characterised by loneliness, hopelessness, and physical and mental decay.[297] In poems from the thirteenth and fourteenth centuries, Saturn is connected not only with old age but also with sorrow, darkness, dryness, and avarice, and sometimes even impotence.[298]

The Icelandic sagas include several examples of vicious fathers full of envy and malice towards sons whom they, in at least a symbolic sense, try to devour.[299] There are echoes of this myth in the narrative of the vampire Þórólfr twist-foot who is fuelled not least by a strong sense of hatred for his own son Arnkell. The undead always seem to hate the living with a vengeance and wish to bring (un)death unto them, their very appearance an embodiment of *forneskja,* the lore of the past. As time eventually devours all, so must the parasitic ghoul infect humans with his demonic nature, "trolling" them and turning them into unspecified demonic others.

The Kronos myth may also to an extent be present in the notion of the primordial giantfather in the Old Norse myths related in *Snorra-Edda.* Snorri Sturluson not only presents Óðinn to us in his *Edda* as the oldest and the mightiest of the gods, god of poets and warriors, the wisest of the gods, and father to them all, but also as the grandson of the giant Bolþǫrn, whose daughter Bestla married Óðinn's father Bor, son of the first human. In spite of this genealogical connection with the highest and the best of gods, Snorri also explicitly states that the giants (variously called "hrímþursar" or "jǫtnar," while the females of the race are called "trollkonur") are evil: "hann var illr ok allir hans ættmenn; þa kavllvm ver hrimþvrsa" (he was evil and all his kin; we call them frost-thurses).[300]

It later becomes apparent that the element of evil characterising the aversion shared between gods and giants is, in fact, one of the fundamental aspects of the version of heathen mythology which is presented in the *Edda*. After the disclosure of the wickedness of Ymir and all of his kin, it is soon revealed that certain unwanted "bergrisar" (stone giants) might cross Bifrǫst, the bridge to the sky, if permitted to do so. And soon after, it is revealed that the primary occupation of Þórr, the strongest of gods and men and Óðinn's most formidable son, is to fight "hrímþursar ok bergrisar" (frost-thurses and stone giants).

Thus, *Snorra-Edda* gradually builds up its narrative of the long-standing antagonism between the gods and the giants, only to be intensified as the narrative of *Gylfaginning*, the first part of the *Edda,* progresses. But at the same time, the audience of *Gylfaginning* is from the outset made aware of the fact that these antagonists are also ancestors of the gods, specifically their grandfathers. Although a somewhat dramatic Us and Them binary is well established in *Snorra-Edda,* there is also found there an uncanny genealogical affinity between the opposed Them and Us.[301]

From our childish point of view, we are in fact all raised by giants, a perspective that may resonate in these myths about gigantic ancestors. But they do not only represent the life they gave to us but also the death which looms over us, an integral part of life. Their death is in a sense also our death, their mortality a bell that sounds across time and which also tolls for us. Thus past and parent are not only vital to us but are also dangerous, the passage of time that permitted our own production will devour us in the end, each of our very beginnings is the beginning also of each of our ends.

My Parent, Myself

THE UNCANNY NATURE OF PAST and parent is well encapsulated in the youngest and strangest of all of the great Sagas of Icelanders, *Grettis saga*. As already mentioned above, Grettir has a strangely contradictory role as both an outlaw and a defender against the dark arts,[302] and thus is he essential to the human society that counts him as only a borderline member. This society needs Grettir but also has reasons to fear him. For them he is a benevolent monster that might prove more dangerous than those enemies he fights and expels.[303]

On the eve of Grettir's supposed readmittance into society, he is finally vanquished by one of his many opponents, though he can only be defeated by the wiles of an uncanny creature from the past. It is indeed his primary antagonist's nanny, whom Grettir himself refers to as a "fjandi" (fiend, or demon),[304] who consequently curses him and sends him an enchanted tree that causes an infection and a fatal illness that enables his persecutors to slay him.[305] The rituals that she performs when enchanting the tree are somewhat reminiscent of the aforementioned witch Ljót's practices: "Hon gekk ǫfug andsœlis um tréit ok hafði þar yfir mǫrg rǫmm ummæli" (She walked backwards and widdershins round the tree and spoke many potent curses).[306] The nanny's queer practices would probably have qualified as *ergi* in the sense of the terms use in *Ynglinga saga*; one can imagine the rear end functioning prominently here, as it had in the witchcraft of Ljót, and for the same reasons, as the abode of the demonic.

This old crone, when first introduced in the saga, is presented as a kind of nearly forgotten relic from the pagan past:

Fóstru átti Þorbjǫrn ǫngull, er Þuríðr hét; hon var mjǫk gǫmul ok til lítils fœr, at því er mǫnnum þótti. Hon hafði verit fjǫlkunnig mjǫk ok margkunnig mjǫk, þá er hon var ung ok menn váru heiðnir; nú þótti sem hon myndi ǫllu týnt hafa. En þó at kristni væri á landinu, þá váru þó margir gneistar heiðninnar eptir. Þat hafði verit lǫg hér á landi, at eigi var bannat at blóta á laun eða fremja aðra forneskju, en varðaði fjǫrbaugssǫk, ef opinbert yrði. Nú fór svá mǫrgum, at gjǫrn var hǫnd á venju, ok þat varð tamast, sem í œskunni hafði numit. Ok svá sem Þorbjǫrn ǫngull var þrotinn at ráðagǫrðum, leitar hann þangat til trausts, sem flestum þótti ólíkligast, en þat var til fóstru sinnar, ok spurði, hvat þar væri til ráða at taka hjá henni.

(Þorbjǫrn the hook had a nanny called Þuríðr. She was very old and of little ability as people saw it. She had been very sorcerous and very magical when she was young and people were heathen. Now it seemed that she would have lost it all. But even though the country was Christian, there remained many of the embers of paganism. It had been the law in this land that it was not forbidden to sacrifice in secret or commit other ancient witchcraft but was punished with lesser outlawry if it became public. Now it happened to many that the hand did as it was accustomed and it became handiest to do as learned in youth. And as Þorbjǫrn was out of ideas he sought trust where it seemed most unlikely and went to his nanny and asked her what he could do.)[307]

The ancient nanny, Þorbjǫrn's surrogate parent, clearly represents "forneskja," that kind of witchcraft which is named for and associated with the age before Christianity's arrival, which is to say with the heathen past. Her grounding in the past and her paranormal powers are intimately connected; she exemplifies witchcraft as an ancient, partly anachronistic, and yet still potent force.

She is pagan since she is aged, having been born and raised before the advent of Christianity in Iceland, just like the ancestors of the sagas' authors. Her knowledge of old magic, eventually of pivotal importance in bringing about Grettir's downfall, is connected to her advanced age, the one foot that she has stuck in the pagan past, the embers of which have still not cooled. Thus, perhaps even despite all appearances, the heathen parent is monstrous and dangerous in this narrative also, no less so than Þórólfr twist-foot in *Eyrbyggja saga*, though in this case not necessarily to her own nearest and dearest. It is implied that only such a monstrous anachronism could defeat Grettir, although in resorting to black magic to defeat the outlaw, Þorbjǫrn and his nanny manage to lose all support from society; even Grettir's sworn enemies cannot condone their "fjǫlkynngi" and "forneskja."[308]

In this narrative, the nanny's aid is presented as a most unlikely cause of the hero's downfall, the crone herself being old and infirm, more or less helpless, and a nearly forgotten relic from the past. However, she is in the possession of an ancient power and this is no mean thing. The past is never dead, like a revenant it survives its own death and can through its magic continue to be disruptive and destructive. Grettir's own mother had feared for his life when she last met him and exclaimed: "fátt er rammara en forneskjan" (few things are stronger than ancient magic).[309] Too noble to be a witch herself, the hero's kind mother still seems to sense the evil of the antagonist's pagan mother wafting through the air.

There is strength in the past; its magic does not vanish so easily. Though the crone is presented as alien in her monstrosity, Þorbjǫrn had originally sought her aid, as the saga has it, since he was governed by old habits: it being handiest to resort to the knowledge picked up in youth. The nanny, out of place in the Christian world though she is, is still strangely familiar. She is that past which originally served as wetnurse to the present, and, in turning to her, Þorbjǫrn is turning back to his roots, an accursed root consequently serving him well as the device causing Grettir his ultimate grief. The past is alien and yet we cannot be entirely alienated from it: our origins are not so easily shed and they must forever remain a part of us despite any wish to relinquish them.

The kind of alien intimacy that the pagan past might hold within a community that has recently turned to Christianity may be inherent in all humanity aware of its own more uncivilized bestial past. As already mentioned above, Þorbjǫrn's nanny is not the only demonic parental figure appearing in the sagas. Human descent from trolls is a more universal theme — the entire past is demonic. And yet is it also familiar; though to be feared the troll may well also be our nanny, the one to whom we go to seek comfort.

Coda: The Ancestor

The medieval Christian Icelander was not a pure invention untainted by a sordid past, but rather as a recent convert he was precisely the opposite. The impulse to venerate their ancestors may have clashed with the acceptance of a new religion, which meant that the ancestors, however revered, where still a part of a murky otherness that must be kept in the closet. In Tove Jansson's *Moominland Midwinter,* the protagonist, young Moomintroll, having woken up accidentally while the rest of his family is in hibernation, discovers several strange winter creatures, including one who lives in a cupboard in the family's bathing-house. In an angry rebellion against his closest winter comrade Too-Ticky, he lets this creature out, only to learn that it is an older type of troll (*Förfadern,* an "ancestor") and, according to Too-Ticky, who had already warned Moomintroll about letting the thing out of the cupboard, it can be very mischievous and unpredictable.

Even though Moomintroll is originally discombobulated by the relationship, never learning to communicate with this strange primitive creature, and having to seek comfort in the family album full of dignified family members, he begins to enjoy its propinquity.[310] In his complex constellation of feelings Moomintroll may represent modern humanity itself, having a firm faith in progress and our own superiority to the dark ages of our past, but nevertheless feeling a strong affinity for the past. This belief in progress was not necessarily shared by thirteenth- and fourteenth-century Icelanders, and yet they too felt themselves superior to their pagan ancestors by virtue of the new and better religion, thus making the past uncanny, at once noble and worthy of admiration but yet also inferior and nebulous.

The strange and primitive thing in the cupboard, which must at all costs be kept in check, may turn out to be our own ancestor, a primitive hidden version of ourselves, that bestial alien yet familiar creature we used to be. We cannot know it, we cannot but know it.

Ties Unravelled

W HY DO WE FIGHT? SUCCESS seems to be the natural answer, but in medieval Norse mythology, success was elusive. The powerful myth of the twilight (or fate) of the gods is actually not really referred to in the sagas or any other surviving literature outside of the *Snorra-Edda* and the Eddic poetry.[311] This myth nevertheless provides the world and its gods with a grand finale in a final battle with the forces of chaos and disruption, a battle which the gods eventually lose, only to be replaced by a new generation of gods. In this mythic cycle, there is an emphasis on the breaking of fetters, and, in particular, of constricted forces becoming free of their bonds and consequently engulfing the world in chaos.[312]

For some reason the Old Norse deities themselves are repeatedly referred to as "bonds" in poetry.[313] In the myths relayed in the *Snorra-Edda*, acting as agents of bondage also seems to be one of their primary functions. The serpent of Miðgarðr, a vicious and fearful beast spawned by Loki and a giantess, is thrown in its infancy into the ocean in order to grow there and become a great fetter tying the whole world together; he remains the god Þórr's constant antagonist and only worthy foe.[314] When the world's end is nigh, it is this boreal leviathan that breaks lose, is unraveled, and comes unto the shore.[315] The gods also spend a great deal of energy and attention tying up this serpent's brother, the Fenrir wolf, a beast no less large and ferocious. This hellhound manages to break out of two fetters before a third is so cunningly devised that it manages to restrain him until the apocalypse.[316] Like his sibling, he too is only waiting, waiting for the doomsday of the present world to escape and to engulf Óðinn himself,[317] a fate revealed to the high god before his own demise and recorded in the poem *Vafþrúðnismál*.[318]

These apocalyptic monsters are all fathered by Loki, whose name perhaps also signifies an affinity with the end of all things. This devious mythological entity has been accepted into the group of the gods although he is clearly a giant and a malefactor,[319] and he too is eventually bound in a cave, his treason having been unmasked. There he awaits the end of the world to gain freedom from his bonds to attack the gods.[320] The survival of humanity depends on the strength of the bonds that contain these monsters; yet we know they are not lasting, ties will always be unravelled and the myths reveal that all bonds will eventually break.

Thus the end of the world was envisioned in the medieval North as a series of bonds inevitably becoming unravelled, and chaos was imagined in the guise of fettered monsters, a serpent, a wolf, and a mischievous trickster equally comfortable in the realms of the gods and the giants,[321] who, above all, must become untied. The ties that truly bind are existential ties, and our very lives depend on them.

The end lies in the severing of ties, a severing which might unleash apocalyptic monsters. Thus the world order is secured by the enslavement of the forces of chaos, indicating that freedom is inherently dangerous, that bonds and fetters and restrictions are essential to survival. Our very existence is envisioned in these myths as a benign kind of slavery wherein the bonds, the gods, have tied our living space together to ensure the kind of control which life itself requires.[322]

In medieval Iceland there was no well-formulated "chaos theory" as such, but there was still an awareness of perpetual change, instability, and unpredictability, not only in the seemingly chaotic weather of the island but also in the social order. One of the functions of trolls is to serve as metaphors for such chaos. A storm may be caused by a witch, the undead refusing to lie still in their graves, there is a nebulous figure on the mountain-ridge that is not supposed to be there. Chaos is threatening in its subversion of control, and even if the chaos of the end always looms over frail humanity, the idea of control remains important for humans going about their everyday business. This kind of control is elusive and yet badly needed, and yet it is life itself.

Gravity

THE ART KNOWN TO ÓÐINN and called *seiðr* is said to carry "mestr máttr" (the greatest force).[323] Magic is might, therein lies its seductive power, and whoever controls it has momentarily left the great multitudes of fortune's fools, those battered by and grounded into nature's elements, taking their place among gods and creators. The allure of magic lies precisely in its promise of the power to override the all-controlling destiny, fates, and limitations that trap man within his own narrow existence. The witch is man as god, an unlimited being, and therein lies both its terror and fascination, just as the undead terrifies by trespassing on the ground of unlimited time.

Existing in the space age, modern man is bound to feel infinitely small contemplating the vastness of his universe, but this feeling of inferiority may not be a wholly modern innovation. In spite of all of the belief systems that place humanity at the centre of creation, individual humans trapped within a fairly limited existence within a vast landscape such as Iceland provides will still, at least on occasion, have felt their smallness in every fibre of their being.[324] The relative dimensions of man and his world, driven home as he stands dwarfed by every mountain, will inevitably not have altogether escaped his attention in spite of all valiant attempts to ignore them.

Thus there is possibly an element of flattery in the constant intervention, some of which has been described above, of paranormal powers into human everyday existence. The occult forces do care, and will visit you in your dreams and inform you of what the future brings for you and those close to you, and they will present you with ominous portents. They will, somewhat like the Olympian gods during the Trojan war, enhance your importance in the scheme of all things through their perpetual interest in your fate despite the individual's seeming insignificance.[325] Any paranormal encounter sublimates human existence, as the occult powers cast a spotlight on the lone human actor and may have transcendental effect on his life. Even a lowly henchman such as Án ricebelly in *Laxdœla saga* may receive visitations from magic women in his sleep, proving his worth exceeds beyond the limited role he assumes within the mundane everyday world.[326]

As noted above, Óðinn the witchfather was said to use his magic to transport himself, indeed fly by his own power as if in a dream — a frequent dream flyer such as the author of this book cannot but feel affinity with the humans who crafted this myth. Gravity can weigh heavily on the human soul, earthbound and exiled from the heavens, the natural abode of the immortals. The ability to fly, even to send your own soul flying while you sleep and thus to be in two places at one, is exhilarating to terrestrials who normally exercise no control over time and space.[327] No less exciting is the power to affect the lives of others, to reach beyond one's own fate and make a difference outside of one's own skin. Óðinn can attain this power through *seiðr*, and he is imitated by those vicious trolls mentioned in the Sagas of Icelanders, such as Kotkell and Gríma, Þorgrímr Nose, not to mention the undead who in their undead state can, if nothing else, finally attain their lifelong ambition to kill, maim, and destroy.

Örvar-Oddr's nemesis Ögmundr may be the greatest troll in the Northern hemisphere. It is implied that his power is hardly of this world, but it is certainly a force to be reckoned with in the human sphere. He has attained this power through magic, presumably like all of the other trolls in saga narratives who cause the medieval Icelandic warriors occasionally to pause in the midst of battle and contemplate that they seem to be fighting against "troll en ekki menn" (trolls and not men).[328] His is an inhuman and grand power, beyond human capacity, and again there is a form of aggrandizement in the paranormal nature of the enemy: Örvar-Oddr alone among the ancient heroes seems to be worthy of such a foe. Thus the troll may paradoxically bring recognition, even consolation, along with horror.

Paranormal powers are the *raison d'être* of the troll. The troll is nothing if not the sorcerous power it yields, a power to be feared and envied and which may even at times be strangely flattering. The troll provides the human with perspective, a much larger perspective. The presence of the troll may thus be a paradoxical aspect of the divine nature of humanity. We may often resemble mere beasts but we are, in fact, divine, and our divinity is proven by the opprobrium of paranormal persecutors that it inspires.

Troll and Control

"They fed it, not with any grain,
but always just with the thought that it might be.
And this assurance gave the beast so much power."[329]

THESE WORDS OF THE POET Rilke refer to the unicorn ("this beast … the one that never was") and not the troll, but the medieval troll was indeed no less than the unicorn nourished by human "thought that it might be." Unlike Rilke's unicorn, however, which arose from "pure love," the troll is awakaned by fear; perhaps more like a nightmare than a dream — a nightmare begotten from the human condition of finding oneself in a world that is beyond our control, but that seems sometimes manageable enough for us to never completely accept an utter lack of authority. Total absorbtion in thought may sometimes be the closest we get to any sense of control and yet immersing ourselves into ourselves also deprives us of mastery. A dreaming human is a strange amalgamation of power and vulnerability. In the dream, existing only within our own minds, we are, in some sense, absolute rulers. And yet, in our sleeping state, we may often feel more vulnerable than ever. Death seems likely to come to us in sleep, in our imagination it is like sleep. In sleep we lose control, but, paradoxically, in sleep, and only there, we are actually in command of our own dream world, which still refuses to obey us.

Accidentally encountering the new, unfamiliar word "trollable" in a book, which turned out to be the latter half of the familiar "uncontrollable" split between two lines, began the author on the track to the idea that there is a strange symbiotic relationship (though no etymological one) between the idea of control and that of the troll. The two rhyming concepts may become one through magic and witchcraft as there is no troll without magic and the essential focus of magic is control. The term control can thus signify both the impotent feelings of a human facing something occult and the primary *raison d'être* of all magical practice: the idea that a human, you or I, may wield the power to exceed her or his limitations and assume control of a universe so much larger than oneself that any reflection on its size inevitably leads to necessary questions of our own significance within it.

Stories about power must always also be stories about the trauma of impotence. The strong presence of magic, the great leveler, in human culture tells its own story about an obsession with power spawned by feelings of impotence. The hope of magic reveals the lack of hope in our existence. Through the realisation of our limitations comes the desire to overcome them, as if by magic.

Why do we see dead people? What function can a troll on a mountain ridge possibly serve? There is no easy answer to such questions, they are impenetrable dilemmas, but possibly anyone who has woken up with a strong feeling of an intruder in the house can attempt to claw at an answer. We all learn soon enough that bad things happen, experiences so horrible that even the scientific mind finds it hard to normalise them. Traumatic experiences are never only of the moment but are internalised and stay with us as an expectation of more and perhaps greater horror to come, perhaps culminating in the dread feeling that one is perhaps, or even unavoidably, unlucky. Having once experienced one's fears will inevitably lead to an expectation, a dread, of more to come; thus trauma can easily be channeled through the troll, our enemy, that potent force always working against us. There is no need for an organised religion of the troll since it springs naturally from any and all dismal experiences. The troll feeds, is nourished, on our fears. If men were in control, they would have no need for magic. Without traumatic experiences, there would be no trolls. If we did not all die, the undead would not pervade our culture.

As evident in many of the narratives explored in this book, the troll has a direct relationship with the inner lives of the humans who experience it. Its relationship with society is more indirect but should be equally evident from the narratives discussed here. The rules, myths, and dogmas of society at large unquestionably have a pivotal role in shaping the troll that the humans fear. The troll is though a human affect, a metaphor of unspecified fears that take form as the troll. In medieval Iceland, the troll was indeed more than a feeling — it was strangely real, as its counterparts are in various other cultures. Its reality though is still the reality of feelings — what else is the troll but feelings? — feelings that man wishes to control but may be crucially and inevitably beyond all control.

Textual Hauntings (endnotes)

1   The well-known propaganda poster in question was originally called *Kultur-Terror* and was made by Norwegian artist Harald Damsleth (1906–1971) for Vidkun Quisling's *Nasjonal Samling* in 1943, but was published under the title *Liberators* in 1944 by the Dutch SS-Storm magazine.

2   According to the somewhat late textual sources from Iceland, from Ari the learned's *Íslendingabók* (c. 1130) onwards, Iceland was settled in the latter half of the ninth century onwards. The Christianisation of Iceland is dated in *Íslendingabók* and though the exact year may be a matter of debate (see, for example, Ólafía Einarsdóttir, *Studier i kronologisk metode i tidlig islandsk historieskrivning* (Stockholm: Natur och kultur, 1964), pp. 72–82), the country is presented as being officially Christianised at the parliament (*alþingi*) around the turn of the first millennium. It should be kept in mind that the early history of Iceland (from 870 to 1050) is a cultural construction created by Icelandic twelfth-, thirteenth-, and fourteenth-century historians working with various types of traditions; however its authenticity is not of paramount importance to this study. On saga origins and the relationship with tradition, see, for example, Gísli Sigurðsson, *The Medieval Icelandic Saga and Oral Tradition: A Discourse on Method*, Publications of the Milman Parry Collection of Oral Literature 2, trans. Nicholas Jones (Cambridge, MA: Milman Parry Collection, distributed by Harvard University Press, 2004); Ármann Jakobsson, "Tradition and the Individual Talent: The 'Historical Figure' in the Medieval Sagas, A Case Study," *Viator* 45.3 (2014): 101–24; on some of the recent developments in the application of memory studies to medieval Icelandic literature, see *Minni and Muninn: Memory in Medieval Nordic Culture,* ed. Pernille Hermann, Stephen A. Mitchell, and Agnes S. Arnórsdóttir (Turnhout: Brepols, 2014). The frequent references to my own work in these endnotes reflect not the author's narcissism (or at least not

only) but also the fact that in some cases, the necessary brevity may be complemented by looking at previous studies wherein the problems dealt with only briefly here are studied at greater length.

3   The sources under analysis here are mostly Sagas of Icelanders or family sagas (on these terms, see Theodore M. Andersson, "Why do Americans say "Family Sagas"?" in *Gudar på Jorden: Festskrift til Lars Lönnroth*, ed. Stina Hansson and Mats Malm (Stockholm: Stehag, 2000), pp. 297-307), often regarded as the most original and singular genre of Icelandic historical writing. These sagas relate events from the early history of Iceland and purport to take place in the ninth, tenth, and eleventh centuries. Though they are clearly engaging with traditional information and even narratives, their eventual composition equally evidently depends on authors who presumably regarded themselves as historians. Their actual dating is uncertain, in most works of reference they are assumed to date from the thirteenth and fourteenth centuries (see, for example, Sverrir Tómasson, "The Middle Ages: Old Icelandic Prose," trans. Gunnþórunn Guðmundsdóttir, in *A History of Icelandic Literature*, History of Scandinavian literatures 5, ed. Daisy L. Neijmann (Lincoln: University of Nebraska Press, 2006), pp. 64-173) whereas the earliest manuscripts are mostly from the fourteenth and fifteenth centuries (Örnólfur Thorsson, "Leitin að landinu fagra: Hugleiðing um rannsóknir á íslenskum fornbókmenntum," *Skáldskaparmál* 1 (1990): 28-53; see also Einar Ólafur Sveinsson, *Ritunartími Íslendingasagna: Rök og rannsóknaraðferð* (Reykjavík: Hið íslenzka bókmenntafélag, 1965); *Dating the Sagas: Reviews and Revisions*, ed. Else Mundal (Copenhagen: Museum Tusculanum, University of Copenhagen, 2013)), and we may now wonder whether the tendency to regard at least the highest regarded of the sagas as coming from the thirteenth century may not be linked to the nationalist idea prevalent during the campaign for Icelandic independence (from the 1830s to 1944) that they were composed before the fall of the Icelandic commonwealth in 1262-64, or at least composed by authors who matured during that era and were thus not raised as subjects of the kings of Norway. If a conservative view is adopted and sagas regarded as only slightly older than their oldest preserved manuscripts unless firm arguments for an older dating are presented, it might result in regarding the sagas as fourteenth-century literature, and as about half of them only exist in manuscripts from the fifteenth century or later, it would not seem to much of a stretch to

also take the fifteenth century in account. In any case, since only 2 or 3 sagas out of roughly 35 exist in manuscript fragments dated before the birth of Dante Alighieri in 1265, and a substantial number of them might well be contemporary to *The Canterbury Tales*, the designation "late medieval" would seem to be proper.

4   The textual sources for the pre-Christian religions of the North are overwhelmingly late, with the eddic poetry, skaldic poetry and Snorri Sturluson's *Edda* all dating from the thirteenth and fourteenth century in their present form, even though a substantial part of the poetry is believed to be considerably older (Christopher Abram, *Myths of the Pagan North: The Gods of the Norsemen* (London and New York: Continuum, 2011), pp. 10-16). This means that scholars wanting to say something significant about the Old Norse mythology are often in fact trying to establish an earlier and ideally more genuine version of the extant myths by "correcting" Snorri and other sources and thus presenting an "asterisk reality" beyond the known textual sources (on the notion of "asterisk reality," see T.A. Shippey, *The Road to Middle-Earth: How J.R.R. Tolkien Created a New Mythology, Revised and Expanded Edition* (Boston and New York: Mariner Books, 2003), pp. 19-23). The issue is extremely complex but it might be a beginning to accept that our main sources concerning the pagan religions are unreliable which does not mean that all beliefs from the thirteenth and fourteenth centuries are unreservedly Christian; there remains the possibility of paganism influencing the dominant new religion in the way of *substratum* languages, to use Graziado Isaia Ascoli's terminology. In this study I make no case for the age of the religious beliefs discussed and nor do I offer an opinion as to whether they were a part of the pre-Christian religions of the early Middle Ages, and yet I would hesitate to call this belief system Christian in any other sense than as an acknowledgement that it co-existed with the Christian hegemonic religion.

5   Throughout the history of Icelandic studies, in particular during the Icelandic independence movement of the nineteenth and early 20th century, there has been a tendency to distinguish between indigenous literature and texts with clear European influences. To my mind, this is a binary that does little justice to thirteenth and fourteenth-century Icelandic literature. Since literature in general was imported to Iceland (the first texts we know of were composed in the early twelfth century), the foreign influences are everywhere. On the other hand, there is no text immune to the local community it is composed in. While

it could be argued that medieval Icelandic texts are varyingly unique, I do not see the European-Icelandic binary is very helpful in my own approach to medieval Icelandic texts and thus it will not be discussed much; on the dynamic of pagan and Christian traditions in Old Icelandic writing, see, for example, Fredrik Paasche, *Hedenskap og kristendom: Studier i norrøn middelalder* (Oslo: H. Aschehoug & co. (W. Nygaard), 1948), and Ásdís Egilsdóttir, "Pagan Poetry meets Christianity," in *Between Paganism and Christianity in the North*, ed. Leszek p. Słupecki and Jakub Morawiec (Rzeszów: Wydawnictwo Uniwersytetu Rzeszowskiego, 2009), pp. 85–92.

6   I argue for the historicity of all Sagas of Icelanders in "History of the Trolls? *Bárðar saga* as an Historical Narrative," *Saga-Book* 25 (1998): 53–71. When I speak of history, I mean, of course, the literary form called history, in which I am much influenced by the writing of Hayden White and Gabrielle Spiegel (see Gabrielle Spiegel, "History, Historicism, and the Social Logic of the Text in the Middle Ages," *Speculum* 65 (1990): 59–86; Hayden White, "The Value of Narrativity in the Representation of Reality," *Critical Inquiry* 7.1 (1980): 5–27) and other modern historians who distinguish between an imagined historical reality and extant historical narrative. The case for comparison with the historical novel is made convincingly by Joseph Harris, "Saga as Historical Novel," in *"Speak Useful Words or Say Nothing": Old Norse Studies by Joseph Harris*, Islandica 53, ed. Susan E. Deskis and Thomas D. Hill (Ithaca, NY: Cornell University Press, 2008), pp. 227–60, and Torfi Tulinius, "Saga as a Myth: The Family Sagas and Social Reality in Thirteenth-Century Iceland," in *Old Norse Myths, Literature and Society: The Proceedings of the 11th International Saga Conference, 2–7 July 2000, University of Sydney*, ed. Geraldine Barnes and Margaret Clunies Ross (Sydney: Centre for Medieval Studies, University of Sydney, 2000), pp. 526–39. Keeping that in mind, it still cannot be ignored that the authors of the Sagas of Icelanders would not have identified themselves in the similar terms as Walter Scott or Alexandre Dumas or other fiction writers from the dawn of the historical novel in the early nineteenth century, although the definition of what they were doing as history rather than historical fiction (see, for example, Preben Meulengracht Sørensen, *Fortælling og ære: Studier i islændingesagaerne* (Aarhus: Aarhus Universitetsforlag, 1993), p. 18) may not change that in essence it is a not dissimilar project that may be seen in historical fiction of the modern age.

ENDNOTES

7 "Og er þeir Ásbjörn riðu vestr Hrútafjarðarháls, sjá þeir tröll eitt mikit, ok fór þat í svig við þá" (*Sturlunga saga*, ed. Jón Jóhannesson, 2 vols. (Reykjavík: Sturlunguútgáfan, 1946), 2: 284). The passage comes from the *Króksfjarðarbók* tradition of this text. All English translations in this book are my own unless otherwise indicated. The phrase "fór í svig" is ambiguous, the term "svig" or "sveigr" referring to a circular or curved motion (like the slalom in skiing), and most Icelanders asked take this passage to mean that the troll is trying to avoid the men.

8 The imagined binary presented here of course owes much to structuralist thinking, as represented in the works of Claude Lévi-Strauss (see, for example, *Anthropologie structural* (Paris: Plon, 1958)) and Algirdas Julien Greimas (see *Sémantique structurale: Recherche de méthode* (Paris: Larousse, 1966)), both of whom were trying to describe the human thought process and the primordial narrative structure which informs the structure of actual narratives.

9 I have argued this extensively in previous studies (see Ármann Jakobsson, "The Trollish Acts of Þorgrímr the Witch: The Meanings of Troll and Ergi in Medieval Iceland," *Saga-Book* 32 (2008): 39–68, and Ármann Jakobsson, "Vad är ett troll? Betydelsen av ett isländskt medeltidsbegrepp," *Saga och sed* (2008): 101–17) and have discussed the primary evidence. There is no room here to discuss all the examples dealt with there but among them is the description of the sorcerer Þorgrímr Nose in *Gísla saga* whose acts are described thus (*Gísla saga Súrssonar*, in *Vestfirðinga sögur*, ÍF VI, ed. Björn K. Þórólfsson and Guðni Jónsson (Reykjavík: Hið íslenzka fornritafélag, 1943), pp. 56–57 (hereafter *Gísla saga*)), and of the ghost Þórólfr twistfoot who is said to be "enn ófúinn ok inn trollsligsti at sjá; hann var blár sem hel ok digr sem naut" (*Eyrbyggja saga*, ÍF IV, ed. Einar Ól. Sveinsson, Matthías Þórðarson, and Ólafur Halldórsson (Reykjavík: Hið íslenzka fornritafélag, 1985), pp. 169–70) when dug up from the earth. As I have duly noted ("The Trollish Acts," p. 53) the semantic field for troll in thirteenth- and fourteenth-century Iceland is not unlike how Frankenstein fared in the popular culture of the twentieth century, where it eventually became customary to refer to both him and his creature as "Frankenstein" (a famous example being the comedy *Abbott and Costello meet Frankenstein* (1948) wherein the protagonists actually meet the creature). In precisely the same way the medieval equivalent of a scientist, the sorcerer, and the spectre awakened by his sorcerous powers, the ghost, are both "troll" in our sources. An interesting example of this is found

in late medieval law codes where it is both forbidden to conjure up a troll and to dine with a troll ("etur madur med trolle eda blandazt bondi mavtv vit hann"; "vekia vp troll;" see *Diplomatarium Islandicum: Íslenzk fornbréfasafn sem hefir inni að halda bréf og gjörninga, dóma og máldaga og aðrar skrár, er snerta Ísland eða íslenzka menn*, ed. Jón Sigurðsson, Jón Þorkelsson, Páll Eggert Ólason, and Björn Þorsteinsson, 16 vols. (Copenhagen: Hið íslenzka bókmenntafjelag, 1857–1972), 2: 241). Lára Magnúsardóttir originally drew my attention to this ban and has suggested that the troll could be a heretic in this instance (on heresy and excommunication in medieval Iceland, see Lára Magnúsardóttir, *Bannfæring og kirkjuvald á Ísland 1275-1550: Lög og rannsóknarforsendur* (Reykjavík: Háskólaútgáfan 2007)). In the law codes, we see that the tendency to merge the witch and her witchcraft is an ancient and venerable one and not merely an instance of the imbecility of twentieth-century popular culture.

10 Following the use of "mikit" in this instance it is perhaps tempting to make the logical leap to assume that trolls are in general large. Such an assumption may not be warranted though since the troll's largeness could easily be relative, and, of course, largeness is always in the eye of the beholder. To nervous men on a mountain ridge any murky shape in the distance will inevatibly loom large.

11 I refer here to J.R.R. Tolkien's aside about scholars who would regard dragons "as a sober zoologist," and his perception of the Beowulf poet as one who "esteemed dragons, as rare as they are dire, as some do still. He liked them—as a poet, not as a sober zoologist; and he had good reason" ("Beowulf: The Monsters and the Critics," *Proceedings of the British Academy* 22 (1936): 253 [245-95]). Tolkien's observation that scholars tend to treat imaginary creatures as if the methods of biology apply has been very influential to this study; see "Unreal Fauna" below, and also Ármann Jakobsson, "The Taxonomy of the Non-Existent: Some Medieval Icelandic Concepts of the Paranormal," *Fabula* 54 (2013): 199–213.

12 In this study I deliberately do not distinguish between various cultural representations of the undead known under diverse terms (see also "Withcraft Epistemology," and Ármann Jakobsson, "Yfirnáttúrlegar ríðingar: Tilberinn, maran og vitsugan," *Tímarit Máls og menningar* 70.1 (2009): 111–21). The reason for this is not only my belief that visions originating in human confabulations should not be taxonomised like actual living animals, but also that I want to create an "estrangement" or "defamiliarization" effect (the "ostraniene" concept invented by Viktor

Shklovsky in his *O teori prozy* (Moscow, 1925), and later used, as "Verfremdungseffekt," by the influential playwright Bertolt Brecht, first in his essay "Verfremdungseffekte in der chinesischen Schauspielkunst" (1936)), i.e., to separate my readers from the preconceptions imposed on them by culture. Other scholars may find it important to keep each cultural entity (e.g. vampire, zombie, and *draugr*) in their own cultural context and of course there is no instance of an Icelandic undead being referred to as a vampire or a zombie in a medieval source but my message would be that it is dangerous to imagine these phenomena as clearly demarcated; consequently any confusion caused by my language use is deliberate, in the hope that this fog, like others, will clear up as the reader journeys further.

13   The concept of the uncanny (*unheimlich* in German) though not originating in his work (see, for example, Ernst Jensch, "Zur Psychologie des Unheimlichen," *Psychiatrisch-Neurologische Wochenschrift* 8.22 (25 Aug. and 1 Sept., 1906): 195-98, 203-05) was nevertheless made famous by Sigmund Freud in his essay "Das Unheimliche" (Sigmund Freud, "Das Unheimliche," *Imago* 5 (1919): 297-324; see also "The 'Uncanny'" in *The Standard Edition of the Complete Psychological Works of Sigmund Freud,* trans. and ed. James Strachey with Anna Freud, 24 vols. (London: The Hogarth Press, 1953-74), 17: 217-52) who does not discuss animate, anthropomorphic others specifically and has recently received further scrutiny by Nicholas Royle, *The Uncanny* (Manchester: Manchester University Press, 2003), who extends the concept beyond its applicability to aesthetics and individual psychology, regarding it as an inherent element of nearly all aspects of modernity and modern life.

14   I use the *North* here and elsewhere in this study mainly since even though the focus is on the plentiful Icelandic sources, I see no reason to frame the topic within the idea of a specific geographical entity or even a political nation state. Iceland as a political entity has little relevance for this study and even less do I wish to cloud the issue by using the term *Icelanders* and thus lead my readers to mistakenly assume a collective identity for all of inhabitants of this relatively large but scarcely populated island in the Atlantic where I have myself spent most of my days. I have frequently noticed that Old Norse scholars not from Iceland (and, of course, nationalistic Icelanders) seem to take this category too much for granted even though recent studies have demonstrated that Icelanders is a very problematic category to use in the high and late Middle Ages; I discuss this further in a

recent review: Ármann Jakobsson, "Nicolas Meylan, *Magic and Kingship in Medieval Iceland: The Construction of a Discourse of Political Resistance*, Studies in Viking and Medieval Scandinavia 3, Turnhout: Brepols 2014. 232 pp. ISBN: 9782503551579 (review)," *Magic, Ritual and Witchcraft* 10 (2015): 247–49; see also Sverrir Jakobsson, "Defining a Nation: Popular and Public Identity in the Middle Ages," *Scandinavian Journal of History* 24 (1999): 191–201.

15 In spite of some exciting developments in the field of cognitive semiotics during the last two decades, the use of scientific vocabulary still seems to me to often add preciously little to the understanding of human brain products that we can gain using our own insights and the traditional vocabulary of the humanities, which of course has the advantage of having been formed and refined through the ages. I realise that any mention of, for example, psychology will lead to demands for usage of recent work generated within the field as it is defined today but I would instead claim the general applicability of the humanities often assumed a century ago; the merits of this book may cast some light on the merit of that claim.

16 There is even a case to be made that all imaginary others are in a sense anthropomorphic others, even dragons or giant spiders which obviously also owe much of their genesis to the animal kingdom. However, some anthropomorphic others, including giants, dwarfs, elves, and trolls, are obviously even closer to humanity than a giant spider and thus their status as *doppelgängers* more obvious. The figure of the *Doppelgänger* figured strongly in eighteenth- and nineteenth-century literature and became in romanticism a popular method of exploring the perceived duality or complexity of human nature. Carl F. Keppler compiled not a history but an "anatomy" of the Double in his important work *The Literature of the Second Self* (Tucson: The University of Arizona Press, 1972), noting the significance of the age-old idea that it entails of "simultaneous differentiation and participation, rendered by this paradox of simultaneous objectivity and subjectivity," and concluded that the flourishing of the literary image of the Double is largely fed by the hunger for "losing the self that one may find in it, of reconciling the opposites of twoness and oneness" (pp. 209–10).

17 The reader may recognise the tagline from the TV series *X-Files* (1993–2002, and recently revived), which contains many traditional troll motifs, updated with aliens. This is but one out of many pop culture references in this study; their main purpose is indeed a kind of defamiliarization in that their desired effect

is to make the audience regroup things formerly kept together or separated and thus establish new connections or disconnections. Also, well-known (and often well-phrased) sentences have a magic of their own which I feel appropriate to the mood of this book.

18   The "recesses of the mind" is a title of an important study of the works of author Guðbergur Bergsson (Birna Bjarnadóttir, *Recesses of the Mind: Aesthetics in the Work of Guðbergur Bergsson,* trans. Kristjana Gunnars (Montreal and Kingston: Queens University Press, 2012)), which has in its own way influenced the present study. I am also influenced by the work of psychologists and psycho-analyists, many of whom have taken folklore very seriously (see, for example, Freud, "the 'Uncanny'"; Ernest Jones, *On the Nightmare,* International psycho-analytic library 20 (Leonard and Virgina Woolf at the Hogarth Press, 1931); Bruno Bettelheim, *The Uses of Enchantment: The Meaning and Importance of Fairy Tales* (New York: Knopf, 1976); David J. Hufford, *The Terror that Comes in the Night: An Experience-Centred Study of Supernatural Assault Traditions* (Philadelphia: University of Pennsylvania Press, 1982)), and for a while they established a new approach to folklore later taken on board by folklorists such as Holbek whose work (through Davíð Erlingsson) has also been a great inspiration for the present study (Bengt Holbek, *Interpretation of Fairy Tales: Danish Folklore in a European Perspective,* FF communications 239 (Helsinki: Suomalainen Tiedeakatemia, 1987), pp. 259–400).

The focus on the observers and their experience is somewhat askew from the main focus of scholarship of the paranormal in the medieval North and may be a reason why this study may add something to the considerable important body of work done in this field by a number of scholars including Dag Strömbäck (*Sejd och andra studier i nordisk själsuppfattning,* Skrifter utgivna av Kungl. Gustav Adolfs akademien 72 (Hedemora: Kungl. Gustav Adolfs Akademien för svensk folkkultur, 2000)), Neil S. Price (*The Viking Way: Religion and War in Late Iron Age Scandinavia* (Uppsala: Uppsala University Press, 2002)), François-Xavier Dillmann (*Les magiciens dans l'Islande ancienne: Études sur la representation de la magie islandaise et de ses agents dans les sources littéraires norroises,* Acta academiae regiae Gustavi Adolphi 92 (Hedemora: Kungl. Gustav Adolfs Akademien för svensk folkkultur, 2006)), Catharina Raudvere (*Kunskap och insikt i norrön tradition: Mytologi, ritualer och trolldomsanklagelser,* Vägar till Midgård 3 (Lund: Nordic Academic Press, 2003)), Clive Tolley (*Shamanism in Norse myth and magic*, FF Communications 296-97, 2 vols. (Helsinki: Academia Scientiarum Fennica, 2009), Stephen A. Mitchell (*Witchcraft and Magic in the Nordic Middle Ages* (Philadelphia: University of Pennsylvania Press, 2011)), and Nicolas Meylan (*Magic and Kingship in Medieval Iceland: The Construction of a Discourse of Political Resistance*, Studies in Viking and Medieval Scandinavia 3 (Turnhout: Brepols, 2014)), each of whose work is variously but not wholly foundational for the present study.

19   Following, for example, Bengt Holbek (see *Tolkning af tryl-leeventyr* (Copenhagen: Nyt Nordisk Forlag Arnold Busck, 1989), pp. 89-91), I do not see this ancient mode of thinking as in any way less subtle than our finite scientific knowledge and grasp of the physical and psychological worlds; thus I would not dismiss even the "conceptualized" histories of the Middle Ages as unintelligent or superstitious; on the contrary they are in my view produced by equally biologically capable minds as ours, perhaps even more so for lack of detachment to the environments from which our minds and sensory functions evolved.

20   Although there is thorough awareness in science of the "observer effect"; see, for example, Massimiliano Sassoli de Bianchi, "God May Not Play Dice, But Human Observers Surely Do," *Foundations of Science* 20.1 (2015): 77-105: "According to the so-called *creation-discovery* view of reality ... our observations (also to be understood as measurements, tests, experiments, experiences, etc.) always involve a double aspect: an aspect of *discovery*, through which we obtain information about what is already present in the system under consideration, prior to our observation, and an aspect of *creation*, through which we literally create (or destroy) what is being observed, by means of the observational process itself" (p. 77).

21   The enduring popularity of the folktales collected by Jón Árnason (first published as *Íslenzkar þjóðsögur og æfintýri safnað hefir Jón Árnason*, ed. Jón Árnason, 2 vols. (Leipzig: J.C. Hinrichs, 1862-64), and in the second scholarly edition, *Íslenzkar þjóðsögur og ævintýri safnað hefir Jón Árnason*, ed. Árni Böðvarsson and Bjarni Vilhjálmsson, 6 vols. (Reykjavík: Þjóðsaga, 1954-61)) has lead to the subsequent publication of smaller volumes bearing titles such as *Huldufólkssögur* (1901), *Útilegumannasögur* (1902), *Tröllasögur* (1905), and *Draugasögur* (1906), all reprinted in 1917-21, with *Galdrasögur* appearing later (1922), and again 1970-74, this time with illustrations by the hugely popular Icelandic artist Halldór Pétursson. These popular editions thus perpetuate the

framework for scholary thought by simplifying the categorisation used in more serious editions. Jón had started his collection
along with the Rev. Magnús Grímsson and together they published a much slimmer volume, *Íslenzk æfintýri,* in Reykjavík in
1852. Magnús died in 1860, leaving Jón alone to finish the larger
edition. On the history and ideology behind Jón Árnason's collection, see Sverrir Jakobsson, "Yfirlit um sögu þjóðsagnasöf-
nunar," in *Íslenskt þjóðsagnasafn,* ed. Ólafur Ragnarsson, Sverrir
Jakobsson, and Margrét Guðmundsdóttir, 5 vols. (Reykjavík:
Vaka-Helgafell, 2000), 5: 7–60.

22   In his prologue — dated October 26th 1861, but only posthumously
published in 1954 having likely not reached the printers in time
for inclusion in the first edition of his work — Jón refers to the
brothers Grimm as the "fathers" of the folktale form ("Formáli
Jóns Árnasonar," in *Íslenzkar þjóðsögur og ævintýri safnað hefir Jón
Árnason,* ed. Árni Böðvarsson and Bjarni Vilhjálmsson, 6 vols.
(Reykjavík: Þjóðsaga, 1954–61), 1: xx [xvii–xxiii]), drawing a parallel between the brothers and Herodotos, the father of history.

23   In his own prologue (see note 22 above) — unlike Guðbrandur
Vigfússon — Jón Árnason does not refer to the Middle Ages at
all but uses his space to describe the origins of this particular
collection and the reawakened interest in folklore in the early
nineteenth century, by which he really means when folktales
suddenly became interesting not only to the uneducated masses
but also to the political and intellectual elite of Iceland.

24   Jón Árnason explains this in his posthumously published prologue ("Formáli Jóns Árnason," 1: xxii), and this is also mentioned in Guðbrandur Vigfússon's prologue to the original edition ("Formáli," in *Íslenzkar þjóðsögur og ævintýri safnað hefir Jón
Árnason,* ed. Jón Árnason, 2 vols. (Leipzig: J.C. Hinrichs, 1862–64),
1: xxxi [v–xxxiii]).

25   The tenth edition of *Systema Naturæ,* originally a 12-page leaflet
published in the Netherlands in 1735, appeared in Stockholm in
two volumes in 1758–59 and is the first to consistently apply binomial nomenclature. All in all, Linné published 12 editions of
this ever-expanding work. The Linnaean biological taxonomy is
still in use but has recently come under criticism for being out of
line with evolutionary theory, see, for example, Marc Ereshef-
sky, *The Poverty of the Linnaean Hiearchy: A Philosophical Study of
Biological Taxonomy* (Cambridge: Cambridge University Press,
2001). The systemization of the natural world did not begin with
Linné and in fact has its roots in antiquity, evident for example in Aristotle's division of "bloodless" and "blooded" animals

in his *De Partibus Animalium*. The earlier editions of Linné's *Systema Naturæ* indeed emerged from taxonomic traditions current in the sixteenth and seventeenth centuries, including the works of Leonhart Fuchs, John Ray, and Joseph Pitton de Tournefort, but as the discoveries of more and more animals and perhaps more importantly more and diverse plant life grew their arrangement became more and more difficult. It was in his *Species Plantarum* (1753) that Linné first established his innovative system binomial nomenclature nomen plant life, which was just a few year later expanded to include both plants and animals in the tenth edition of his *Systema Naturæ* (see David Quammen, "Linnaeus: A Passion for Order," in *Systema Naturæ 250: The Linnean Ark,* ed. Andrew Polaszek (Boca Raton: CRC Press, 2010), pp. 5–9). Interestingly, each of the first five editions of *Systema Naturæ* includes a small section devoted to the description of what Linné refers to as [*Animalia*] *Paradoxa* (Paradoxical creatures), variously including, for example, the Hydra, the Unicorn, the Phoenix, and the Dragon, but also the Pelican, the Antelope, and the Shrinking Frog. In subsequent editions of the work some of these creatures — or at least the names used to describe them — were integrated into the taxonomic system describing the natural world while others were dismissed entirely (see Sandra Knapp, "Fact and Fantasy," *Nature* 415 (2002): 479).

26   The "paradigm" concept comes from Thomas S. Kuhn's, *The Structure of Scientific Revolutions,* Foundations of the Unity of Science, International Encyclopedia of Unified Science 2.2, 2nd edn. (Chicago: University of Chicago Press, 1970), pp. 43–51, 174–91. Michel Foucault uses the term "episteme" to refer to a similar strategic apparatus that defines the conditions of the possibility of all knowledge (see *Les mots et les choses: Une archéologie des sciences humaines* (Paris: Gallimard, 1966)).

27   Cf. Grimm's categories in his *Deutsche Mythologie* (Göttingen: Der Dieterichschen Buchhandlung, 1835) where the corresponding categories *Riesen, Gespenster,* and *Zauberei* all appear in the volume's table of contents.

28   See mainly Ármann Jakobsson, "Identifying the Ogre: The Legendary Saga Giants," in *Fornaldarsagaerne, myter og virkelighed: studier i de oldislandske fornaldarsögur Norðurlanda,* ed. Annette Lassen, Agneta Ney and Ármann Jakobsson (Copenhagen: Museum Tusculanums Forlag, University of Copenhagen, 2009), pp. 181–200, and the examples provided therein. See also Martin Arnold, "Hvat er Tröll nema Þat? ['What is a Troll but That?']: The Cultural History of the Troll," in *The Shadow-Walkers: Jacob*

Grimm's Mythology of the Monstrous, ed. Tom Shippey (Tempe, AZ: Arizona Center for Medieval and Renaissance Studies, 2005), pp. 111–55.

29 This comment appears in the second prologue of Guðbrandur's Þorláksson's *Ein ny Psalma Bok: Med morgum Andligum Psalmû, Kristelegû Lofsaunguum og Vijsum, skickanlega til samans sett og Auken og endurbætt* (Holum i Hiallta Dal, 1589), unpaginated. On the cultural context, see Eric S. Bryan, "The Moon Glides, Death Rides: Pejoration and Aborted Otherworldly Journeys in "The Dead Bridegroom Carries off his Bride," (ATU 365), *Integrité* (forthcoming, 2017).

30 Antti Aarne's (1867–1925) classification system first appeared in his *Verzeichnis der Märchentypen mit Hülfe von Fachgenossen Ausgearbeitet,* FF Communications 3 (Helsinki: Suomalaisen Tiedeakatemian, 1910), and was later revised, translated, and expanded by Stith Thompson (1885–1976) in the second and third editions of that same volume (*The Types of the Folktale: Antti Aarne's Verzeichnis der Märchentypen, Translated and Enlarged,* FF Communications 74 (Helsinki: Suomalaisen Tiedeakatemian, 1928); *The Types of Folktale: A Classification and Bibliography: Antti Aarne's "Verzeichnis der Märchentypen,"* Translated and Enlarged, 2nd ed., FF Communications 184 (Helsinki: Academia Scientiarum Fennica, 1961)). In this system, each fairytale has been given its own AT-number, which may be said to correspond to the binomial nomenclature used to categorise all living species. Thompson went on to construct his own classification system, which appeared in his own monumental *Motif-Index of Folk Literature: A Classification of Narrative Elements in Folk-Tales, Ballads, Myths, Fables, Mediæval Romances, Exempla, Fabliaux, Jest-Books, and Local Legends,* 6 vols. (Bloomington: Indiana University Press, 1932–36); 2nd ed. (Bloomington: Indiana University Press, 1955–58).

31 Guðbrandur Vigfússon, "Formáli," p. v.

32 As a scholarly reaction to these tendencies, the "Retrospective Methods Network," founded in Uppsala in 2009 by Eldar Heide of Bergen and others, takes a strong stance against using "late evidence in the same naïve way as the scholars of the early twentieth century" according to their website (http://www.helsinki.fi/folkloristiikka/English/RMN/index.htm). This network concentrates on late material rather than the nineteenth-century classifications that I am criticising and aims for critical debate on such terms and classifications, similar to the present study; see Eldar Heide, "More Inroads to Pre-Christian Notions,

after All? The Potential of Late Evidence," in *Á austrvega: Saga and East Scandinavia, Preprint Papers of the 14th International Saga Conference*, ed. Agneta Ney, Henrik Williams, and Fredrik Charpentier Ljungqvist, 2 vols. (Gävle: Gävle University Press, 2009), 2: 361–68; cf. Matthias Egeler, "A Retrospective Methodology for Using Landnámabók as a Source for Religious History of Iceland? — Some Questions," *The Retrospective Methods Network Newsletter* 10 (2015): 78–92.

33 See mainly Ármann Jakobsson, "The Extreme Emotional Life of Vǫlundr the Elf," *Scandinavian Studies* 78 (2006): 227–54; Ármann Jakobsson, "Beware of the Elf!: A Note on the Evolving Meaning of Álfar," *Folklore* 126 (2015): 215–23.

34 Like the term "troll," the concept of "álfr" is clearly much less semantically constricted in the Middle Ages than it later was in the days of Jón Árnason, and early twenty-first-century elves are different still from the elves presented in the folk material of the seventeenth, eighteenth, and nineteenth centuries, having been incorporated into a new paradigm of the paranormal mostly defined by new age beliefs and spiritism. Thus the elves in Jón Árnason's collection are usually the same size as humans and essentially our "doubles" while twenty-first-century elf enthusiasts tend to depict them as much smaller and essentially different. Modern media reporting about the consistent Icelandic belief in elves tends to conflate the elves from nineteenth-century folk belief with those twenty-first-century elves that psychics and mediums claim to communicate with and who are promoted partly by spiritualists and new age believers, and partly by the tourist industry (see Ármann Jakobsson, "Beware of the Elf!" pp. 217–18).

35 Ármann Jakobsson, "Vampires and Watchmen: Categorizing the Mediaeval Icelandic Undead," *Journal of English and Germanic Philology* 110 (2011): 284 [281–300].

36 *Harðar saga Grímkelssonar eða Hólmverja saga*, in *Harðar saga*, ÍF XIII, ed. Þórhallur Vilmundarson and Bjarni Vilhjálmsson, (Reykjavík: Hið íslenzka fornritafélag, 1991), p. 39 (hereafter *Harðar saga*); see also *Saga af Hrómundi Greipssyni*, in *Fornaldar sögur Nordrlanda eptir gömlum handritum*, ed. C.C. Rafn, 3 vols. (Copenhagen, 1829–30), 2: 368 (hereafter *Hrómundar saga*).

37 This allusion to *The Highlander* is not totally frivolous since the paranormal duel between Ögmundr and Oddr is an ages-old battle of nearly immortal warriors, and the Highlander's unforgettable antagonist The Kurgan would have been defined as a troll in the literature discussed in the present study.

38 *Örvar-Odds saga*, ed. R.C. Boer (Leiden: E.J. Brill, 1888), p. 131
    (hereafter *Örvar-Odds saga*). The version of the saga cited here is
    attested in the fifteenth-century parchment manuscript AM 343
    4to, and others stemming from it. A shorter and likely older ver-
    sion of the same saga is attested in the fourteenth-century man-
    uscripts Stock. Perg. 7 4to and AM 344 4to, which are thought
    to have independently drawn upon a now lost thirteenth-
    century original. R.C. Boer produced a critical edition of the
    shorter version of the saga based on his transcriptions of both
    manuscripts — printed on facing pages — and included variants
    and supposed interpolations from the later, longer version of
    the saga in his notes. Boer also explored the various relations
    between the different manuscripts attesting the different ver-
    sions of the saga in his lengthy introduction and also produced
    a manuscript stemma tracing both versions back to a no longer
    extant thirteenth-century original (see R.C. Boer, "Einleitung,"
    in *Örvar-Odds saga*, ed. R.C. Boer (Leiden: E.J. Brill, 1888), pp. i–
    lii). A few years later Boer produced a second edition of the saga,
    though here the main text was drawn only from the manuscript
    Stock. Perg. 7 4to, with variants from AM 344 4to provided in the
    notes (*Örvar-Odds saga*, Altnordische Saga-Bibliothek 2, ed. R.C.
    Boer (Halle: M. Niemeyer, 1892)).

39 *Örvar-Odds saga*, pp. 126, 190. Ögmundr is more prominent in
    the younger than in the older version of the saga, although the
    seeds of the fuller characterization with which he is provided in
    the younger version of the saga are somewhat discernable in the
    older tradition wherein, for example, Ögmundr is described as
    "svartr á hárslit, ok hekk flóki svartr mikill ofan fyrir andlitit ...
    Allr var hann ok svartr í andliti nema augu ok tenn" and he and
    his men — who are described to be just like him to look at — are
    said to "líkari trǫllum [jǫtnum] en mǫnnum fyrir vaxtar sakir ok
    allrar illzku" (*Örvar-Odds saga*, pp. 90–91).

40 Apart from the word "blót," in other late medieval sources often
    indicating sacrifice, one can only imagine what the ritual en-
    tailed but it is certainly a possibility that Ögmundr was killed
    and then reanimated. When it comes to rituals of witchcraft, the
    sagas are often vague, and it is, of course, a matter of debate to
    what extent rituals depicted in sagas accurately reflect actual
    practices and if those practices are actual ancient heathen prac-
    tices. While these question are outside the scope of the present
    study, it seems likely that the sagas are in this, like narrative
    tends to do in general, at least attempting to mediate some real-
    ity and it is not unlikely that thirteenth and fourteenth-century

rituals of unofficial folk beliefs, at least in some cases, harked back to pre-Christian times. How can a modern scholar then decide what is ancient and what not? That question I leave to others, see, for example, Jón Hnefill Aðalsteinsson, *Blót í norrænum sið: Rýnt í forn trúarbrögð með þjóðfræðilegri aðferð* (Reykjavík: Háskólaútgáfan, 1997), pp. 189–220.

41   *Örvar-Odds saga*, p. 133.

42   *Örvar-Odds saga*, pp. 90, 91, 131.

43   "Andi" is a word well known from Christian religious literature, denoting both good spirits connected with divinity and evil spirits from the netherworld (see see, "andi," *Ordbog over det norrøne prosasprog*, 2010, retrieved from http://onp.ku.dk). As previously indicated (see note 4 above), Christianity and various pre-Christian and non- or un-Christian belief systems co-exist in one stew in thirteenth- and fourteenth-century narrative sources from Iceland and it depends on each medieval author how rigourously the official religion will be used to explain paranormal phenomena. All Icelandic late medieval literature is permeated with clerical learning and the word "andi" in this otherwise fairly secular narrative provides a good example of this (see Jonas Wellendorf, "Ecclesiastical Literature and Hagiography," in *The Routledge Research Companion to the Medieval Icelandic Sagas*, ed. Ármann and Sverrir Jakobsson (Oxford/New York: Routledge, 2017), pp. 48–58). In 1953, Turville-Petre had famously described the influence of the learned literature on the later sagas thus: "the learned literature did not teach the Icelanders what to think or what to say, but it taught them how to say it" (E.O.G. (Gabriel) Turville-Petre, *Origins of Icelandic Literature* (Oxford: Clarendon Press, 1953), p. 142), and the matter of learned influence on the sagas has been fundamental to the research of diverse scholars of the 1960s onwards, with Hermann Pálsson and Lars Lönnroth being two of the most influential.

44   While devil, demon, and spirit have their place within the Christian religion, ghost and troll have traditionally been seen as folk belief terms. The opposition might be false, though, as they all co-exist within the psyche of late medieval Icelanders (though representing the human race rather than their nation). Torfi H. Tulinius has drawn attention to the possibility of Ögmundr symbolising death and further conjectures that the emphasis on him reflects the importance of death in the worldview of people in the fifteenth century, following the plague (*The Matter of the North: The Rise of Literary Fiction in Thirteenth-Century Iceland*, Viking Collection 13, trans. Randi C. Eldevik (Odense: Odense

University Press, 2002), pp. 163–64). As already indicated in the present study, the relationship between paranormal apparitions and death might be seen as ubiquitous, but Ögmundr, as an undead, is a potent statement of the spectre of death.

45   Cf. G.W.F. Hegel's statement: "The first act, by which Adam established his lordship over the animals, is this, that he gave them a name, i.e., he nullified them as beings on their own account, and made them into ideal [entities]" (*System of the Ethical Life (1802–3) and First Philosophy of Spirit (Part III of the System of Speculative Philosophy, 1803–4)*, ed. and trans. H.S. Harris and T.M. Knox (Albany: State University of New York Press, 1979), pp. 221–22).

46   Neikter's study has recently been republished by Krister Östlund and Carl Frängsmyr, see in particular Ármann Jakobsson, "Medeltidens trollbegrepp," In Jacob Fredrik Neikter, *Om människans historia: Avhandlingar Om klimatets inverkan & Om den urgamla trollnationen*, ed. Krister Östlund and Carl Frängsmyr (Stockholm: Atlantis, 2013), pp. 291–98.

47   Very often this is unstated since the idea is so general and universal that it is unnecessary to state it; the present author is used to coming up against an audience that is assuming he is using these terms to denote clearly defined groups of individuals that are comparable to races or species; in fact a question founded on that premise will emerge every single time. The most extensive recent study of trolls is John Lindow, *Trolls: An Unnatural History* (London: Reaktion Books, 2014), who is well aware of the complexities of the concept which he traces from *Snorra-Edda* to the internet-age, and yet even he sees trolls primarily as "'nature beings'; that is, beings who were encountered in nature" (p. 9), whereas the present author sees the primary medieval meaning as witchcraft, the witch and the undead thus being the main examples of trolls, and both can be encountered in the homestead as well as in nature (see "Troll on Your Doorstep").

48   As reflected in Tolkien's "zoologist" comment (see note 11 above).

49   *Bárðar saga Snæfellsáss*, in *Harðar saga*, ÍF XIII, ed. Þórhallur Vilmundarson and Bjarni Vilhjálmsson, (Reykjavík: Hið íslenzka fornritafélag, 1991), pp. 101–2 (hereafter *Bárðar saga*). See also Ármann Jakobsson, "The Good, the Bad, and the Ugly: Bárðar saga and Its Giants," *Mediaeval Scandinavia* 15 (2005): 1–15.

50   *Eddukvæði*, ed. Jónas Kristjánsson and Vésteinn Ólason, ÍF Goðakvæði and Hetjukvæði, 2 vols. (Reykjavík: Hið íslenzka fornritafélag, 2014), 1: 294; *Edda Snorra Sturlusonar*, ed. Finnur Jónsson (Copenhagen: Gyldendal, 1931), 20–21. One may note the

dwarf Alvíss in the poem *Alvíssmál* who takes on the typical role of the unwanted paranormal suitor, usually assigned to giants and berserks and later to trolls and ogres, see, for example, Ármann Jakobsson, "The Hole: Problems in Medieval Dwarfology," *Arv* 61 (2005): 61 [53–76].

51   *Edda Snorra Sturlusonar*, pp. 12–16; see also Ármann Jakobsson, "The Good, the Bad, and the Ugly," pp. 3–4, and "Identifying the Ogre," pp. 186–87.

52   The brilliant and inspired scholar Lotte Motz (1922–1997) attempted to distinguish between giant types, arguing that the medieval giant was a mixture of four older categories of supernatural Others and that this mixed heritage was reflected in the various terms used: *tröll*, *jötunn*, *risi*, and *þurs* ("The Families of Giants," *Arkiv för nordisk filologi* 102 (1987): 216–36). As a theory, this is excellent but the sources provide little support for it, yielding instead confusion and uncertainty and a random distribution of terms not at all in accordance with the "original meaning" postulated by Motz. These terms and their distribution are presented succinctly by Katja Schulz in her monograph, *Riesen: Von Wissenshütern und Wildnisbewohnern in Edda und Saga* (Heidelberg: Winter, 2004), p. 39, wherin she also discusses each term thoroughly.

53   *Bergbúa þáttr*, in *Harðar saga*, ÍF XIII, ed. Þórhallur Vilmundarson and Bjarni Vilhjálmsson, (Reykjavík: Hið íslenzka fornritafélag, 1991), pp. 439–50. *Bergbúa þáttr* appears on the leaves 4r–4v of the late fourteenth-century manuscript AM 564 a, the so-called Pseudo-Vatnshyrna (see Stefán Karlsson, "Um Vatnshyrnu," *Opuscula* 4 (1970): 279–303; John McKinnell, "The Reconstruction of Pseudo-Vatnhyrna," *Opuscula* 4 (1970): 304–37), which also contains *Kumlbúa þáttr*, another short narrative centred around a paranormal encounter. The two have become somewhat intertwined in twentieth-century works of reference, possibly because of their shared existence in this and other manuscripts. Of the latter, *Bergbúa þáttr* exists in seventeenth-century copies by Árni Magnússon (AM 555 h 4to and AM 564c 4to), Jón Eggertsson (Sth. papp. fol. no. 67), and Jón Gizurarson (AM 165 m fol.), in the saga book AM 426 fol. from roughly the same time, and in AM 560c 4to, dated to 1707, which was used for Guðbrandur Vígfusson first published edition of *Bergbúa þáttr* in his *Barðarsaga Snæfellsass, Viglundarsaga, Þórðarsaga, Draumavitranir, Volsaþáttr* (Copenhagen: Nordiske Literatur-Samfund, 1860), pp. 123–28. The title *Bergbúa þáttr*, in fact, makes its first appearance only in the aforementioned late seventeenth-century manuscript

AM 426 fol., and neither does the word "bergbúi" (known from *Bárðar saga* and other medieval sources) appear in the narrative itself (the being in the cave seemingly refers to itself as a "bjargálfr" instead). *Bergbúa þáttr* has received scant scholarly attention until very recently (see, for example, Oren Falk, "The Vanishing Volcanoes: Fragments of Fourteenth-century Icelandic Folklore," *Folklore* 118 (2007): 7-8 [1–22]; Daniel Sävborg, "Avstånd, gräns och förundran: Möten med de övernaturliga i islänningasagan," in *Greppaminni: Rit til heiðurs Vésteini Ólasyni sjötugum*, ed. Margrét Eggertsdóttir, Árni Sigurjónsson, Guðrún Ása Grímsdóttir, Guðrún Nordal, and Guðvarður Már Gunnlaugsson (Reykjavík: Hið íslenska bókmenntafélag, 2009), pp. 337-39 [323-49]; Ralph O'Connor, "Astronomy and Dream Visions in Late Medieval Iceland: *Stjörnu-Odda draumr* and the Emergence of Norse Legendary Fiction," *JEGP* 111 (2012): 490-97 [474-512]). One reason why *Bergbúa þáttr* remained relatively little known is that, following Guðbrandur's edition of the narrative, it was not published again until 1946 when Guðni Jónsson included it in the fourth volume of his *Íslendinga sögur*, ed. Guðni Jónsson, 13 vols. (Reykjavík, 1946-49), 4: 389-400. Since then it has been included in *Íslendingasögur* anthologies based on the 1986 *Svart á hvítu* edition (*Íslendinga sögur*, ed. Jón Torfason, Sverrir Tómasson, Örnólfur Thorsson, Bragi Halldórsson, Kristján Eiríksson, and Bergljót Soffía Kristjánsdóttir, 2 vols. (Reykjavík: Svart á hvítu, 1986), 2: 2086-90), as one of the so-called *Íslendingaþættir*. As mentioned above, Þórhallur Vilmundarson included it in volume 13 of the *Íslenzk fornrit* series, along with *Harðar saga* and *Bárðar saga*, making use of both the vellum manuscript and six paper manuscripts preserving the story.

54   While the "stage-directions" indicate a threefold repetition of the poem, it's contents are recorded only once in the narrative as it now survives (*Bergbúa þáttr*, pp. 443-50). In his introduction to the tale, Þórhallur Vilmundarson ("Formáli," in *Bergbúa þáttr*, edited by Þórhallur Vilmundarson and Bjarni Vilhjálmsson, cciii-ccxii) is clear but brief and mostly focuses on geography and landscapes, and, like all twentieth-century scholars who paid the narrative any attention at all, he is far more interested in the poem contained within it than the *þáttr* as a whole ("Formáli," in *Harðar saga*, ÍF XIII, ed. Þórhallur Vilmundarson and Bjarni Vilhjálmsson, (Reykjavík: Hið íslenzka fornritafélag, 1991), pp. cciii-ccxii [v-ccxxviii]). The poem contained within the narrative, the so-called *Hallmundarkviða*, which was independently edited and published by Finnur Jónsson in

his *Den norsk-islandske skjaldedigtning*, 2 vols. (Copenhagen and Christiania: Gyldendal, 1912-15), B (2): 226-29, and which is currently being prepared by Tarrin Wills for publication in the *Skaldic Poetry of the Scandinavian Middle Ages* series, assumed that title only in a nineteenth century. Guðbrandur Vigfússon refers to the poem using this name in the foreword to his 1860 edition containing the *þáttr* ("Fortale," in *Barðarsaga Snæfellsass, Viglundarsaga, Þórðarsaga, Draumavitranir, Volsaþáttr* (Copenhagen: Nordiske Literatur-Samfund, 1860), p. viii [iii-xvii]). It also appears in nineteenth-century manuscripts and may originate in an episode in *Grettis saga* describing Grettir's encounter with the cave-dweller Hallmundr who recites six stanzas in the *fornyrðislag* metre that are given this heading (*Grettis saga*, ÍF VII, ed. Guðni Jónsson (Reykjavík: Híð íslenzka fornritafélag, 1936), pp. 203-4). The modern scholars who use the name to describe the verses appearing in Bergbúa þáttr perhaps see it as another version of this poem. The poem itself has usually been dated to the thirteenth century and is generally thought to be older than the prose narrative that frames it, although it is nowhere independently preserved outside of its frame. Guðmundur Finnbogason drew attention to the *kviða*, and was, like Þórhallur Vilmundarson, mostly interested in both landscape and the volcanic eruption apparently depicted in the poem, and in a way this approach is typical of how the sagas have been interpreted for the last 400 years, continuing even to this day ("Hallmundarkviða," *Skírnir* 109 (1935): 172-81). The leading trend here follows the one famously argued against by J.R.R. Tolkien in his "Beowulf: The Monsters and the Critics," — who was discussing only Beowulf studies of the late nineteenth and early twentieth centuries — wherein the determined "source value" of the sagas tends to attract scholars' attention far more than their literary value.

55 On the importance of conversion narratives within the Sagas of Icelanders, see, for example, Preben Meulengracht Sørensen, *Fortælling og ære*, pp. 187-89; Bernadine McCreesh, "Structural patterns in the Eyrbyggja saga and other sagas of the Conversion," *Mediaeval Scandinavia* 11 (1978-79): 271-80; Katrín Jakobs-dóttir, "Á mörkum gamals og nýs: Um kristnitökuna í Íslendin-gasögunum," *Mímir* 49 (2001): 44-55.

56 It complicates the generic definition of a saga that more or less all Icelandic prose narratives from c. 1100 to c. 1500 may, at least on occasion, be referred to as sagas, including translations of chivalric narratives, such as the *chansons de geste*, which in the

North end up as *Karlamagnús saga,* and hagiographic narratives such as the *vitae* of Blaise and Lawrence, in the North known as, respectively, *Blasíus saga* and *Laurentíus saga.* This fact should be noted but may not be a great stumbling block for understanding of the present study where most of the narratives discussed are Sagas of Icelanders.

57 Only four Sagas of Icelanders exist in preserved thirteenth-century manuscripts. In addition, ten sagas exist in fourteenth-century manuscripts, whereas the earliest manuscripts of fourteen of the Sagas of Icelanders come from the fifteenth century, and four do not appear in any extant medieval manuscript; see, for example, Örnólfur Thorsson, "Leitin að landinu fagra," p. 35.

58 In fact, every extant written text of a Norse myth may be referred to as reception, from Tacitus to court poetry to the *Edda* of Snorri Sturluson, composed during the thirteenth century. None of these texts comes to us directly from a heathen culture, they all provide an outsider's view. Snorri's *Edda* was written two centuries after Iceland became officially Christian. The eddic poetry is preserved in manuscripts from the thirteenth century or later. The Norse gods also make frequent appearances in legendary sagas and Sagas of Icelanders, also not composed in the heathen era. Even the skaldic poetry, though some of it may date from before the Christianization of Iceland, comes to us through its inclusion in the kings' sagas from the twelfth, thirteenth, and fourteenth centuries, works pervaded by the Christian religion. What about archaeological remains? There are pictures on stones that have been purported to depict Völundr the smith or Sigurðr slayer of Fáfnir. But how do we know it is them and not other dragonslayers or aeronautical smiths? Thirteenth-century written texts have thus provided the framework for every interpretation of an artefact from the pre-Christian age, as well as our understanding of ancient place-names. There is, actually, no escape from the Christian reception of the heathen religion (see, for example, Ármann Jakobsson, "'Er Saturnús er kallaðr en vér köllum Frey': The Roman Spring of the Old Norse Gods," in *Between Paganism and Christianity in the North,* ed. Leszek P. Słupecki and Jakub Morawiec (Rzeszów: Wydawnictwo Uniwersytetu Rzeszowskiego, 2009), p. 159 [158–64].

59 In Iceland a snowstorm is possible more or less any time though unexpected from June to September. *Bergbúa þáttr* thus relates strongly to the Icelandic experience of insignificant humanity dwarfed by the excesses of the elements of nature.

60   While the servant joins him in this, Þórðr is clearly the instiga-
     tor and one may imagine that only he does the sign in the proper
     frame of mind, the servant being overwhelmed by his fears.
61   The emphasis seems to be on the strong dichotomy between
     the (holy) church service they miss, the expected encounter in-
     tended to bring comfort, and the (unholy) paranormal event, the
     unexpected encounter which brings discomfort, they receive
     instead. The cave, as an unholy location, then serves as a coun-
     terpart to the holy location of the church, reminding those who
     seek its safety perhaps of the thin red line between condemna-
     tion and salvation and the courage required of the individual on
     that particular line.
62   On this element in classical narrative, see Yulia Ustinova, *Caves
     and the Ancient Greek Mind: Descending Underground in the Search
     for Ultimate Truth* (Oxford: Oxford University Press, 2009).
63   This is used to a great effect in Joan Lindsay's novel *Picnic at
     Hanging Rock* (London: Chatto & Windus, 1967) and even more
     effectively in Peter Weir's film of the same name (1975).
64   The relationship between medieval humans and stone has only
     just now begun to be explored in detail, see Jeffrey Jerome Co-
     hen, *Stone: An Ecology of the Inhuman* (Minneapolis, MN: Uni-
     versity of Minnesota Press, 2015). Cohen's work seems to spring
     from recent developments in the fields of both ecotheory and
     object oriented ontology (OOO), which may promise interesting
     and yet unrealised insights into the literature of medieval Ice-
     land.
65   How present is the monster? As demonstrated recently by Rich-
     ard Cole ("Towards a Typology of Absence in Old Norse Litera-
     ture," *Exemplaria* 28 (2016): 137–60), there is considerable ambi-
     guity in both presence and absence.
66   Originally proposed in his *Jenseits des Lustprinzips* (Leipzig, Vi-
     enna, and Zurich: International Psycholanalytischer Verlag,
     1920; see also "Beyond the Pleasure Principle," in *The Standard
     Edition of the Complete Psychological Works of Sigmund Freud*,
     trans. and ed. James Strachey with Anna Freud 24 vols. (London:
     The Hogarth Press, 1953–74), 18: 7–64), Freud saw repetition as
     representing an urge to restore an earlier state of things, an es-
     sentially thanatic impulse.
67   A reminder perhaps of the "economy" of many a paranormal
     encounter; see Timothy R. Tangherlini, "Barter and Games: Eco-
     nomics and the Supernatural in Danish Legendry," *Arv* 54 (1998):
     41–62.

68　Few modern science fiction authors have equalled H.P. Lovecraft (1890–1937) in creating a sense of doom and frail humanity in their work. It is precisely this lack of control I find relevant to some of the narratives discussed in the present study.

69　Ármann Jakobsson, "Beware of the Elf!," 216.

70　While kennings that refer to the pagan mythology are common in skaldic poetry, they are not ubiquitous and there is a great deal of variation in how often they are used. Nine mythological references in twelve stanzas constitute a relatively significant presence of the pagan heritage in one poem; on heathen mythological kennings and their aesthetic function in skaldic poetry, see, for example, Bjarne Fidjestøl, "Pagan Beliefs and Christian Impact: The Contribution of Skaldic Studies," in *Viking Revaluations: Viking Society Centenary Symposium 14–15 May 1992*, ed. Anthony Faulkes and Richard Perkins (London: Viking Society for Northern Research, 1992), pp. 100–20; Guðrún Nordal, *Tools of Literacy: The Role of Skaldic Verse in Icelandic Textual Culture of the Twelfth and Thirteenth Centuries* (Toronto, Buffalo, and London: University of Toronto Press, 2001); Judy Quinn, "The 'Wind of the Giantess': Snorri Sturluson, Rudolf Meissner and The Interpretation of Mythological Kennings Along Taxonomic Lines," *Viking and Medieval Scandinavia* 8 (2012): 207–59; Erin Michelle Goeres, *The Poetics of Commemoration: Skaldic Verse and Social Memory, c. 890–1070* (Oxford: Oxford University Press, 2015).

71　In Herman Melville's *Moby-Dick, or The Whale* the importance of the survivor is expressed in the epilogue: "The drama's done. Why then here does any one step forth? — Because one did survive the wreck" (Herman Melville, *Moby-Dick, or The Whale* (New York, 1851), p. 635). The logic of any catastrophe narrative is that there is a survivor since else the narrative itself is logically impossible, and yet that does little to alleviate the audience's concerns, possibly since doom has not been evaded, only postponed. An escape from death cannot be permanent. As also expressed by Melville, there is great loneliness in escape.

72　Perichoresis is a term coined by early medieval theologians trying to describe the relationship between the individual members of the holy trinity (father, son, and holy ghost); see, for example, Lane G. Tipton, "The Function of Perichoresis and the Divine Incomprehensibility," *Westminster Theological Journal* 64 (2002): 289–306; Emmanuel Durand OP, "Perichoresis: A Key Concept for Balancing Trinitarian Theology," in *Rethinking Trinitarian Theology: Disputed Questions and Contemporary Issues in Trinitar-*

THE TROLL INSIDE YOU

ian Theology, ed. Giulio Maspero and Robert J. Wozniak (London and New York: T & T Clark International, 2012), pp. 177–92.

73 An early twenty-first-century audience is perhaps unlikely to read about menacing doubles and an uncanny ancestral core without thinking of a more modern cave scene, when Luke Skywalker enters a paranormal cave in *The Empire Strikes Back,* encounters Darth Vader, beheads him and, when unmasking him, sees his own face. The power of this scene, which the present author loathed when first seeing the film at the age of eleven, may rest in how it refers to the uncanny *doppelgänger* element in all troll narratives; the ancestral relationship itself will be discussed in more detail later in this study (see "My Parent, Myself").

74 The topic of borders and the place of monsters outside them is not a focal point of the present study. I have touched on the geographical location of the other in "Where Do the Giants Live?" *Arkiv för nordisk filologi* 121 (2006): 101–12, and return to the topic again near the end of this work, see "Ties Unravelled."

75 Davíð Erlingsson, "Saga gerir mann: Hugleiðing um gildi og stöðu hugvísinda," *Skírnir* 166 (1992): 321–45. The man-making function of narrative is not unrelated to the etiological or foundation narrative (see, for example, Mircea Eliade, *Myth and Reality,* World Perspective 31, trans. Willard Trask (New York: Harper & Row, 1963)) the main function of which is to establish a past that explains the present. This is, of course, a foundation principle of structuralist narrative theory (see note 8 above).

76 The dismissal of the paranormal is a theme in some of the prologues to the distinguished *Íslenzk fornrit* editions of the Sagas of Icelanders, for example (see further Ármann Jakobsson, "King Arthur and the Kennedy Assassination: The Allure and Absence of Truth in the Icelandic Sagas," *Scandinavian-Canadian Studies* 22 (2015): 12–25). The most prominent approach is to simply ignore it, or dismiss it as insignificant, seeing the realistic depictions in the sagas as their core. Davíð Erlingsson has discussed this in his article "Fótaleysi göngumanns: Atlaga til ráðningar á frumþáttum táknmáls í sögu af Hrólfi Sturlaugssyni, ásamt formála," *Skírnir* 170 (1996): 341–48 [340–356].

77 The term "game-changer" is documented as early as 1962 — in the *Brainerd Daily Dispatch* — and refers (in its extended use outside of a sporting context) to "an event, idea, or procedure that produces a significant shift in the current way of thinking about or doing something" ("game-changer," *Oxford English Dictionary,* 2016, retrieved from http://oed.com). This usage may be

influenced by Wittgenstein's *Sprachspiel* (language game) concept, which certainly permeates modern culture (originates in his *Philosophische Untersuchungen* (*Philosophical Investigations*), dated to 1936–1948 but first published in 1953).

78   Such a traditional notion is attested in Einar Ólafur Sveinsson's evaluation of the sagas attitude towards reality as a kind of "heroisk realisme" ("Íslendingasögur," *Kulturhistorisk leksikon for nordisk middelalder fra vikingetid til reformationstid* 7 (1962): 496–513), and also in W.P. Ker's assertion that the sagas' distinction amongst medieval literature might rest on the large proportation that they give to the "meanness of reality" (*Epic and Romance: Essays of Medieval Literature* (London: Macmillan, 1908), p. 200–201).

79   See Davíð Erlingsson, "Fótaleysi göngumanns."

80   *Fóstbrœðra saga*, in *Vestfirðinga sǫgur*, ÍF VI, ed. Björn K. Þórólfsson and Guðni Jónsson (Reykjavík: Hið íslenzka fornritafélag, 1943), p. 128.

81   *Fóstbrœðra saga*, p. 157. On the *doppelgänger* motif in the saga of these blood-brothers, see Ármann Jakobsson, "Dr Jekyll and Mr Hyde in Medieval Iceland: Saga realism and the sworn brothers," in *Medieval & Modern: An Interdiscliplinary Collection of Essays,* ed. Christopher Crocker, Dustin Geeraert, and Elizabeth Anne Johnson (forthcoming, 2018).

82   However, paranormal beings do often speak in verse; in fact there are several examples of such poems, which are, more commonly, single stanzas, as seen in Finnur Jónsson's *Den Norsk-islandske Skjaldedigtning,* where many of them are categorised as anonymous verse (see A (1), pp. 174–87, 419–31, 602–7), or "uægte vers" (non-original verse) from the sagas (see A (2), pp. 198–221, 430–61).

83   The textual history of the sagas of Óláfr Tryggvason is complicated (see Ólafur Halldórsson, "Formáli," in *Færeyinga saga, Óláfs saga Tryggvasonar eptir Odd munk Snorrason,* ÍF 25, ed. Ólafur Halldórsson (Reykjavík: Hið íslenzka fornritafélag, 2006), pp. lxxxi-clxxxiv [v–clxxxv]; Theodore M. Andersson, "The First Icelandic Kings' Saga: Oddr Snorrason's Óláfs saga Tryggvasonar or the Oldest Saga of Saint Óláfr?" *Journal of English and Germanic Philology* 103 (2004): 139–55; Sverre Bagge, "The Making of a Missonary King: The Medieval Accounts of Olaf Tryggvason and the Conversion of Norway," *Journal of English and Germanic Philology* 105 (2006): 473–513). Two sagas seem to have been composed in Þingeyrar around 1200, possibly originally in Latin and then in Icelandic translation, one by Gunnlaugur Leifsson (d. 1219), now

lost, the other Oddr's, which now exists in three thirteenth-century manuscripts (AM 310 4to, Holm. Perg 18 4to and the fragments DG 4–7) (see Ólafur Halldórsson, "Formáli," pp. cxliii–clii). Oddr's history of Óláfr served as an important source for *Heimskringla*'s version of the story and for the more voluminous fourteenth-century versions of *Óláfs saga Tryggvasonar in mesta* (see *Óláfs saga Tryggvasonar en mesta*, Arnamagnæanæ Series A, 1–3, ed. Ólafur Halldórsson, 3 vols. (Copenhagen: Munksgaard, 1958–2000)). Oddr Snorrason of Þingeyrar is a fairly nebulous figure (see Ólafur Halldórsson, "Formáli," clxxxiii–clxxxiv) and nothing really known about him apart from some genealogical information and this text, which means that we know more about his inner life as expressed textually than what there otherwise exists of biographical data.

84 In the manuscript AM 310 4to, the king and his men are rather said to be in *Naumudalr* (Namdalen) at this stage of the narrative (*Óláfs saga Tryggvasonar eptir Odd munk Snorrason*, in *Færeyinga saga, Óláfs saga Tryggvasonar eptir Odd munk Snorrason*, ÍF 25, ed. Ólafur Halldórsson (Reykjavík: Hið íslenzka fornritafélag, 2006), p. 290 (hereafter *Óláfs saga Tryggvasonar*).

85 *Óláfs saga Tryggvasonar*, p. 291.

86 "Þeir heyrðu at eitt tók til orða ok mælti — þat leizk þeim sem vera mundi foringi trǫllanna: „Vita munu þér at Óláfr konungr er kominn í heruð vár ok ætlar á morgun upp at ganga ok sœkja hingat til byggða várra ok flæma oss á braut." Þá svarar annat trǫll: „Þat horfisk illa til, því at ek mun segja yðr at eitt sinn bar okkarn fund saman. Ek átta byggð í Gaulardal suðr skammt frá Hákoni jarli vin mínum, ok varð mér óhaglig skipti er sjá kom í staðinn, því at vit jarl áttum saman margan félagsskap. Ok eitt sinn er konungsmenn léku nær byggð minni þótti mér illt háreisti þeira, ok óþokki var mér at þeim, ok réðumk ek í leikinn með þeim svá at þeir sá mik eigi, ok skilðum ek svá við þá at brotin var hǫnd á einum. Ok annan dag þá braut ek fót á ǫðrum, ok þótit mér þá mjǫk vænliga horfask. Ok enn þriðja dag kom ek til leiks, ok ætlaða ek þá at gera þeim hríð einhverjum. Ok er ek tók hǫndum um einn, þá greip sá at síðum mér, ok þótti mér brenna undir hans átaki, ok vilda ek gjarna undan, en þess var eigi kostr, ok vissa ek þá at konungr var þar. Ok alls staðar þess er hann fór hǫndum um mik, þá brann ek, ok hefi ek aldregi jafn vesæll orðit, ok varð þat loks at ek leitaða niðr í jǫrðina, ok fór ek síðan á braut ok norðr hingat." Þá mælti annarr djǫfull: „Ek kom þar sem konungr var á veizlu, ok vilda ek gera honum svik með drykk, ok brá ek á mik konulíki fagrar, ok stóð ek með horn

á trapizu ok vel búin. Ok um kveldit er konungr sá mik, rétti hann til mín hǫndina ok til hornsins, ok hugða ek þá gott til. Ok er hann tók við horninu, þá laust hann í hǫfuð mér ok svá mikit hǫgg at ek hugða at haussinn mundi brotna, ok varð ek þá at neyta ennar neðri leiðar, ok hefi ek slíkt af fengit okkrum fundi." Ok þá mælti et þriðja trǫll: „Ek vil segja yðr hvé mér fór. Ek kom í þat herbergi er konungr hvíldi ok byskup í annarri rekkju, ok brá ek á mik konusýn vænnar. Konungr mælti: „Þú kona! Gakk ok klá fót minn." Ok svá gerða ek, ok kló ek fœtr hans, ok lét ek vaxa í kláðann mjǫk. Síðan sofnaði konungr, ok þá gægðumk ek upp yfir hann, ok ætlaða ek þá at styrma yfir honum. Ok í því þá rak byskup bók á meðal herða mér, ok varð mér svá illt við at hvert bein brotnaði, ok varð ek þá at neyta ennar neðri leiðar. En byskup vakði konung ok beiddisk at sjá fótinn, ok var þá komit í drep, ok skar byskup ór flekkinn, ok gerðisk þá heilt eptir. Nú má ek slíkar minjar hans hafa." Ok er þeir hǫfðu þetta heyrt fóru þeir aptr til skipa. En um morguninn sǫgðu þeir konungi ok byskupi slíkt er þeir hǫfðu sét ok heyrt, ok þeir kǫnnuðusk við um þetta. En konungr bað at eigi skyldi þeir svá optar gera ok kvað þetta hættu vera mikla at fara svá. Ok síðan gengu þeir upp ok støkkðu vatni ok fóru með sǫngum ok eyddu þar skrímslum ǫllum. Ok eptir þat fór konungr til Þrándheims með miklum veg" (*Óláfs saga Tryggvasonar,* pp. 291–94).

87   In both fairytales and the Icelandic sagas, a lack of wonder is a literary convention, which may have enhanced the sense of wonder or danger that the audience were supposed to feel but is nevertheless not mentioned. In this the sagas resemble oral narrative, in particular fairytales whose protagonists seem unable to feel fear; see, for example, Max Lüthi, *The European Folktale: Form and Nature,* trans. John D. Niles (Philadelphia: Institute for the Study of Human Issues, 1982), p. 7.

88   It is interesting to note that modern accounts of alien abductions share certain connections with older narratives concerning encounters with demonic others, and of such narratives Joseph Laycock has written that even if "we cannot personally experience the presence of an angel, demon, or alien, we can still benefit from such encounters vicariously, provided the experiencer's story is sufficicently credible" ("Carnal Knowledge: The Epistemology of Sexual Trauma in Witches' Sabbaths, Satanic Ritual Abuse, and Alien Abduction Narratives," *Preternature* 1 (2012): 123 [100–29]).

89   In the manuscript AM 310 4to the narrator does not refer to "skrímslum ǫllum" (all monsters) in the penultimate sentence

of the passage corresponding to the one cited above but rather "djǫfuligum vélum" (devilish viles) (*Óláfs saga Tryggvasonar*, p. 294).

90 As noted, this does not necessarily make the monsters less objectionable to the humans. One may keep in mind the "uncanny valley" concept from roboticist Masahiro Mori (see "The Uncanny Valley," *IEEE Robotics & Automation Magazine* 19.2 (1970): 98–100), who explored the revulsion felt by humans to a robot whose appearance has become less distinguishable from a human; cf. Sarah Bienko Eriksen, "Traversing the Uncanny Valley: Glámr in Narratological Space," *Paranormal Encounters in Iceland, 1150–1400*, ed. Ármann Jakobsson and Miriam Mayburd (forthcoming, 2018).

91 This study is mostly concerned with textual sources so the word "text" is used in the traditional sense here although I acknowledge the twentieth-century usage of a text as any object that can be examined using the interpretative tools fashioned for textual interpretation. The problem of interpreting the paranormal by other means than spoken or written human language is deftly examined in Steven Spielberg's film *Close Encounters of the Third Kind* (1977) where Roy Neary (Richard Dreyfuss) finds himself trying to shape a unique-looking mountain preying on his mind out of various items in his household, including toothpaste and mashed potatoes.

92 This narrative of a troll acting as an illusionist will not be explored much in this study (apart from "Popular"). However, the question of to which degree all paranormal power is an illusion is very pertinent to it and will continue to hover over it.

93 The power to maim may be linked to the power of healing often attributed to paranormal figures. The theme of paranormal beings and medical knowledge has been explored by Alaric Hall (*Elves in Anglo-Saxon England: Matters of Belief, Health, Gender and Identity*, Anglo-Saxon studies 8 (Woodbridge and Rochester: Boydell Press, 2007), pp. 96–156) and Davíð Erlingsson ("Fótaleysi göngumanns," pp. 348–56), who focused, respectively, on elves and dwarfs. As canny readers may already have discerned, the present author attributes little significance to what medical knowledge is ascribed to various species, the main point is that medical knowledge is rendered paranormal and so is all the imagined power and control over the volatile and vulnerable human body that comes with it. As indicated elsewhere in this study, illness and death and the fear of such transformation are fundamental to concepts of paranormal control; on this re-

lationship, see Alaric Hall, "'Þur sarriþu þursa trutin': Monster-Fighting and Medicine in Early Medieval Scandinavia," *Asclepio: Revista de Historia de la Medicina y de la Ciencia*, 61.1 (2009): 195–218.

94　This phrase ("neðri leiðin") appears only in the S-version of *Óláfs saga* (represented by the manuscript Holm. perg. 18 4to), where it is lacking in the A-version (in the manuscript AM 310 4to). Both manuscripts date from 1250–1300. The relationship between the infernal nature of the demonic and the rear end of humanity has been explored by Davíð Erlingsson ("Frá hrópi til saurs, allrar veraldar vegur," *Árbók Hins íslenzka fornleifafélags* 91 (1994): 137–48) and will be explored further in this study ("Co-prophagy in the Fields"). The congruity between the view of the cosmos and the human body (the microcosm theory) (see, for example, A. J. Gurevich, *Categories of Medieval Culture*, trans. G. L. Campbell (London: Routledge & Kegan Paul, 1985), pp. 41–91) does mean that there is an uncanny relationship between man and the dark forces since the everyday physical environment of any human (including his own anus and excrement) becomes charged with an aura of otherness believed to be essentially demonic.

95　As this study is more concerned with conceptualisations of the paranormal rather than its rituals (unlike the many other fine studies of Old Icelandic magic and witchcraft referred to at various points in these endnotes, including Strömbäck, *Sejd*; Price, *The Viking Way*; Dillmann, *Les magiciens dans l'Islande ancienne*; Raudvere, *Kunskap och insikt i norrön tradition*; Tolley, Shamanism in Norse myth and magic; Mitchell, *Witchcraft and Magic in the Nordic Middle Ages*; and Meylan, *Magic and Kingship in Medieval Iceland*), I will not dwell here on ways imagined to be useful in driving out dark forces. Many are mentioned in the present text such as decapitation of corpse, burning of corpse, putting the face between the buttocks.

96　Among these enemies are not only the aforementioned trolls but pagans, witches, giants, and even the god Óðinn himself, in disguise (*Óláfs saga Tryggvasonar*, pp. 232–36, 249–54, 281–82).

97　There is an inherent tension in the fact that a narrative that is so concerned with the fight against the occult forces also imagines Christianity itself as paranormal and thus an ideal opponent of paranormal evil, not yet another paranormal belief system but the truth itself. In thirteenth- and fourteenth-century Christianisation narratives from Iceland, there are several instances of Christ being (erroneously) identified by ignorant people as yet another paranormal figure closely akin to the pagan deities (see, for example, *Þorvalds þáttr víðfǫrla*, in *Biskupa sögur*, ÍF XV–XVII, ed. Ólafur Halldórsson, Peter Foote, Guðrún Ása Grímsdóttir, Ásdís Egilsdóttir, and Sigurgeir Steingrímsson, 3 vols. (Reykjavík: Hið íslenzka fornritafélag, 1998–2003), 1(2): 62).

98 This is given an ironical twist in the Þiðrandi episode of *Óláfs saga Tryggvasonar in mesta* (see also "The Confidence of Youth") wherein the prophet Þorhallr sees the hills open and "huert kuikvendi byr sinn bagga bæði sma ok stor ok gera fardaga" (all creatures great and small are packing their backs and preparing to move) (*Óláfs saga Tryggvasonar en mesta*, 2: 150; see also *Af Þiðranda ok dísunum*, in *Biskupa sögur*, ÍF XV–XVII, ed. Ólafur Halldórsson, Peter Foote, Guðrún Ása Grímsdóttir, Ásdís Egilsdóttir, and Sigurgeir Steingrímsson, 3 vols. (Reykjavík: Hið íslenzka fornritafélag, 1998–2003), 1(2): 125).

99 See, for example, Torfi H. Tulinius, "Revenants in Medieval Icelandic Literature," *Caietele Echinox* 21 (2011): 58–74; Jonas Wellendorf, *Kristileg visionslitteratur i norrøn tradition* (Oslo 2009), pp. 63–65. A psychological approach to the paranormal is still fairly uncommon among medievalists and folklorists whereas psychologists have been dealing with medieval and folklore evidence since the genesis of the subject (see note 18 above).

100 On zombies, see Ármann Jakobsson, "Vampires and Watchmen," and on the incubi, see Ármann Jakobsson, "Yfirnáttúrlegar ríðingar;" cf. note 2 above.

101 See also note 12 above.

102 See, in particular, Mircea Eliade, *Le chamanisme et les techniques archaïques de l'extase* (Paris: Payot, 1951).

103 See, for example, François-Xavier Dillmann, "Seiður og shamanismi í Íslendingasögunum," *Skáldskaparmál* 2 (1992): 20–33, and *Les magiciens dans l'Islande ancienne*, pp. 269–308. In his criticism Dillmann uses the strict definition provided by Laszló Vajda ("Zur phaseologischen Stellung des Schamanismus," *Ural-Altaische Jahrbucher* 31 (1959): 456–85) rather than Eliade's open one. In his *Shamanism in Norse Myth and Magic*, Clive Tolley has since made a better case for the appropriateness of the term shamanism by undertaking a close comparison of various types of shamanism, including the Norse type.

104 Stephen A. Mitchell uses both the Latin and the Germanic terms in his *Witchcraft and Magic in the Nordic Middle Ages*, with a focus on the Greco-Roman and Christian heritage, while Richard Kieckhefer uses the Latin term in his *Magic in the Middle Ages* (Cambridge and New York: Cambridge University Press, 1989).

105 *Eyrbyggja saga*, p. 165.

106 See Dag Strömbäck, *Sejd*, pp. 160–90; Hilda E. Davidson, "Shape-changing in the Old Norse Sagas," in *A Lycanthropy Reader*, ed. Charlotte Otten (Syracuse: Syracuse University Press, 1986), pp. 142–60; Aðalheiður Guðmundsdóttir, "The Werewolf in Medieval Icelandic Literature," *Journal of English and Germanic Philology* 106 (2007): 277–303.

107 *Heimskringla I–III*, ÍF XXVI–XXVIII, ed. Bjarni Aðalbjarnarson, 3 vols. (Reykjavík: Hið íslenzka fornritafélag, 1941), 1: 18 (hereafter *Heimskringla*).

108 *Þorleifs þáttr jarlsskálds*, in *Eyfirðinga sǫgur*, ÍF IX, ed. Jónas Kristjánsson (Reykjavík: Hið íslenzka fornritafélag, 1956), p. 225; *Vǫlsunga saga ok Ragnars saga loðbrókar*, STUAGNL 36, ed. Magnus Olsen (Copenhagen: Samfund til udgivelse af gammal nordisk litteratur, 1906–8), p. 12.

109 See, for example, *Fóstbrœðra saga*, p. 165; *Vatnsdœla saga*, ÍF VIII, ed. Einar Ól. Sveinsson (Reykjavík: Hið íslenzka fornritafélag, 1939), p. 60; *Heiðarvíga saga*, in *Borgfirðinga sǫgur*, ÍF III, ed. Sigurður Nordal and Guðni Jónsson (Reykjavík: Hið íslenzka fornritafélag, 1938), p. 303.

110 See, for example, *Þorskfirðinga saga eða Gull-Þóris saga*, in *Harðar saga*, ÍF 13, ed. Þórhallur Vilmundarson and Bjarni Vilhjálmsson (Reykjavík: Hið íslenzka fornritafélag, 1991), p. 183 (hereafter *Þorskfirðinga saga*); *Vatnsdœla saga*, pp. 69–70. See also Ármann Jakobsson, "The Trollish Acts."

111 *Bárðar saga*, pp. 103, 163; *Gísla saga*, p. 70; *Grettis saga*, p. 262; *Sörla saga sterka*, in *Fornaldar sögur Nordrlanda eptir gömlum handritum*, ed. C.C. Rafn, 3 vols (Copenhagen, 1829–30), 3: 444. The reason for not including a single-word translation after each term is that I do not wish to emulate the confidence trick of a lexicographer and lull my audience into a false sense of security about the firmly established meanings of medieval words, some of which only exist in a handful of texts, where their meaning is far from clarified.

112 In *Grettis saga*, it is said that "þó at kristni væri á landinu, þá váru þó margir gneistar heiðninnar eptir. Þat hafði verit lǫg hér á landi, at eigi var bannat at blóta á laun eða fremja aðra forneskju" (p. 245). In fact, the saga claims that it is after Grettir's death that a law is passed that all "forneskjumenn" (sorcerers) are outlawed (pp. 268–69) and it is made clear that to kill people through the use of "gørningar" is considered to be wicked (p. 268). In *Hallfreðar saga*, the parallel is made between "forneskju ok illum átrúnaði" (ancient lore and evil beliefs) (Hallfreðar saga, in

Vatnsdœla saga, ÍF VIII, ed. Einar Ól. Sveinsson (Reykjavík: Hið íslenzka fornritafélag, 1939), p. 153). In *Brennu-Njáls saga*, the relapsed pagan Bróðir uses "forneskju" sorcery to divine the outcome of a battle (Brennu-Njáls saga, ÍF XII, ed. Einar Ól. Sveinsson (Reykjavík: Hið íslenzka fornritafélag, 1954), p. 449).

113   *Heimskringla*, 2: 124; *Eddukvæði*, 2: 283, 303.

114   *Eyrbyggja saga*, p. 148.

115   *Galdrar* is plural, *galdr* in the singular. The word is related to the verb *gala* "screech," originally a strong verb and declinated *gala-gól-gólu-galit*.

116   Cf. Catharina Raudvere, *Kunskap och insikt i norrön tradition*, p. 43.

117   *Eddukvæði*, 2: 437–39; see also *Eddukvæði*, 1: 353, 2: 366; *Edda Snorra Sturlusonar*, pp. 104, 192; *Heimskringla*, 1: 13, 19.

118   *Laxdœla saga*, ÍF V, ed. Einar Ólafur Sveinsson (Reykjavík: Hið íslenzka fornritafélag, 1934), p. 99. Similarly, in *Grettis saga*, Þuríðr — fostermother of Þorbjörn ǫngull (see "My Parent, Myself") — is said to recite her magic ("kvað yfir galdra"), clearly emitting some kind of sound in the process (p. 250).

119   See, respectively, Eyjólfr Valgerðarson, "Lausavísa 1," in *Poetry from the Kings' Sagas 1: From Mythical Times to c. 1035*, Skaldic Poetry of the Scandinavian Middle Ages 1, ed. Diana Whaley, 2 vols. (Turnhout: Brepols, 2012), 1: 276; *Egils saga Skalla-Grímssonar*, ÍF II, ed. Sigurður Nordal (Reykjavík: Hið íslenzka fornritafélag, 1933), p. 206 (hereafter *Egils saga*); *Gunnlaugs saga ormstungu*, in *Borgfirðinga sǫgur*, ÍF III, ed. Sigurður Nordal and Guðni Jónsson (Reykjavík: Hið íslenzka fornritafélag, 1938), p. 92 (hereafter *Gunnlaugs saga*); *Edda Snorra Sturlusonar*, p. 239; *Eyrbyggja saga*, p. 45; *Morkinskinna*, ÍF XXIII-XXIV, ed. Ármann Jakobsson and Þórður Ingi Guðjónsson (Reykjavík: Hið íslenzka fornritafélag, 2011), 2: 219; see also Rudolf Meissner, *Die Kenningar der Skalden: Ein Beitrag zur skaldischen Poetik* (Bonn and Leipzig: Kurt Schroeder, 1921), pp. 186-91, 196-97. Meissner categorizes there various types of noise, typical of early twentieth-century taxonomies, which focused on the specific and the variations, sometimes not paying enough attention to the essential sameness or confluence of such categories.

120   See, for example, *Bárðar saga*, p. 103; *Dorotheu saga in Heilagra manna søgur*, ed. C.R. Unger, 2 vols. (Kristiania/Oslo 1877), 1: 324; *Gaungu-Hrólfs saga*, in *Fornaldar sögur Nordrlanda eptir gömlum handritum*, ed. C. C. Rafn, 3 vols. (Copenhagen, 1829-30), 3: 273; *Grettis saga*, p. 262; *Hrólfs saga kraka og Bjarkarímur*, STUAGNL 32,

ed. Finnur Jónsson (Copenhagen: Samfund til utgivense af gammel nordisk litteratur, 1904), p. 84 (hereafter *Hrólfs saga kraka*).

121 See, for example, *Heimskringla*, 1: 311; *Hrólfs saga kraka*, p. 95.

122 See, for example, *Þorleifs þáttr jarlsskálds*, p. 225; *Jóns saga Hólabyskups ens Helga*, Arnamagnæanæ Series A, 14, ed. Peter Foote, (Copenhagen: C.A. Reitzels Forlag, 2003), p. 84.

123 *Eyrbyggja saga*, p. 28.

124 This word is used about pagan supernatural entities (*Edda Snorra Sturlusonar*, p. 61), sorcerous kings of old (*Gaungu-Hrólfs saga*, p. 282), and about saga age witches in Iceland (*Bárðar saga*, pp. 120, 126; *Flóamanna saga*, in *Harðar saga*, ÍF XIII, ed. Þórhallur Vilmundarson and Bjarni Vilhjálmsson (Reykjavík: Hið íslenzka fornritafélag, 1991), p. 265; *Harðar saga*, pp. 49, 65, 67; *Kormáks saga*, in *Vatnsdœla saga*, ÍF VIII, ed. Einar Ól. Sveinsson (Reykjavík: Hið íslenzka fornritafélag, 1939), p. 290; *Laxdœla saga*, pp. 95, 99, 100).

125 See, for example, *Gaungu-Hrólfs saga*, p. 241; *Heimskringla*, 1: 138.

126 See, for example, *Sturlaugs saga starfsama* in *Fornaldar sögur Norðrlanda eptir gömlum handritum*, ed. C.C. Rafn, 3 vols. (Copenhagen, 1829–30), 3: 625; *Gaungu-Hrólfs saga*, p. 351; *Katerine saga* in *Heilagra manna søgur*, ed. C.R. Unger, 2 vols. (Kristiania/Oslo 1877), 1: 404.

127 The term appears both in the indigenous sagas and those "sagas" that are translations of Christian hagiographic narratives (see *Agnesar saga meyiar* in *Heilagra manna søgur*, ed. C.R. Unger, 2 vols. (Kristiania/Oslo, 1877), 1: 18; *Lucie saga* in *Heilagra manna søgur*, ed. C.R. Unger, 2 vols. (Kristiania/Oslo 1877), 1: 435).

128 *Heimskringla*, 1: 19–20.

129 The term is used as a synonym of "galdrar" without any elaboration in *Dorotheu saga* (p. 324), and in *Þorleifs þáttr jarlaskálds* (p. 207), of "gørningar" in *Gísla saga* (p. 37), and "konstir" in *Gaungu-Hrólfs saga* (p. 237n1).

130 This diversity in language use is partly caused by the literary mode of the sagas; they are history, at the time a genre in some ways closer to modern poetry than modern science, complete with an affinity for variety, imagery, and allusion. Old Norse scholars have nevertheless often fallen prey to the lack of specificity of the language of the sagas, sometimes too freely declaring obscure or contradictory passages to be corruptions or uninformed interpolations, where they may have been better served to follow the advice of the classicist Eduard Fraenkel who advised that, when exploring ancient texts, "[e]very possible effort should be made to understand a difficult passage; but when a

careful examination of the language and the style has produced no indication of a corruption and yet the sense remains obscure, then there may be a case, not for putting a dagger against the passage, but for admitting the limits of our comprehension" ("Preface," in Aeschylus, *Agamemnon*, ed. Eduard Fraenkel, 3 vols. (Oxford: The Clarendon Press, 1950), I: ix).

131 Snorri appears or is at least mentioned in several Sagas of the Icelanders, a supporting character in some but a leading figure in others (including *Njáls saga, Laxdœla saga, Eyrbyggja saga, Kristni saga, Heiðarvíga saga, Gísla saga,* and also *Ölkofra þáttr*). His "fame" is indeed attested in *Eyrbyggja saga* itself wherein the narrator remarks that Snorri "[k]emr ... ok víða við sǫgur aðrar en þessa" (p. 180). Snorri is also mentioned in Ari's *Íslendinga-bók* from the early twelfth century (*Íslendingabók* in *Íslendinga-bók, Landnámabók,* ÍF I, ed. Jakob Benediktsson (Reykjavík: Hið íslenzka fornritafélag, 1968), p. 4 (hereafter *Íslendingabók*)) and in *Landnámabók* (*Landnámabók,* in *Íslendingabók, Landnámabók,* ÍF I, ed. Jakob Benediktsson (Reykjavík: Hið íslenzka fornri-tafélag, 1968), pp. 109, 110, 114, 118, 119, 123, 125, 126, 128, 141, 146, 166, 180, 181, 182, 183, 226 (hereafter *Landnámabók*)), in Snorri's *Heimskringla* (1: 7) and as an ancestor of many of the notables in *Sturlunga saga* (1: 52, 53, 55, 64), which is not surprising when it is considererd that he is reputed to have fathered at least 19 chil-dren (*Eyrbyggja saga,* pp. 185–86). He is one of a handful of saga characters whose exact age is known as he is said to have died in his 68th year (*Laxdœla saga,* p. 226). It is thus safe to say that few personalities from the sagas are so well attested as historical figures. He is indeed a "historical figure" in both senses of the word, as he probably existed outside of texts and that he is the subject of many historical narratives. On his nickname, see note 159 below.

132 The idea that the parliament of 999 or 1000 was pivotal in the Christianization of Iceland is present already in Ari's *Íslendinga-bók* (c. 1130) and is a staple in most Christianization narratives whenceforth. Scholars have argued that the Christianization of Iceland was actually a much more gradual process and did not only concern chieftains and magnates (see, for example, Hjalti Hugason, *Kristni á Íslandi I: Frumkristni og upphaf kirkju* (Rey-kjavík: Alþingi, 2000), pp. 7–11) and in this they have much sup-port from some of the late thirteenth- and fourteenth-century Christianization narratives (see Ármann Jakobsson, "Two Old Ladies at Þváttá and 'History from Below' in the Fourteenth Century," in *Scandinavia and Christian Europe in the Middle Ages.*

Papers of The 12th International Saga Conference, Bonn/Germany, 28th July–2nd August 2003, ed. Rudolf Simek and Judith Meurer (Bonn: University of Bonn, 2003), pp. 8–13, and "The Friend of the Meek: The Late Medieval Miracles of a Twelfth-century Icelandic Saint," in *The Making of Christian Myths in the Periphery of Latin Christendom (c. 1000-1300)*, ed. Lars Boje Mortensen (Copenhagen: Museum Tusculanum, 2006), pp. 135-51).

133 *Kristni saga*, in *Biskupa sögur*, ÍF XV-XVII, ed. Ólafur Halldórsson, Peter Foote, Guðrún Ása Grímsdóttir, Ásdís Egilsdóttir, and Sigurgeir Steingrímsson, 3 vols. (Reykjavík: Hið íslenzka fornritafélag, 1998-2003), 1(2): 33. In the fourteenth-century *Óláfs saga Tryggvasonar en mesta* his same remark is rendered, "hueriu voro guðin reið. þa er her bran iǫrðin sem nu stǫndum ver" (What angered the gods when the lava burned that we are standing on now?) (2: 191).

134 Sigfús Blöndal, "Goden Snorri Thorgrimsson: Et 900-aars minde," *Dansk-Islandsk Samfunds Aarbog* (1931): 80 [68-87].

135 The synthesis of these two variants would be "Hverju reiddust goðin, þá er hraunið brann, sem nú stöndum vér á?" as reported by Jónas Jónsson in his influential *Íslandssaga*, aimed at 10-12 year old schoolchildren (first edition 1915, eighth edition in two volumes 1967-1968, volume I repr. 1976, p. 100), and this is the version that Icelanders of the twentieth century learned by heart, including the present author.

136 A Google search reveals several examples from 2010 and 2011, in some cases connected with volcanic eruptions and other natural phenomena but on others simply with great events of national significance; cf. "Orð hans á kristnitökuþinginu um hraunið og reiði goðanna hafa nú flogið um landið og jafnvel út yfir hafið um níu alda skeið, og virðast ekki að því komin enn að detta dauð niður" (Matthías Þórðarson, "Hvað Snorri goði sagði: Tvær athugasemdir við 145. kap í Njáls sögu," *Árbók Hins íslenzka fornleifafélags* (1920): 8 [8-13]).

137 Gunnar Benediktsson, "Hverju reiddust goðin?" *Tímarit Máls og menningar* 41 (1980): 366-78.

138 Þorleifur Einarsson, *Jarðfræði: Saga bergs og lands* (Reykjavík: Mál og menning, 1968), p. 10. To Þorleifur, Snorri provides an example of medieval man's understanding of the laws of nature and (to a degree) the dynamics of volcanic eruptions. This sentiment is sometimes also attributed to noted geologist Sigurður Þórarinsson who became somewhat of a culture hero in Iceland in the 1950s and 1960s but I have not been able to locate such a statement in his many and varied articles.

139 I am critical of this idea of scientific progress, following the late twentieth-century postmodern tradition exemplified by such thinkers as Kuhn and Foucault; see note 26 above.

140 Most Icelandic scholars of the twentieth century were both Christians and rationalists and thus were in favour of organised religion but despised superstition. It is illuminating to see this "dance" performed in Einar Ólafur Sveinsson's history of the thirteenth century wherein he depicted his saga-writing magnate heroes as weatherbitten rationalists who respected religion, acknowledged some forms of superstition, but were above all moderate in everything (see *Sturlungaöld: Drög um íslenzka menningu á þrettándu öld* (Reykjavík: Nokkrir Reykvíkingar, 1940)). It is only in the twenty-first century that the scientist as atheist is established as a cultural phenomenon, not least with the work of Richard Dawkins (see *The God Delusion* (London: Bantam, 2006)).

141 Jón Helgason, "Höfuðlausnarhjal," in *Einarsbók: Afmæliskveðja til Einars Ól. Sveinssonar 12. desember 1969*, ed. Bjarni Guðnason, Halldór Halldórsson, and Jónas Kristjánsson (Reykjavík: Nokkrir vinir, 1969), p. 156 [156–76].

142 Lars Lönnroth, on the other hand, has suggested that "the literary magic of the saga has very little to do with realism" in the normal sense of that word ("Saga and jartegn: The Appeal of Mystery in Saga Texts," in *Die Aktualität der Saga: Festschrift für Hans Schottmann*, ed. Stig Toftgaard Andersen (Berlin: de Gruyter, 1999), p. 123 [111–123]; on earlier saga scholars selectiveness is describing the realism or authenticity of medieval Icelandic writing, see also Ármann Jakobsson,"Tradition and the Individual Talent," and "Hvað á að gera við Landnámu?: Um hefð, höfunda og raunveruleikablekkingu íslenskra miðaldasagnarita," *Gripla* 26 (2015): 7–27.

143 From the days of Church Fathers into the Middle Ages — largely under the influence of Augustine — miracles "were wonderful acts of God shown as events in this world, not in opposition to nature but as a drawing out of the hidden working of God within a nature that was all potentially miraculous" (Benedicta Ward, *Miracles and the Medieval Mind: Theory Record and Event 1000–1215* (Philadelphia: University of Pennsylvania Press, 1982), p. 3).

144 Óðinn's portrayal in the sagas is a good example, see Annette Lassen, *Odin på kristent pergament: En teksthistorisk studie* (Copenhagen: Museum Tusculanums Forlag, University of Copenhagen, 2011).

145 This battle is only mentioned within *Brennu-Njáls saga* itself (see Einar Ól. Sveinsson, "Formáli," in *Brennu-Njáls saga*, ÍF XII, ed. Einar Ól. Sveinsson (Reykjavík: Hið íslenzka fornritafélag, 1954), pp. xvii–xxi [v–clxiii]) and may be regarded as of dubious historical authenticity since it is unlikely that all the other sources, including *Kristni saga* and many other Sagas of Icelanders, that relate the events of the early eleventh century would ignore an event of such magnitude.

146 *Brennu-Njáls saga*, pp. 405–6. It should be noted that the particular mention of these two men belonging to Flosi's party is found in the X-grouping of manuscripts, but not for example in the version of *Brennu-Njáls saga* attested in *Möðruvallabók* (*Brennu-Njáls saga*, pp. 406n1).

147 Although the Sagas of Icelanders relate 200–400 year old events they often clearly refer to a context known to their audience but which has since been lost, mostly information regarded as public knowledge but linguistic changes may also sometimes have an impact on modern comprehension of the sagas.

148 Matthías Þórðarson, "Hvað Snorri goði sagði," pp. 8–10.

149 The nickname "kroppinskeggi" is linked only to those two men (Finnur Jónsson, "Tilnavne i den islandske Oldlitteratur," *Aarbøger for nordisk Oldkyndighed og Historie* (1907), p. 208 [161–381]). The present author has elsewhere discussed the aesthetic effect of historical "corrections" in thirteenth-century sagas which may serve to further enhance the credibility of the historians who use them by demonstrating their critical standpoint (Ármann Jakobsson, *A Sense of Belonging: Morkinskinna and Icelandic Identity c. 1220*, The Viking Collection 22, trans. Fredrik Heinemann (Odense: University Press of Southern Denmark, 2014), pp. 297–305. On medieval "imperfection" authorial tropes, see further Sverrir Tómasson, *Formálar íslenskra sagnaritara á miðöldum: Rannsókn bókmenntahefðar* (Reykjavík: Stofnun Árna Magnússonar, 1988), pp. 149–260.

150 *Íslendingabók*, pp. 8–9.

151 On Þingvellir as sacrosanct space, see, for example, Jón Hnefill Aðalsteinsson, *Hið mystíska X* (Reykjavík: Háskólaútgáfan, 2009), pp. 211–20.

152 The paranormal in *Njáls saga* has been discussed by several scholars and demonstrated to play a large role in the saga. However, like in many of the sagas (including, for example, *Egils saga*; see Ármann Jakobsson, "Beast and Man: Realism and the Occult in Egils saga," *Scandinavian Studies* 83 (2011): 38–41 [29–44]), the sagas seem to appeal both to the faithful and the skepti-

cal, leaving room for interpretation (see also Ármann Jakobsson, "The Taxonomy of the Non-existent," pp. 202–07; Lars Lönnroth, "Saga and jartegn"). In the terms adopted by Rory McTurk in his exploration of the "supernatural" in *Njáls saga,* it is such events of specifically Christian significance that are described in "objectivist statements," while others may be conveyed primarily through "subjectivist statements" ("The Supernatural in Njáls saga: A Narratological Approach," *Saga-Book* 23 (1990–93): 28–45), not dismissing them outright but rather seeming to leave considerable room for interpretation.

153 Matthías Þórðarson, "Hvað Snorri goði sagði," p. 10.

154 Though not referring to either of these scenes specifically, according to William Ian Miller Snorri goði "is consistently portrayed from saga to saga as an operator, as cunning, as self-interested in the extreme, and as ruthless about pursuing his interests as anyone in the family sagas" (*'Why Is Your Axe Bloody?': A Reading of Njáls saga* (New York: Oxford University Press, 2014), p. 270).

155 Stephen Kern has recently explored causality as a cultural phenomenon, contesting that "the question behind all other questions is the "why?" of human experience" (*A Cultural History of Causality: Science, Murder Novels and Systems of Thought* (Princeton: Princeton University Press, 2004), p. 1).

156 As previously noted (see note 131 above), Snorri goði appears in a variety of thirteenth- and fourteenth-century sources which, given the temporal distance between the age of the sources and that of his life, may not be useful for the scholar who wants to establish secure facts about Snorri's life but can, on the other hand, be extremely useful in determining how thirteenth- and fourteenth-century historiographers created meaning when presenting events of the tenth and eleventh centuries; on the similar case of Skapti Þóroddsson, see Ármann Jakobsson, "Tradition and the Individual Talent."

157 On miracles, magic, and the paranormal in medieval Christendom more generally, see Benedicta Ward, *Miracles and the Medieval Mind.*

158 *Eyrbyggja saga,* pp. 150–51. The word "exorcist" is certainly well-known in medieval Iceland, appearing, for example, as a loan-word (*exorcizta*) in a version of *Martinus saga* (see *Martinus saga II* in *Heilagra manna søgur,* ed. C.R. Unger, 2 vol. (Kristiania/Oslo, 1877), 1: 577.

159 Goði is a nickname, referring to Snorri's role as a *pontifex maximus,* priest-chieftain, of his region. Little is known about the ac-

tual religious role of the goði, and how long it lasted whereas the
secular role of this office, participating in both the local and the
national parliament, is often referred to in the Sagas of Icelanders. For a thorough investigation of this institution, see Gunnar
Karlsson, *Goðamenning: Staða og áhrif goðorðsmanna í þjóðveldi
Íslendinga* (Reykjavík: Heimskringla, 2004), pp. 369–410.

160 This includes also Óláfr the Peacock, for example, who will be
discussed later ("Immigrant Song").

161 On the category of the "wondrous," as opposed to good and evil,
see Francis Dubost, *Aspects fantastiques de la littérature narrative
médiévale (XIIe-XIIIe s.): L'autre, l'ailleurs, l'autrefois*, 2 vols. (Gene-
va: Slatkine, 1991), whom Torfi Tulinius has referred to in his insightful study of Grettis saga ("Framliðnir feður: Um forneskju
og frásagnarlist í Eyrbyggju, Eglu og Grettlu," in *Heiðin minni:
Greinar um fornar bókmenntir*, ed. Haraldur Bessason and Baldur
Hafstað (Reykjavík: Heimskringla, 1999), pp. 283–316).

162 See note 131 above.

163 *Laxdæla saga*, p. 39.

164 *Laxdæla saga*, p. 39.

165 Jonathan Evans ("As Rare As They are Dire: Old Norse Dragons,
Beowulf, and the Deutsche Mythologie," in *The Shadow-Walkers:
Jacob Grimm's Mythology of the Monstrous*, ed. Tom Shippey (Tempe, AZ: Arizona Center for Medieval and Renaissance Studies,
2005), pp. 207–69) has discussed this relation between dragons
and ghosts. Since Evans believes that Nordic dragons mainly
symbolize the greed for gold and its influence, he feels they are
very close to ghosts, especially mound-dwellers (some dragon
stories are quite similar to those of mound-dwellers; see, for
example, *Þorskfirðinga saga*, pp. 185–88), but these dragons are
perhaps not quite typical). The Old Norse words *dreki* and *draugr*
are rather similar, even though there is no proof of their relation. Norse sources indicate that dragons are no less symbolic of
fear and threat than of the greed for gold (see, Ármann Jakobsson, "Enter the Dragon: Legendary Saga Courage and the Birth
of the Hero," in *Making History: The Legendary sagas*, ed. Martin
Arnold (University College London: Viking Society for Northern
Research, 2010), pp. 33–52), which certainly applies to ghost stories as well.

166 When it comes to younger Icelandic folktales, Jón Árnason categorizes a special group of misers ("maurapúkar") whose undead
presence is explained by their wishes to guard their possessions
(*Íslenzkar þjóðsögur og ævintýri*, 1: 264–80). This notion is also
exemplified in Old Icelandic writing in the story of the dragon

Fáfnir; see *Vǫlsunga saga ok Ragnars saga loðbrókar,* pp. 33–36; cf. Andrew McGillivray, "The Best Kept Secret: Ransom, Wealth, and Power in Völsunga saga," *Scandinavian Studies* 87 (2015): 365–82.

167 No causal relationship is presented overtly in the saga between Hrappr and Kjartan's later tragic death. However, this event is foreshadowed in the saga by a wide range of prophecies and warnings and it is more than likely that the medieval audience was meant to see the occult origins of the Hjarðarholt farmstead as one more in this ominous sequence of events.

168 Another Víga-Hrappr shows up much later in the saga, when Helgi Harðbeinsson is attacked; he claims to be from Breiðafjörðr and is described as "lítill vexti ok allkviklátur; hann var margeygur furðuliga" (small and somewhat restless, and his eyes darted strangely into all directions) (*Laxdœla saga,* p. 190). We cannot tell whether this Hrappr has anything more than the name in common with the former, but he seems to be a rather garrulous person who "segir mart, en spurði fás" (says a lot but asks little) and boasts of his valour in the impending attack. In the event, he is the first to attack Helgi, who kills him easily. If this is what is left of the ghost of the former Hrappr, it is certainly no longer threatening which is much in keeping with the whole tone of this "Helgi part" of *Laxdœla saga* (pp. 186–93) where formerly tragic and poignant events from the saga seem to repeat themselves, this time as farce.

169 The monster always returns, according to Jeffrey Jerome Cohen's interesting analysis of the cultural role of monsters ("Monster Culture (Seven Theses)," in *Monster Theory: Reading Culture,* ed. Jeffrey Jerome Cohen (Minneapolis, MN: University of Minnesota Press, 1996), pp: 4–6 [3–25]). This is also a theme in the Þórólfr twistfoot narrative of *Eyrbyggja saga* (see "Please! Let Me In!") wherein numerous measures taken fail to expel the troll.

170 *Laxdœla saga,* p. 40.

171 *Laxdœla saga,* pp. 68–69.

172 The present author dealt with this theme in a short story about a resilient guest who ends up being accidentally killed and then returns as a ghost, composed as a by-product of this book; see Ármann Jakobsson, "Gesturinn," *Stína* 10.2 (2015): 26–31.

173 *Heiðreks saga: Hervarar saga ok Heiðreks konungs,* STUAGNL 48, ed. Jón Helgason (Copenhagen: Samfund til udgivense af gammel nordisk litterature, 1924), p. 24 (hereafter *Heiðreks saga*).

174 See Ármann Jakobsson, "The Specter of Old Age: Nasty Old Men in the Sagas of Icelanders," *Journal of English and Germanic Philology* 104 (2005): 297–325.

175 Paul Barber, *Vampire, Burial, and Death: Folklore and Reality* (New Haven: Yale University Press, 1988), pp. 34–36; on the possible relationship between mental or spiritual disintigration and the undead in medieval Iceland, see, for example, Kirsi Kanerva, "Disturbances of the Mind and Body: Effects of the Living Dead in Medieval Iceland," in *Mental (dis)Order in Later Medieval Europe*, ed. Sari Katajala-Peltomaa and Susanna Niiranen (Leiden and Boston: Brill, 2014), pp. 219–42.

176 These mound-breaking motifs may be found in various medieval Icelandic narratives, incuding, for example, *Hrómundar saga*, pp. 368–71; *Heiðreks saga*, pp. 17–33; *Grettis saga*, pp. 56–61; *Harðar saga*, pp. 40–44; *Bárðar saga*, pp. 167–68; *Flóamanna saga*, pp. 255–56; *Flateyjarbók: En samling af norske konge-sagaer med indskudte mindre fortællinger om begivenheder i og udenfor Norge samt annaler*, ed. Guðbrandur Vigfússon and C.R. Unger, 3 vols. (Christiania: Malling, 1860–68), 2: 9. Jonas Wellendorf has analysed stories of mound-dwellers and their anthropological premises in medieval Scandinavia ("Ideologi og trosforestillinger i Ólafs þáttr Geirstaðálfs: Om jordfundne genstande og rituelle højbrud," *Nordica Bergensia* 29 (2003): 147–69. Many of the mound-breaking motifs reappear in stories of mummies from the twentieth century, mainly the idea that those who disturbed mummies were often cursed. This is depicted, for example, in the film *The Mummy* from 1932, where Boris Karloff plays the main role. The inspiration came from sensational newspaper reports about the curse connected to the mummy of the Egyptian pharaoh Tutankhamun, who was discovered by the archaeologists Howard Carter and Lord Carnarvon in 1923. In fact these stories, told by word of mouth, were unfounded.

177 *Laxdœla saga*, pp. 84–85.

178 On this topic, see, for example, Christopher Crocker, *Situating the Dream: Paranormal Dreams in the Íslendingasögur*, PhD dissertation (Reykjavík, 2016).

179 As Hollywood made Thomas Andrews, architect of *The Titanic*, say, in the anagnorisis moment of the fittingly colossal 1997 film about the doomed gargantuan ship. In a large cinema in Iceland that year, the present author and his brother were the only ones who laughed during this dramatic moment.

180 The phrase "Computer says no" was made famous by unhelpful functionary Carol Beer (played by David Walliams), a recurring

character in the British comic TV series, *Little Britain* (2003–6). Doubtless many readers, as well as the author, will feel that this character represents fairly well various real-life functionaries.

181 The reciprocity of paranormal figures is a fairly ubiquitous folklore phenomenon, see also the "Grateful Dead" folktale (AT 505), and others.

182 *Sturlunga saga*, 1: 521.

183 See, for example, Ármann Jakobsson, "Enabling Love: Dwarfs in Old Norse-Icelandic Romances," in *Romance and Love in Late Medieval and Early Modern Iceland: Essays in Honor of Marianna Kalinke*, Islandica 54, ed. Johanna Denzin and Kirsten Wolf (Ithaca: Cornell University Library, 2008), pp. 183–206.

184 An exception might be Bárðr Snæfellsáss who is said to be a "heitguð" (a *hapax legomenon* in Old Icelandic writing) (*Bárðar saga*, p. 119). With regard to dreams, for example, Paul Schach has noted that the "the vast majority of dreams in Old Icelandic literature are sinister, foreboding adversity and disaster" ("Symbolic Dreams of Future Renown in Old Icelandic Literature," *Mosaic* 4.4 (1971): 52 [51–73]).

185 A similar narrative of a dream that seems to illustrate the guilt of the dreamer is Flosi's haunting paranormal dream of a mountain man who summons the dreamer's followers whose deaths are clearly Flosi's responsibility, at least in his own subconsciousness (*Brennu-Njáls saga*, pp. 336–38; see also Christopher Crocker, "To Dream is to Bury: Dreaming of Death in Brennu-Njáls saga," *Journal of English and Germanic Philology* 114 (2015): 261–91.

186 See Ármann Jakobsson, "The Hunted Children of Kings: A Theme in the Old Icelandic Sagas," *Scandinavica* 43 (2004): 5–27.

187 The textual history of *Óláfs saga Tryggvasonar en mesta* is complicated. It is attested in as many as eleven extant fourteenth- and early fifteenth-century manuscripts, including the famous *Flateyjarbók* (GKS 1005 fol.) and there is some variation between these many different versions of the text. For comprehensive details on the manuscripts and the different versions of *Óláfs saga Tryggvasonar en mesta*, see Ólafur Halldórsson, "Indledning," in *Óláfs saga Tryggvasonar en mesta*, Arnamagnæanæ Series A, 1–3, ed. Ólafur Halldórsson, 3 vols. (Copenhagen: Munksgaard, 1958–2000), 3: xvii–cccxxiii [vii–cccxxiii].

188 *Af Þiðranda ok dísunum*, p. 121. This same event is referred to in *Brennu-Njáls saga* wherein, of the same Þiðrandi, "þann er sagt er, at dísir vægi" (*Brennu-Njáls saga*, p. 239). On the episode's ideological stance towards the past, see Merrill Kaplan, "Prefigura-

tion and the Writing of History in Þáttr Þiðranda ok Þórhalls," *Journal of English and Germanic Philology* 99 (2000): 379–94.

189 See "dís," *Ordbog over det norrøne prosasprog*, 2010, retrieved from http://onp.ku.dk. There are only a few instances of the word in Old Norse texts, mostly in late texts, all fairly vague as to the actual identity of these "dísir" although they have been much theorised about; see, for example, Dag Strömbäck, *Tidrande och Diserna — Ett Filologiskt-Folkloristiskt Utkast* (Lund: Carl Blom, 1949); Folke Ström, *Diser, Nornor, Valkyrjor: Frukbarhetskult och sakralt kungadöme i Norden* (Stockholm: Almquist & Wiksell, 1954); Karen Bek-Pedersen, *The Norns in Old Norse Mythology* (Edinburgh: Dunedin, 2011), pp. 41–48.

190 On the fylgjur phenomenon, see Zuzana Stankovitsová, "Following up on Female Fylgjur: A Re-Examination of the Concept of Female fylgjur in Old Norse Literature," in *Paranormal Encounters in Iceland 1150–1400*, ed. Ármann Jakobsson and Miriam Mayburd (forthcoming, 2018); William Friesen, "Family Resemblances: Textual Sources of Animal Fylgjur in Icelandic Saga," *Scandinavian Studies* 87 (2015): 255–80.

191 See, for example, Ármann Jakobsson, *A Sense of Belonging*, pp. 317–19.

192 See Ármann Jakobsson, "Enter the Dragon," pp. 33–52.

193 The mass murder of teenagers and young adults, often connected to their recently awakened and massive interest in romance, sex, and copulation, is a mainstay of the so-called "slasher films" which often feature a main antagonist who is some kind of a monster or an undead, i.e., a troll (on this genre and its social significance, see Carol J. Clover, *Men, Women, and Chain Saws: Gender in the Modern Horror Film* (Princeton: Princeton University Press, 1992)). From teenagers just hitting puberty to young adults, youngsters are also often a "channel" for paranormal activity (with Regan in *The Exorcist* perhaps the most notorious example), often in a less innocent way than younger children that also figure prominently in such narratives (i.e., in *Poltergeist* (1982), written by Spielberg and directed by Tobe Hooper), usually as more unambiguous victims.

194 *Eyrbyggja saga*, p. 93.

195 Anonymous saga characters have not been the subject of much scrutiny but will be examined in the present author's forthcoming book among other supporting saga characters and marginal people in the sagas. One observation that can safely be made about anonymous characters is that they are primarily defined by their role or function in the narrative and are not what E.M.

Forster would have defined as "round characters" in his *Aspects of the Novel* (New York: Harcourt, Brace and Company, 1927), pp. 103–18. It still seems inevitable that people who repeatedly read or hear the narrative will eventually start to wonder about them and they thus do have an important function in creating a more replete illusion of reality in the narrative. The idea of the "secret life" of anonymous characters was explored in the "henchmen" scenes of the film *Austin Powers: International Man of Mystery* (1997) where the narrative suddenly breaks off to show friends and family members of anonymous henchmen killed, stock figures that usually meet their end in films without expectation of audience empathy.

196 Youths do not only have the dual role of victims and possible perpetrators of paranormal phenomena but are also prominent witnesses to them, as evidenced by several saga narratives, including a haunting episode in *Brennu-Njáls saga* where an otherwise unknown Hildiglúmr, living in the vicinity, sees a "gandreið" just before the climactic burning of Njáll and is severly affected by his vision (pp. 320–21); see also Ármann Jakobsson, "'I See Dead People': The Externalisation of Paranormal Experience in Medieval Iceland," in *Paranormal Encounters in Iceland 1150–1400*, ed. Ármann Jakobsson and Miriam Mayburd (forthcoming, 2018).

197 See, Dillmann, *Les magiciens dans l'Islande ancienne*, pp. 332–35, 432–39, 527–37, 577–78; Raudvere, *Kunskap och insikt i norrön tradition*, pp. 186–95. *Eyrbyggja saga* is a saga of the Snæfellsnes region, often dated to around 1250, which means that it was composed, in its present form, in the death throes of that system which is often referred to as the Icelandic commonwealth. The oldest surviving manuscript of the saga is AM 162 E fol. from the thirteenth century (for a detailed discussion of the manuscripts, see *Eyrbyggja saga: The Vellum Tradition*, Editiones Arnamagnæanæ, Series A, 18, ed. Forrest S. Scott, (Copenhagen: C. A. Reitzels Forlag, 2003), pp. 1*–143*). Einar Ólafur Sveinsson has argued that the saga was probably composed around 1220 ("Formáli," in *Eyrbyggja saga*, ÍF IV, ed. Einar Ól. Sveinsson, Matthías Þórðarson, and Ólafur Halldórsson (Reykjavík: Hið íslenzka fornritafélag, 1985), pp. xliii–lii [v–lxvi]). Bjarni Guðnason has, on the other hand, argued that *Eyrbyggja saga* was several decades younger, composed around 1265 (*Túlkun Heiðarvígasögu*, Studia Islandica 50 (Reykjavík: Bókmenntafræðistofnun Háskóla Íslands, 1993), pp. 220–23). For my purposes in this study, the exact dating of the saga is irrelevant.

198 On Þórólfr and his nature as a ghost, see Ármann Jakobsson, "The Spectre of Old Age: Nasty Old Men in the Sagas of Icelanders," *Journal of English and Germanic Philology* 104 (2005): 322–25 [297–325].

199 *Eyrbyggja saga*, p. 28.

200 The study of magic is a well-known saga theme (see Hermann Pálsson, *Úr landnorðri: Samar og ystu rætur íslenskrar menningar*, Studia Islandica 54 (Reykjavík: Bókmenntafræðistofnun Háskóla Íslands, 1997), pp. 131–40; François-Xavier Dillmann, *Les magiciens dans l'Islande ancienne*, pp. 591–94). In *Bárðar saga*, it is said that Bárðr studied magic with the mountain-dweller Dofri in Norway (p. 103). Unlike Gunnlaugr, he survived but the saga is vague on the subject of his use of magic, and whether he is, in fact, to be considered human at all (see Ármann Jakobsson, "The Good, the Bad, and the Ugly," pp. 7–10). Somewhat similarly Gunnhildr konungamóðir, in *Heimskringla*, claims to have been housed with two Finnar to "nema kunnostu," but in this case it is the student who brings about her teachers' deaths (1: 135).

201 The Icelandic proverb reads, "eru ok opt flǫgð í fǫgru skinni" (*Eyrbyggja saga*, pp. 28–29).

202 *Eyrbyggja saga*, pp. 34, 36

203 Cf. Sean B. Lawing, "Re-membering Auðr's Hand in *Eyrbyggja saga*" (forthcoming).

204 As William I. Miller has noted ("Dreams, Prophecy and Sorcery: Blaming the Secret Offender in Medieval Iceland," *Scandinavian Studies* 58 (1986): 110–16 [101–23]), they would in any case be ideal scapegoats for whatever has taken place.

205 The narrative closely parallels an episode in *Brennu-Njáls saga* in which Þráinn Sigfússon hides Hrappr from the wrath of Earl Hákon (pp. 216–20). On the ritualistic nature of this event, see Jón Hnefill Aðalsteinsson, *Blót í norrænum sið*, pp. 151–53.

206 The evil eye of the sorcerer is a well-known theme from other sagas, such as *Laxdæla saga* (pp. 107, 109) and *Vatnsdæla saga* (p. 70); see also *Gísla saga*, p. 60, and the examples found in Hermann Pálsson, *Úr landnorðri*, pp. 151–53.

207 In *Landnámabók* he is said to have died soon afterwards (p. 112).

208 Katla is a recognizable witch's name from *Harðar saga*, where it is used as a sobriquet (p. 63; see also Dillmann, *Les magiciens dans l'Islande ancienne*, pp. 381–83). The name is derived from the masculine name Ketill—a name that Torfi H. Tulinius has convincingly argued is extremely important as a structural element in *Egils saga* (*The Enigma of Egill: The Saga, the Viking Poet, and Snorri Sturluson*, Islandica 57, trans. Victoria Cribb (Ithaca,

NY: Cornell University Press, 2014), pp. 24–31, 86–88) — which also means "kettle," an instrument that can be used for brewing magic potions (Finnur Jónsson, "Tilnavne i den islandske Oldlitteratur," p. 289; Erik Henrik Lind, *Norsk-isländska personbinamn från medeltiden* (Uppsala: Lundequistska bokhandeln, 1920–21), p. 191). Katla's name alone may thus reveal her to be a sorceress, a somewhat undignified one, unlike her counterpart Geirríðr, whose name suggests a Valkyrie, Geir- ("spear") being a popular prefix of Valkyrie-names, including, for example, the names Geirskǫgul, Geirǫnul, Geirahǫð (*Eddukvæði*, 1: 299, 373, 375; *Edda Snorra Sturlusonar*, p. 40; see also Guðrún Kvaran and Sigurður Jónsson, *Nöfn Íslendinga* (Reykjavík: Heimskringla, 1991), p. 241). The second part of her name (-ríðr) refers to the act of "riding," and it is notably the case that Valkyries may occasionally be seen "riding" in Eddic texts (*Eddukvæði*, 1: 298).

The connection between witches and "riding" is indeed well known throughout various phases of history (see, for example, Valerie I.J. Flint, *The Rise of Magic in Early Modern Europe* (Oxford: Clarendon Press, 1991), pp. 116–26; Elliot Rose, *A Razor for a Goat: A Discussion of Certain Problems in the History of Witchcraft and Diabolism* (Toronto: University of Toronto Press, 1962), pp. 106–29), and according to Éva Pócs such creatures — which she somewhat sweepingly refers to as *moras* — "are generally human beings who are able to send their souls out at night while in a trance. Thus they can make journeys by assuming the shapes of animals (snakes, butterflies, mice, hens, cats). They infiltrate peoples dwellings as incubi, confinement demons, or even as vampires, and they 'ride upon' or torment people" (Between the *Living and the Dead: A Perspective on Witches and Seers in Early Modern Age*, trans. Szilvia Rédey and Michael Webb (Budapest: Central European University Press, 1999), p. 32), mentioning also that another name for the *mora* is "night-goer" (p. 46). I have discussed various categories of dark creatures that seem to somewhat fall under this description and whose main purpose it is to craze their victims and transport them to a different world in another study (Ármann Jakobsson, "Yfirnáttúrlegar ríðingar"). Bearing some similarity to Pócs's work, G. David Keyworth has recently drawn attention to the affinities, among others, between Icelandic ghosts and Eastern European vampires, generally concluding that the only distinguishing feature of the eighteenth-century vampires from Eastern Europe is their apparent thirst for blood ("Was the Vampire of the Eighteenth Century a Unique Type of Undead-corpse?" *Folklore* 117 (2006):

241–60; cf. William Sayers, "The Alien and Alienated as Unquiet Dead in the Sagas of the Icelanders," in *Monster Theory: Reading Culture*, ed. Jeffrey Jerome Cohen (Minneapolis: University of Minnesota Press, 1996), pp. 242–263).

209 *Eyrbyggja saga*, pp. 28–30.

210 *Brennu-Njáls saga*, pp. 37–38.

211 Sverrir Jakobsson has discussed the figure of the saga that has prophetic gifts but is never defined as a witch in his article "Galdur og forspá í ríkisvaldslausu samfélagi," in *Galdramenn: Galdrar og samfélag á miðöldum*, ed. Torfi H. Tulinius (Reykjavík: Hugvísindastofnun, 2008), pp. 73–84. The benevolence of these characters is usually stressed, reminding us of the strong relationship between witchcraft and malice also mentioned in the depiction of Óðinn as witch (see "The Witchfather").

212 See, for example, *Brennu-Njáls saga*, p. 57.

213 It has been remarked recently (see, for example, Ármann Jakobsson, "Masculinity and Politics in Njáls saga," *Viator* 38 (2007): 191–215; Theodore M. Andersson, *The Growth of the Medieval Icelandic Sagas (1180–1280)* (Ithaca, NY: Cornell University Press, 2006), pp. 183–203) that *Brennu-Njáls saga* in many ways subverts saga ideals and commonplaces. In making the main protagonist and hero a magical figure, the saga is again going against the grain, at least to some degree.

214 Whether to designate Njáll's ancestry as undistinguished is a matter of debate. According to *Brennu-Njáls saga*, Njáll is the son of Ásgerðr, one of a few female settlers in Iceland (pp. 55–56) whereas in *Landnámabók*, he is listed as her grandson (p. 344). While his name is Irish, his family comes from Norway according to *Landnámabók* and there is no mention of any Irish roots there. Nothing indicates that Njáll's ancestors are of noble stock although it could be argued that anyone who acquired the status of settler in *Landnámabók* could be said to belong to the elite of Iceland. That being said, Njáll's ancestry is clearly less distinguished than that of some of the other wise magnates of the saga, such as Gizurr the White or Hallr of Síða.

215 *Grágás* ("Grey Goose") is the name used for collections of Icelandic laws from the commonwealth period, before the 1270s. The name is not contemporary and of uncertain significance and these laws should perhaps not be regarded as a unified body of law. The laws probably only existed in human memory and oral recitation before the early twelfth century when they were written down. *Brennu-Njáls saga* stages many legal disputes and Njáll, along with many other great legal minds appearing in the

narrative, is clearly a representative of that system of law codes of uncertain contours that is now called *Grágás*; see Miller, 'Why Is Your Axe Bloody?,' pp. 126–31.

216 *Laxdœla saga*, p. 95.

217 *Laxdœla saga*, p. 99.

218 *Laxdœla saga*, pp. 105–6.

219 The word appears twice in the saga, first when it is explained that people could still (in the thirteenth century) see the remains of Hrútr's temple and it is called "Trollaskeið" (*Laxdœla saga*, p. 48), and again when a supporting character called Auðunn festargarmr angers the sage Ósvífr who promptly predicts his imminent demise at sea by saying "þú ... munt fara í trollendr [trolla hendr] í sumar" (you ... will go to the trolls [or troll's hands] in the summer) (p. 159). The fluidity of the term troll is well exemplified here since in neither case does it seem likely that it refers to a specific paranormal race, in the first clearly connected with pagan deities and those who worship them (later redefined as witches) and in the other with death at sea, and possibly also pagan, possibly aquatic gods who may collect the sea-dead.

220 *Laxdœla saga*, p. 65.

221 Sverrir Jakobsson, "Strangers in Icelandic Society 1100–1400," *Viking and Medieval Scandinavian* 3 (2007): 144 [141–57].

222 The trope is well-known, for example, from the novels of Philip Roth (see *The Dying Animal* (Boston: Houghton Mifflin, 2001)). In addition to *Eyrbyggja saga*, the first part of *Brennu-Njáls saga* has a similar narrative, wherein Hrútr Herjólfsson enters into the service of Queen Gunnhildr, the Mrs Robinson of medieval Scandinavia, and soon becomes her paramour (pp. 11–20).

223 On the theme of "fearless youth" and its significance to a late medieval audience, see Ármann Jakobsson, "Enter the Dragon," pp. 42–47.

224 Cf. Dillmann, *Les magiciens dans l'Islande ancienne*, p. 439.

225 See, for example, *Laxdœla saga*, pp. 95, 99, 106–9; see also Dillmann, *Les magiciens dans l'Islande ancienne*, pp. 505–47; Catharina Raudvere, *Kunskap och insikt i norrön tradition*, pp. 142–54. While "seiðr" generally seems to be interpreted as a magic ritual in the sagas under consideration here, its original meaning could have been much wider, possibly the basis of the whole order ("siðr") of society in which case it would be natural enough that post-conversion society interpreted it as magic; this has been suggested to me by Davíð Erlingsson to whom this book is dedicated.

226 *Sagan af Herrauði ok Bósa*, in *Fornaldar sögur Nordrlanda eptir gömlum handritum*, ed. C.C. Rafn, 3 vols. (Copenhagen, 1829–30), 3: 196; see also Stephen Mitchell, "Gender and Nordic Witchcraft in the Later Middle Ages," *Arv* 56 (2000): 9–11 [7–24].

227 Freud, "The 'Uncanny,'" p. 241.

228 John McKinnell has analysed narratives of heroes and giantesses in the legendary sagas wherein the latter serve as surrogate mothers, sexual partners and supernatural aides, sometimes even mistaking the hero for a child in the beginning (see, for example, *Örvar-Odds saga*, pp. 127–28), which is a continuing trope in such narratives (see John McKinnell, *Meeting the Other in Norse Myth and Legend* (Cambridge: D.S. Brewer, 2005)). According to McKinnell, the giantess may represent the dual nature of the mother in the life of a teenager or a young adult, as an ogress and a figure of benevolent authority (pp. 172–96). Helga Kress has analysed these narratives in terms of gender warfare while also highlighting their symbolic nature (*Máttugar meyjar: íslensk fornbókmenntasaga* (Reykjavík: Háskólaútgáfan, 1993), pp. 119–35).

229 All human death may seem to represent our own personal death, which effectively ends the world from our point of view, and the very past itself, in its vulnerability, will thus always be, at least in a tinypart, abhorrent to us, an abhorrence that may in narrative be transferred to ancestors, including parents, possibly providing fuel for generational conflict myths (see, for example, Ármann Jakobsson, "A Contest of Cosmic Fathers: God and Giant in Vafþrúðnismál," *Neophilologus* 92 (2008): 263–77).

230 See, for example, Rudolf Meissner, *Die Kenningar der Skalden*, pp. 116–26, 202–8.

231 *Edda Snorra Sturlusonar*, p. 14.

232 Margaret Clunies Ross contends that while Óðinn's matrilineal ancestry is traced to giants, his patrilineal ancestry is not, contributing to a "de-emphasis of the gods' kinship with the giants," but notes also that it is through the giants, perhaps his maternal uncle, that Óðinn might gain his spiritual or mystical knowledge (*Prolonged Echoes: Old Norse Myths in Medieval Northern Society*, Viking Collection 7, 10, 2 vols. (Odense: Odense University Press, 1994–98), 1: 57, 227–28). The relationship between Óðinn and the sibyl in Völuspá is also far from clear (see *Eddukvæði*, 1: 291, 298, 318); on the dynamics of their verbal exchange, see Jacob Malone, *Vessel and Voice: A Cognitive Semiotic Approach to the Prophetic Voice of Vǫluspá*, MA thesis (Reykjavík, 2015).

233 *Heimskringla*, 1: 19.

234 *Edda Snorra Sturlusonar,* pp. 8, 10, 17, 20, 22, 25, 27, 28, 34, 36, 38, 43, 88; see also Ármann Jakobsson, "Óðinn as Mother: The Old Norse Deviant Patriarch," *Arkiv för nordisk filologi* 126 (2011): 5–16.

235 On the medieval European context of the eheumeristic narrative of the gods in *Ynglinga saga* and *Snorra-Edda,* see, for example, Anthony Faulkes, "Descent from the gods," *Mediaeval Scandinavia* 11 (1978–1979): 92–125.

236 *Heimskringla,* 1: 18.

237 Óðinn's life in the medieval Christian sources has been dealt with extensively by Annette Lassen (see *Odin på kristent pergament*).

238 Although the Old Norse gods are positioned as the "other" in most Sagas of Icelanders and legendary sagas, as discussed by Lassen (see note 237 above), in the myths found in *Snorra-Edda's Gylfaginning* and *Skáldskaparmál,* they become the norm, taking effectively the place of regular and often fallible humanity against the forces of otherness.

239 Óðinn's appearance is often described as resembling that of an old man, in *Vǫlsunga saga* for example (cf. Lassen, *Odin på kristent pergament,* pp. 55–58) so he provides a good exampe of a deity that is essentially modelled on humanity.

240 The character Þorgrímr Nose, termed "seiðskratti" ("witch," or "warlock") in this narrative (*Gísla saga,* p. 37), is hired to curse Gísli (pp. 56–57), this curse is blamed for Gísli's misfortune (pp. 69, 84) and Þorgrímr is duly killed in revenge (p. 60), with a bag over his head, clearly to ward off the aforementioned "evil eye" of the troll, but then he is stoned to death, like Kotkell and Gríma. The magic that Þorgrímr performs is called "seiðr" (p. 56) and is said to be performed "með allri ergi ok skelmiskap" (pp. 56–57), while later reference is made to "þess trollskapar, er Þorgrímr nef hafði haft í seiðinum, ok atkvæða" (p. 69). In this instance, this "trollskapr" seems to be a part of the magic ritual of the witch, along with the undefined "ergi" he acts out. His execution is narrated briefly. Gísli kills Þorgrímr to avenge an old woman who had been helpful to the former, but who had been killed by Gísli's adversary Bǫrkr. Both witch killings seem unquestionably justifiable by their very acts.

241 Apart from Loki's attempt, described in the poem *Lokasenna* (v. 24), when he claims that Óðinn has acted as a witch (or, more precisely, as a vala, a sibyl or seeress): "En þik síða kóðu / Sámseyju í, / ok draptu á vétt sem vǫlur; / vikta líki / fórtu verþjóð yfir, / ok hugða ek þat args aðal" (*Eddukvæði,* 1: 413) ("But you, they say, practised seid on Samsey, / and you beat on the drum

as seeresses do, / in the likeness of a wizard you journeyed over mankind, / and that I thought the hallmark of a pervert") (*The Poetic Edda*, trans. Carolyne Larrington (Oxford: Oxford University Press, 2014), p. 85). In this stanza and with his accusation, Loki is countering Óðinn's claim that Loki has carried children in his womb like a woman, so it seems evident that "seiðr" and sorcery are very unmanly, almost up to par with bearing children.

242 See note 214 above.
243 For the case of Njáll as the modest hero of the saga, see Ármann Jakobsson, "Masculinity and Politics in Njáls saga." It has also been argued that he may be regarded as a master manipulator and, thus, perhaps even a modest villain (Kristján Jóhann Jónsson, *Lykillinn að Njálu* (Reykjavík: Vaka-Helgafell, 1998), pp. 46–49, 158; Yoav Tirosh, "Víga-Njáll: A New Approach toward Njáls saga," *Scandinavian Studies* 86 (2014): 208–26; Miller, '*Why Is Your Axe Bloody?*,' pp. 70, 144–47, 160–61, 165–69, 246–47). These interpretations need not be mutually exclusive.
244 *Brennu-Njáls saga*, p. 264. The verse is also attested in *Íslendingabók* (p. 15), *Kristni saga* (p. 26), and in *Óláfs saga Tryggvasonar* (p. 246; see also *Óláfs saga Tryggvasonar en mesta*, 2: 162). Though only the versions of the verse attested in *Njáls saga* and *Ólafs saga* refer to Óðinn.
245 See, for example, *Brennu-Njáls saga*, pp. 261, 264, 269, 274, 328–29, 331.
246 *Brennu-Njáls saga*, pp. 328–29.
247 *Sturlunga saga*, 1: 114; see also Ármann Jakobsson, "Hversu argur er Óðinn?: Seiður, kynferði og Hvamm-Sturla," in *Galdramenn: Galdur og samfélag á miðöldum*, ed. Torfi H. Tulinius (Reykjavík: Hugvísindastofnun, 2008), pp. 51–71.
248 *Gísla saga*, pp. 56, 69. On the meaning of the terms "ergi" and "trollskapr" see Ármann Jakobsson, "The Trollish Acts," "Vad är ett troll?" "Hvað er tröll?" and "Hversu argur er Óðinn?"; see also Preben Meulengracht Sørensen, *Norrønt nid: Forestillingen om den umandige mand i de Islandske sagaer* (Odense, 1980); Gunnar Karlsson, "Karlmennska, drengskapur, bleyði og ergi," in *Bókmentaljós: Heiðursrit til Turið Sigurðardóttir*, ed. Dagný Kristjánsdóttir, Malan Marnersdóttir, Leyvoy Joensen, and Anfinnur Johansen (Tórshavn: Faroe University Press, 2006), pp. 371–86.
249 The term "troll" is perhaps most commonly used today with respect to internet activity where it is used to refer to those who stir up discord and deliberately upset people, with the apparent purpose of ruining the discussion and drawing it off topic (and

gained wide currency during the meteoric rise and subsequent fall of "alt-right troll" Milo Yiannopoulos in 2015–17). Its etymology is often related to the fishing technique "trolling," its primary meaning thus being to "draw away" which is closely connected to many of the oldest meanings of the verb "troll" that are connected with movement and turning (see "troll," *Oxford English Dictionary*, 2016, retrieved from http://oed.com; see also Terence H. Wilbur, "Troll: An Etymological Note," *Scandinavian Studies* 30 (1958): 137–39; Þorfinnur Skúlason, "Ótti Emilíu," *Mímir* 43 (1996): 69–75). However, the internet troll is also curiously attached to the demonic medieval troll discussed in this book; thus modern users should not hesitate to refer to that cultural phenomenon when they discuss internet trolls. Like its medieval counterpart, the internet troll is usually nameless, faceless, hostile, and fiendish, and decisively othered; there are no known societies for internet trolls.

250 On Grettir's ambiguous status in the narrative itself, see in particular Robert Cook, "The Reader in Grettis Saga," *Saga-book* 21 (1982–85): 133–54.

251 On outlaws and outlawry in medieval Iceland, see Gabriel Turville-Petre, "Outlawry," in *Sjötíu ritgerðir helgaðar Jakobi Benediktssyni 20. Júlí 1977*, ed. Einar G. Pétursson and Jónas Kristjánsson, 2 vols. (Reykjavík: Stofnun Árna Magnússonar á Íslandi, 1977), 2: 769–78; Marion Poilvez, "Access to the Margins: Outlawry and Narrative Spaces in Medieval Icelandic Outlaw Sagas," *Brathair* 12.1 (2012): 115–36; Joonas Ahola, *Outlawry in the Icelandic family sagas*, PhD dissertation (Helsinki, 2014). On the monstrosity of outlaws, see Rebecca Merkelbach, "Engi maðr skapar sik sjálfr: Fathers, Abuse and Monstrosity in the Outlaw Sagas," in *Bad Boys and Wicked Women: Antagonists and Troublemakers in Old Norse Literature*, ed. Daniela Hahn and Andreas Schmidt (Munich: Herbert Utz Verlag, 2016), pp. 59–93.

252 *Grettis saga*, pp. 130, 211.

253 *Grettis saga*, pp. 209–17. The terms used here are "trollagangr," "reimleikar," "aptrgangar," "trollkona," "jǫtunn," and "óvættir"; on the usefulness of calling them "zombies," see note 12 above.

254 See Ármann Jakobsson, "The Fearless Vampire Killers: A Note about the Icelandic Dragur and Demonic Contamination in Grettis Saga," *Folklore* 120 (2009): 307–16.

255 *Grettis saga*, p. 184. Þórir, however, later chastizes Þorbjǫrn, implicitly calling him *ódáðamaðr* (an unvirtuous man) and *fordæða* (a sorceror), for using *galdr* and *fjǫlkynngi* to bring about Grettir's death (p. 264).

256 *Brennu-Njáls saga*, p. 298; see also Ármann Jakobsson, "Some Types of Ambiguity in the Sagas of the Icelanders," *Arkiv för nordisk filologi* 119 (2004): 38–42 [37–53].

257 See Ármann Jakobsson, "Masculinity and Politics in *Njáls saga*." Further study by Miriam Mayburd has revealed the interesting possibility of a connection between inter-gender space and magical practice in medieval Icelandic writing ("'Helzt þóttumk nú heima í millim ...': A Reassessment of Hervör in Light of Seiðr's Supernatural Gender Dynamics," *Arkiv för nordisk filologi* 129 (2014): 121–64).

258 *Brennu-Njáls saga*, pp. 112–14, 229; see also William Sayers, "Njáll's Beard, Hallgerðr's Hair and Gunnarr's Hay: Homological Patterning in *Njáls saga*," *Tijdschrift voor Skandinavistiek* 15 (1994): 5–31; William Ian Miller, "Why Is Your Axe Bloody?" pp. 102–6. The accusation is that the beards of the Njálssynir have been cultivated by manure, which means that they supposedly smeared faeces into their faces. There is no accusation of actual coprophagy but once excrement is on one's face, its proximity to the mouth is uncomfortable.

259 For further reading on this topic, see William Ian Miller, *The Anatomy of Disgust* (Cambridge, MA. and London: Harvard University Press, 1997), pp. 89–108.

260 The human body (man as microcosm) as a metaphor for the universe is a strong theme in the medieval worldview (see note 94 above) and is actually mentioned in the Icelandic translation of the *Elucidarius* (*Elucidarius in Old Norse Translation*, Rit Stofnun Árna Magnússonar á Íslandi 36, ed. Evelyn Scherabon Firchow and Kaaren Grimstad (Reykjavík: Stofnun Árna Magnússonar, 1989), pp. 39–41; see also *Alfræði íslenzk: Islandsk encyclopædisk litteratur*, STUAGNL 37, 41, 45, ed. Kristian Kålund and Natanael Beckman, 3 vols. (Copenhagen: 1908–18), 3: 93). It is an essential part of the relationship between anus and inferno discussed, for example, by Davíð Erlingsson ("Frá hrópi til saurs").

261 *Vatnsdæla saga*, p. 50.

262 On various aspects of and paralells to this magic ritual, see in particular Terry Gunnell, "'Magical Mooning' and the 'Goatskin Twirl': 'Other' Kinds of Female Magical Practices in Early Iceland," in *Nordic Mythologies: Interpretations, Intersections, and Institutions*, ed. Timothy R. Tangherlini (Berkeley and Los Angeles: North Pinehurst Press, 2014), pp. 133–53. It is also a well-known trope from legendary sagas that ogres wear shirts not long enough to cover their genitals and buttocks; in fact this indecency is perhaps the most striking characteristic of wild ogres

encountered in those narratives (see Ármann Jakobsson, "Identifying the Ogre," p. 192).

263　The Old Icelandic *móðr* is usually glossed in dictionaries as any
kind of emotional uproar: anger, grief, upset, etc. (see, for example, "móðr," *Ordbog over det norrøne prosasprog*, 2010, retrieved
from http://onp.ku.dk). There may though be no clear separation of the body and soul in how *móðr* is understood (see Ármann Jakobsson, "Beast and Man," pp. 38–41).

264　This ability to turn the earth around is also noticeable in the
Laxdœla saga episode when Hallbjǫrn and Stígandi, sons of Kotkell, are captured (pp. 106–7). Why do these magicians possess
the "evil eye"? Is it an attribute they have gained by magic or a
part of their very nature? Can these two even be separated? The
sagas do not explain this.

265　There is no shortage of such parasitic monsters in modern culture, including, for example, the ringwraiths in Tolkien's *The
Lord of the Rings*, or the dementors in J.K. Rowling's *Harry Potter*
series. The defining factor of these monsters is that they prey
on their victims from within, by establishing some contact with
their own souls or moods and thus work like a parasite from
within. On parasitic monsters in medieval Icelandic and popular
culture, see Ármann Jakobsson, "Yfirnáttúrlegar ríðigar."

266　*Eyrbyggja saga*, p. 81; see also Ármann Jakobsson, "The Specter of
Old Age," and William Sayers, "The Alien and Alienated," p. 258.

267　*Eiríks saga rauða*, in *Eyrbyggja saga*, ÍF IV, ed. Einar Ól. Sveinsson, Matthías Þórðarson, and Ólafur Halldórsson (Reykjavík:
Hið íslenzka fornritafélag, 1985), pp. 214–16; see also *Eiríks saga
rauða, texti Skálholtsbókar* AM 557 4to, in *Eyrbyggja saga*, ÍF IV, ed.
Einar Ól. Sveinsson, Matthías Þórðarson, and Ólafur Halldórsson (Reykjavík: Hið íslenzka fornritafélag, 1985), pp. 417–19.

268　As Torfi H. Tulinius has suggested, Glámr is anti-social, even
demonic, long before his eventual development into a zombie
("Framliðnir feður," pp. 293–97).

269　*Eyrbyggja saga*, pp. 91–92, 92n2; *Grettis saga*, pp. 121–22. Two of
those are Old Kárr (*Grettis saga*, p. 58) and Raknarr the Viking
(*Bárðar saga*, p. 167); see also *Egils saga*, p. 174, and Torfi H. Tulinius, *The Enigma of Egill*, pp. 113–14.

270　*Eyrbyggja saga*, pp. 93–95, 115, 169–70.

271　See "The Confidence of Youth." The metamorphosis of troll victims into the entourage of the monster, and a monster too, eerily recalls the spread of sexual abuse today, with many of the
perpetrators being past survivors of the same crime. One may
also recall the story of Elmer Wayne Henley and David Brooks

(still imprisoned in Texas) who while only in their teens assisted Houston mass murderer Dean Corll in abducting, torturing, and killing children, teenagers, and young adults from 1970 to 1973. Their dual role as victims and perpetrators may be troubling for the conscience of those involved with modern justice but is very familiar to those acquainted with folk traditions, exemplified in the story of Þórólfr's hauntings, in which case the question of guilt and innocence is left open.

272 *Biskupa sögur*, ed. Jón Sigurðsson and Guðbrandur Vigfússon, 2 vols. (Copenhagen: S.L. Möller, 1858–78), 1: 604–8.

273 *Eyrbyggja saga*, pp. 169–70.

274 Among others, Víga-Hrappr, when Óláfr the Peacock digs him up long after his death (*Laxdœla saga*, p. 69).

275 See *Eyrbyggja saga*, p. 169; "inn trollsligsti at sjá" (cf. Ármann Jakobsson, "The Trollish Acts," p. 54, and "Vad är ett troll?" p. 106).

276 *Grettis saga*, p. 112.

277 The colour blue and its demonic aspect have yet to be explored in more detail by the present author. Also relevant is the description of the "vǫlubein" (bones of a witch) in *Laxdœla saga* that are "blá ok illilig" (blue and evil looking) and related to sorcery (p. 224). It is widely known that the strangely honourable main antagonist Brennu-Flosi in *Brennu-Njáls saga* also becomes "blár sem hel" (blue as Hell) when Hildigunnr enrages him (p. 292), and one might certainly postulate a hellish aspect of his fury. It is questionable whether Christian listeners of the story clearly distinguished between Hel (the goddess of the dead) and Hell, or whether this is one more clue that the ghost hails from the devil himself. In the oldest Norse sources Hel is mainly referred to as a person (the goddess of death) rather than as a place (the domain of death) (see Chris Abram, "Hel in Early Norse Poetry," *Viking and Medieval Scandinavia* 2 (2006): 1–29). When it comes to the period of the composition of *Njáls saga,* however, the person and the place may have become interchangeable.

278 *Grettis saga*, pp. 107–23. When Glámr defeats the monster of Forsæludalr he is infected and takes on her role, but it is said "við þá meinvætti hefir aldri vart orðit síðan" (that ogre has never appeared since) (p. 112).

279 Consequently Grettir and Glámr are doubles, as scholars have previously noted (Sayers, "The Alien and Alienated," p. 254; Ármann Jakobsson, "The Fearless Vampire Killers"), and together illustrate how monster and hero, good and evil, are essentially intertwined.

280 *Harðar saga*, p. 39; see also *Þorskfirðinga saga*, p. 183, wherein, of a man called Agnarr berserkr, it is said "eigi vitum vér, hvárt hann tryllist dauðr eðr kvikr."

281 *Laxdœla saga*, p. 39; *Flateyjarbók*, 2: 7.

282 See Ármann Jakobsson, "The Spectre of Old Age," pp. 323–25.

283 The phrase originates with Simone De Beauvoir's remark that, "On ne naît pas femme: on le devient" (*Le Deuxième Sexe*, 2 vols. (Paris: Gallimard, 1949), 2: 13).

284 See, for example, *Hálfdanar saga Eysteinssonar*, Altnordische Saga-Bibliothek 15, ed. Franz Rolf Schröder (Halle a. S.: Niemeyer, 1917), p. 139; *Heiðarvíga saga*, pp. 303–4.

285 There are, in medieval Icelandic writing, examples of people becoming entrolled ("tryllisk") and becoming a serpent (*Hulda: Sagas of the kings of Norway 1035–1177, manuscript no. 66 fol. In the Arnamagnæan collection*, Early Icelandic manuscripts in facsimile 8, ed. Jonna Louis-Jensen (Copenhagen: Rosenkilde og Bagger, 1968), p. 23r), or a dog ("Viktors saga ok Blávus," in *Late medieval Icelandic romances*, Editiones Arnamagnæanæ, Series B, 20–24, ed. Agnete Loth, 5 vols. (Copenhagen: Munksgaard, 1962–65), 1: 31), indicating that an animal metamorphosed from human state is essentially a troll, and perhaps even that such metamorphosis is essential to the troll.

286 *Orms þáttr Stórólfssonar*, in *Harðar saga*, ÍF XIII, ed. Þórhallur Vilmundarson and Bjarni Vilhjálmsson, (Reykjavík: Hið íslenzka fornritafélag, 1991), p. 401; see also, for example, *Harðar saga*, p. 28, and *Hávarðar saga Ísfirðings*, in *Vestfirðinga sögur*, ÍF VI, ed. Björn K. Þórólfsson and Guðni Jónsson (Reykjavík: Hið íslenzka fornritafélag, 1943), p. 293. This could be interpreted as classic litotes or understatement (for example, "not too shabby"), a very well known stylistic feature of medieval saga writing (see Lee M. Hollander, "Litotes in Old Norse" *PMLA* 53 (1938): 1–33). But there may also be echoes here of apophasis in which the paranormal entity is described negatively, with the focus on precisely what it is not since there can be no precision as to what it in fact is. C.S. Lewis was a proponent of apophatic or negative theology and uses it, famously, in his Narnia books where the divine figure of Aslan is often said to be "not a tame lion" (see also C.S. Lewis, *Miracles: A Preliminary Study* (New York: Macmillan, 1947; rev. 1960)).

287 *Heimskringla*, 1: 18.

288 See Ármann Jakobsson, "Beast and Man," pp. 36–43. See also note 189 above.

289 I have explored the relationship between dragons and humans elsewhere (see Ármann Jakobsson, "Enter the Dragon," and "Talk to the Dragon: Tolkien as Translator," *Tolkien Studies* 6 (2009): 27-39). Even though dragons are not as obviously human doubles as anthropomorphic others, a dragon metamorphosed from a human is still strangely familiar, and in both *Völsunga saga* and modern literature (such as Tolkien's *The Hobbit*), there is a case to be made for seeing the dragon as a parental figure.

290 Ármann Jakobsson, "A Contest of Cosmic Fathers," pp. 273-75. The family relationship of the gods and the giants has been an important feature of most of the giant studies of the last half a century or so, see, for example, Marlene Ciklamini, "Óðinn and the Giants," *Neophilologus* 46.2 (1962): 145-58, "Grettir and Kettil hængr, the giant-killers," *Arv* 22 (1966): 136-55, and "Journeys to the Giant Kingdom," *Scandinavian Studies* 40.2 (1968): 95-110; Lotte Motz, "The Rulers of The Mountain: A Study of the Giants of the Old Icelandic Texts," *Mankind Quarterly* 20 (1979-80): 393-416, "Giantesses and their Names," *Frühmittelalterliche Studien* 15 (1981): 495-511, "Giants in Folklore and Mythology: A New Approach," *Folklore* 93 (1982): 70-84, "Giants and Giantesses: A Study in Norse Mythology and Belief," *Amsterdamer Beiträge zur älteran Germanistik* 22 (1984): 83-108, "Old Icelandic Giants and their Names," *Frühmittelalterliche Studien* 21 (1987): 295-317, and "The Families of Giants," *Arkiv för nordisk filologi* 102 (1987): 216-236; Gro Steinsland, *Det hellige bryllup og norrøn kongeideologi: en analyse av hierogami-myten i Skírnismál, Ynglingatal, Háleygjatal og Hyndluljóð* (Oslo: Solum, 1991); Else Mundal, "Forholdet mellom gudar og jotnar i norrøn mytologi i lys av det mytologiske namnematerialet," *Studia anthroponymica Scandinavica* 8 (1990): 5-18, "Austr sat in aldna ...: Giantesses and female powers in Vǫluspá," in *Mythological Women: Studies in Memory of Lotte Motz*, ed. Rudolf Simek and Wilhelm Heizmann (Vienna: Fassbaender, 2002), pp. 185-95, and "Sigurðr hrísi eller Sigurðr risi?" *Nordica Bergensia* 29 (2003): 5-13; Katja Schulz, *Riesen: Von Wissenhütern und Wildnisbewohneern in Edda und Saga* (Heidelberg: Winter, 2004); Ingunn Ásdísardóttir, *Jötnar í eddukvæðum og Snorra-Eddu*, PhD dissertation (Reykjavík, forthcoming 2017).

291 Marina Warner, *No Go the Bogeyman: Scaring, Lulling, and Making Mock* (London: Chatto & Windus, 1998), pp. 48-77. Warner quotes George Devereux on the likelihood of parents killing their children ("The Cannibalistic Impulses of Parents," *The Psychoanalytic Forum* 1 (1966): 114-24). Both myths are an inversion of the act of sexual intercourse, the beginning of life, In the Kro-

nos myth it is Gaia who inserts "a phallus into the male mouth as a form of food and thereafter the children are born through the mouth in the form of vomit" (Edmund Leach, *Lévi-Strauss* (London: Fontana, 1970), p. 81). Murderous parents are usually male although female perpetrators of such acts seem to attract a disproportionate degree of attention and have long inspired the cultural phenomenon of the "woman who kills her children" (see Jennifer Jones, *Medea's Daughters: Forming and Performing the Woman Who Kills* (Columbus, Ohio: Ohio State University Press, 2003)). Jones argues that while atypical, the cultural phenomenon of the women who kills children speaks "to a culture engaged in a fierce debate about women who leave their children to fend for themselves as they "selfishly" pursue their own desires" (p. 75).

292 *Hauksbók udgiven efter de Arnamagnæanske håndskrifter no. 371, 544 og 675, 4° samt forskellige papirshåndskrifter af Det kongelige nordiske oldskrift-selskab*, ed. Finnur Jónsson (Copenhagen: Kongelige nordiske oldskrift-selskab, 1892–96), p. 158.

293 *Heimskringla*, 1: 47–50; see also Samson Eitrem, "König Aun in Uppsala und Kronos," in *Festskrift til Hjalmar Falk 30. desember 1927* (Oslo: Aschehoug, 1927), 245–61; Joseph Harris, "Sacrifice and Guilt in Sonatorrek," in *Studien zum Altgermanischen: Festschrift für Heinrich Beck*, Ergänzungsbände zum Reallexikon der Germanischen Altertumskunde 11, ed. Heiko Uecker (Berlin: Walter de Gruyter, 1994), p. 180 [173–96]. Mostly the sacrificed children in Old Icelandic writing are male but there is also the attempted sacrifice of Helga in *Gunnlaugs saga*, ostenibly attributed to a different concern (p. 55–58) and the sacrifice of Iphigenia in the legends of the Troy wars parallels Aun's sacrifices, even though longevity does not seem to be the main concern.

294 Warner, *No Go the Bogeyman*, pp. 57–59. Warner argues that this conflation unconsciously collates with the father's intention, the metaphor being that the hours are inexorably swallowed up as time rolls on. Cf. Raymond Klibansky, Erwin Panofsky, and Fritz Saxl, *Saturn and Melancholy: Studies in the History of Natural Philosophy, Religion and Art* (London: Nelson, 1964), pp. 177, 185

295 Klibansky et al., *Saturn and Melancholy*, pp. 127–35.

296 *Alfræði íslenzk*, 3: 34.

297 Klibansky et al., *Saturn and Melancholy*, pp. 148–49; J.A. Burrow, *The Ages of Man: A Study in Medieval Writing and Thought* (Oxford: Clarendon Press, 1986), p. 54.

298 Klibansky et al., *Saturn and Melancholy*, pp. 186, 191; see also Peter Brown and Andrew Butcher, *The Age of Saturn: Literature and*

History in the Canterbury Tales (Oxford: Blackwell, 1991), pp. 212–36.

299 See Ármann Jakobsson, "The Spectre of Old Age," pp. 312–15.

300 *Edda Snorra Sturlusonar*, p. 13.

301 The giant origins af Óðinn are referred to in skaldic poetry, for example, in Arnórr Þórðarson's *Magnússdrápa*, in the kenning "Allnǫttfǫrull marr víís Yggjar áleggjar," where the *marr* (steed) of the "víf Yggjar áleggjar" is a wolf, the wife is a female giant, and the "áleggjar Yggr" (the Odin of the river-limb) is a giant (see *Morkinskinna*, 1: 67; *Magnússdrápa*, ed. Diana Whaley, in *Skaldic Poetry of the Scandinavian Middle Ages II: Poetry from the Kings' Sagas I–II*, ed. Kari Ellen Gade (Turnhout: Brepols, 2009), 1: 221). There also exist in skaldic poetry the kennings fjall-Gautr and grjót-Móði where the giant is connected to stone and mountain. One wonder if it would be possible to thus merge the high god (and his grandson Móði) and the main antagonists of the gods in a kenning if it were not for the pre-existing family relationship of Óðinn to the giants (see note 290 above). The descent of a human protagonist (hero) from the giants is a theme in several sagas of Icelanders, kings' sagas and legendary sagas, most notably in the sagas of the Hrafnistumenn, *Ketils saga hængs*, *Gríms saga loðinkinna*, and *Örvar-Odds saga*, tales of ancestors on the periphery (see Arngrímur Vídalín, "'Er þat illt at þú vilt elska tröll þat': Hið sögulega samhengi jöðrunar í Hrafnistumannasögum," *Gripla* 24 (2013): 173–210), but also in *Egils saga* which begins with Kveld-Úlfr, Egills paternal grandfather, whose maternal uncle is Hallbjǫrn hálftroll in Hrafnista, father of Ketill hœngr. It soon becomes apparent that Kveld-Úlfr has a wolfish streak, indeed it is suggested in *Egils saga* that Kveld-Úlfr and his family are actual shapeshifters, although the saga never settles the issue, as if the saga author challenges those who would like to do so to believe in the shapeshifters, whereas others are allowed to see the constant references to wolves as metaphors (Ármann Jakobsson, "Beast and Man," pp. 37–38). The family may or may not be superhuman and that may owe something to their kinsman Hallbjǫrn hálftroll. The word troll suggests witchcraft and paranormal beings and its usage might indicate that Hallbjǫrn, like the giant Bǫlþorn, is another disreputable heathen ancestor that Old Norse heroes so often possess. According to *Ketils saga hængs*, Hallbjǫrn was a troublesome father. Ketill does not receive much affection from his father, who criticizes him for lying in the kitchen and not contributing much to the work at the farmstead. Indeed the first third of the saga relates of Ketill's

THE TROLL INSIDE YOU

attempt to impress his father, whose trollish character does not
seem prominent. It is nevertheless evident that he has made
friends with some neighbourhood "jǫtnar" and "troll" who are
both primitive and cannibalistic. The perceived cannibalism of
the troll may be one of the reasons why having food with a troll
is expressively forbidden in Norse law codes (see note 9). Somewhat contradictoraly, Hallbjǫrn opposes his son's relationship
with the giantess Hrafnhildr Brunadóttir, wants Ketill to marry
a human girl from the vicinity, and calls Hrafnhildr a "troll" repeatedly to belittle her. This might seem strange, coming from
a "hálftroll" but perhaps characteristic of the ambiguous states
of "jǫtnar" and "troll" in medieval Icelandic narratives. In *Ketils
saga hœngs*, Ketill acquires a second father in Bruni, Hrafnhildr's
father, who takes him under his wing and aids him with all the
supernatural power at his disposal. Ketill is thus armed with
both a good and a bad giant father and this ambiguity about ancestry is characteristic of the Old Norse textual project of the
late Middle Ages, usually classified as legendary sagas, although
that defintion, like most medieval generic definitions, is problematic. The fostering (rather than blood kinship) by giants is
an important theme in various sagas (see Hilda R. Ellis (Davidson), "Fostering by Giants in Old Norse Sagas," *Medium Aevum*
10 (1941): 70–85), including narratives concerning King Haraldr
fairhair, the semi-legendary ninth-century ancestor of Norwegian kings (see, for example, Bruce Lincoln, *Between History and
Myth: Stories of Harald Fairhair and the Founding of the State* (Chicago: The University of Chicago Press, 2014)), and in mythological narratives such as *Vǫluspá*, or *Vafþrúðnismál* that stages the
generational conflict without an actual blood relationship being
present (see Ármann Jakobsson, "A Contest of Cosmic Fathers").
302 See Ármann Jakobsson, "The Fearless Vampire Killers."
303 The benevolent monster is a powerful theme throughout human
cultures, making an appearance in modern film narratives such
as the *Rambo* series (1982–1988 and 2008), where the protagonist sometimes resembles a superhuman force which is terrible
when unleashed unless under control by the forces of good, and
perhaps even more prominently in the *Hellboy* series (originally
a comics series but filmed in 2004, with a sequel appearing in
2008) the protagonist of which is literally infernal although partially tamed and then utilised by the forces of good.
304 *Grettis saga*, p. 248.
305 *Grettis saga*, pp. 249–50. The relationship between the norns (or
fates) and trees is strong in the extant sources, as they seem to

carve their prophecies in wood and are pictured living at one of the roots of the world-tree Yggdrasill (*Eddukvæði*, 1: 295–96, 310–11; see Karen Bek-Pederson, *The Norns in Old Norse Mythology*, pp. 75, 92). There is also in the Old Norse sources a relationship between man and tree that is evident, for example, in the double meaning of the word "draugr," meaning both "wooden log" and "undead human" (see Ármann Jakobsson, "Vampires and Watchmen," pp. 281–85, 299) but also in poems such as *Hávamál* and *Sólarljóð* where the human is likened to a tree and so are his individual body parts, such as the tongue.

306 *Grettis saga*, p. 250.

307 *Grettis saga*, pp. 245–46.

308 *Grettis saga*, pp. 264, 268.

309 *Grettis saga*, p. 224.

310 Tove Jansson, *Moominland Midwinter*, trans. Thomas Warburton (New York: Farrar, Straus and Giroux, 1992), pp. 73–83.

311 *Edda Snorra Sturlusonar*, pp. 70–76; Eddukvæði, 1: 302–6, 313–15. On the proliference of this myth, see Kolfinna Jónatansdóttir, *Ragnarök*, PhD dissertation (Reykjavík, forthcoming 2017). The apocalypse is called "ragna røk" (fate or end of the gods) in *Vǫluspá* (*Eddukvæði*, 1: 302, 314), but "ragna raʋkr" or "ragna rauckur" (twilight of the gods, famously used by Richard Wagner) in the various *Snorra-Edda* manuscripts (*Edda Snorra Sturlusonar*, p. 70). The former term is usually seen as more original but both are attested only in thirteenth-century texts.

312 *Edda Snorra Sturlusonar*, pp. 70–72; Eddukvæði, 1: 302–6, 313–15, 416, 448. On the fetter-theme in apocalyptic narrative, see further Kolfinna Jónatansdóttir, "Er í bǫndum skal bíða ragnarøkrs": um fjötraðar óvættir sem losna í ragnarökum," (forthcoming). The bondage theme appears in *Snorra-Edda*, Saxo's *Gesta Danorum*, and the eddic poems *Vǫluspá*, *Lokasenna*, and *Baldursdraumar*. As noted by W.P. Ker, this myth of the end of the world remarkably ends in victory for the forces of chaos and the destruction of all the major gods: "The winning side is Chaos and Unreason; but the gods, who are defeated, think that defeat is not refutation" (*The Dark Ages* (New York: Charles Scribner's sons 1904), p. 58). One may wonder how the remaining gods will fare in the new world, or if they will possibly become the new troublesome ancestors.

313 The poetic term "bǫnd" indicating the gods appears in *Snorra Edda*, along with "hǫpt" which also means bonds and gods (Edda Snorra Sturlusonar, pp. 165–66). This poetic word also appears in *Hávamál* (st. 109), and is used by such ninth- and tenth-cen-

tury skaldic poets as Þjóðólfr ór Hvini, Egill Skalla-Grímsson, Eyvindr skáldaspillir, Einarr skálaglamm, Úlfr Uggason, Steinunn Refsdóttir, and Tindr Hallkelsson whose poetry is largely preserved in thirteenth- and fourteenth-century prose sagas.

314 *Edda Snorra Sturlusonar,* pp. 34, 60–63, 71–72, 75. In the *Hauksbók* version of *Vǫluspá,* this serpent is referred to as the "ribbon of the earth" (*lindi jarðar*), indicating its role in tying the world together (*Eddukvæði,* 1: 314). The line is actually almost illegibile but Prof. Jón Helgason in Copenhagen read it by ultraviolet light and the *Hauksbók* stanza made an appearance in his edited version of *Vǫluspá* in 1951 (*Eddadigte I: Vǫluspá-Hávamál, Nordisk filologi 4,* ed. Jón Helgason (Copenhagen: Munksgaard, 1951), pp. 12, 39–40).

315 *Edda Snorra Sturlusonar,* p. 72. Apolyptic monsters are frequently in serpent shape but may also be giants such as the Biblical Gog and Magog who were conflated into the giant Gogmagog (or Geomagog) in Geoffrey of Monmouth's *Historia regum Britanniae* (c. 1136) (*Historia regum Britanniae,* ed. Jacob Hammer (Cambridge, MA: The Mediaeval Academy of America, 1951), pp. 39–40).

316 *Edda Snorra Sturlusonar,* pp. 35–38.

317 *Edda Snorra Sturlusonar,* p. 72.

318 *Eddukvæði,* 1: 363–66; see Ármann Jakobsson, "A Contest of Cosmic Fathers"; Andrew McGillivray, *Preparing for the End,* PhD dissertation (Reykjavík, 2015), pp. 171–74.

319 In *Vǫluspá,* Loki (presumably) is referred to as a "jǫtunn" (*Eddukvæði,* 1: 303 (see also note 46. vísa)) and in Snorri's *Edda,* he is said to be the son of a giant (*Edda Snorra Sturlusonar,* p. 34). There is also the possibility that Loki and the illusionist giant Útgarða-Loki are actually the same mythological character. The case is made in Ármann Jakobsson, "Loki og jötnarnir" in *Greppaminni: Rit til heiðurs Vésteini Ólasyni sjötugum,* ed. Árni Sigurjónsson, Guðrún Ása Grímsdóttir, Guðrún Nordal, Guðvarður Már Gunnlaugsson, and Margrét Eggertsdóttir (Reykjavík: Hið íslenska bókmenntafélag, 2009), pp. 31–41.

320 *Edda Snorra Sturlusonar,* pp. 68–70; see also *Eddukvæði,* 1: 299–300, 303, 421, 448. This story has strong echoes of the Greek Prometheus myth first attested in Hesiod's *Theogony.* Like Prometheus Loki is bound to rocks and there is an element of repetition about the punishment of both. Prometheus has an eagle to torture him and similarly Loki has a nadder whose poison falls on him now and then; his spasms being the aetiological explanation of earthquakes.

321　The meaning of the name Loki (possibly "the one who closes") might suggest that this connection with the world's end is a fundamental mythological function (see, for example, Kurt Schier, "Loki og Heimdallur: Athugasemdir um eðli og uppruna tveggja torræðra goða," in *Heiðin minni: Greinar um fornar bókmenntir*, ed. Haraldur Bessason and Baldur Hafstað (Reykjavík: Heimskringla, háskólaforlag Máls og menningar, 1999), pp. 25–46). Even the fates (or norns) themselves are sometimes connected to fetters, cutting men's lives short by severing ties, although Karen Bek-Pedersen has demonstrated that the examples are both few and ambiguous (*The Norns in Old Norse Mythology*, pp. 123–64)

322　In this role the Norse gods play a role similar to that of the Persian rug owned by Jeffrey "The Dude" Lebowski in the film *The Big Lebowski* (1998) by Joel and Ethan Cohen, the main usefulness of which lay in the fact that "it really tied the room together."

323　*Heimskringla*, 1: 19.

324　Any anthropocentric world view which casts man as the lord of the world, made in God's own image, has to contend with the human experience of being alone in the wilderness, in an environment that dwarfs you. How can we sustain the illusion of centrality on such an occasion? On the other hand, being confined within our own bodies, how can we not?

325　*The Iliad*, presumably composed in the eighth century BC and attributed to Homer since the fifth century BC, relates the destruction of Troy four or five centuries earlier. However, the work only exists in manuscripts from the Middle Ages. In the poem and its sequel, *The Odyssey*, the gods (Zeus, Athena, Poseidon, et al.) are depicted as active participants in the wars and other concerns of human dignitaries, thus indubitably enhancing the glory of the affairs and the participants.

326　*Laxdæla saga*, pp. 149, 155. Án ricebelly is an aging henchman of Óláfr the Peacock and his son Kjartan Ólafsson. Before the fatal attack on Kjartan, he has an ominous dream about a woman who takes out his guts and replaces them with rice. In the battle he is wounded and is taken for dead but wakes up again and is miraculously cured, possibly by the intervention of this dream woman. Before he had been ridiculed for the dream and called ricebelly; such scorn is never directed at the dreams of the ruling class but in the sagas, even lowly henchmen can acquire importance through dreams (cf. Christopher Crocker, "Even a Henchman Can Dream: Dreaming at the Margins in *Brennu-Njáls saga*," in *Paranormal Encounters in Iceland 1150–1400*, ed. Ármann Jakobsson and Miriam Mayburd (forthcoming, 2018)).

327 The present author is frequently able to fly in dreams, usually by jumping in the air and not coming down again, and has thus experienced the thrill of being airborne by your own power and able to cross greater distances and be unhampered by various ground problems. It is a kind of exhilaration that is hard to describe. One Old Icelandic term used to describe such feelings is *svefnför*, although there is no particular reference to flight in the second element of the compound word, *för* (a journey), though it does convey the notion of some kind of physical displacement taking place during sleep (*svefn*) (see *Bjarnar saga Hitdælakappa*, in *Borgfirðinga sǫgur*, ÍF III, ed. Sigurður Nordal and Guðni Jónsson (Reykjavík: Hið íslenzka fornritafélag, 1938), p. 196; *Gísla saga*, pp. 75, 94, 110). The word also appears in *Ála saga flekks*, dated to the early fifteenth century, when it is said that the eponymous Áli one night "lætr þá illa í svefni, ok eru svefnfarir hans bæði harðar ok langar" (then lay poor in sleep, and his *svefnfarir* are both difficult and long), and indeed he later remarks upon waking that during the night a *trǫllkona* had appeared before him while he was sleeping (*Drei lygisǫgur: Egils saga einhenda ok Ásmundar berserkjabana, Ála Flekks saga, Flóres saga konungs ok sona hans*, Altnordische Saga-Bibliothek 17, ed. Åke Lagerholm (Halle a. S.: Niemeyer, 1927), pp. 105-6); see also Christopher Crocker, *Situating the Dream: Paranormal Dreams in the Íslendingasögur*, PhD dissertation (Reykjavík, 2016), pp. 82–83.

328 See, for example, *Grettis saga*, p. 184; *Finnboga saga*, in *Kjalnesinga saga*, ÍF XIV, ed. Jóhannes Halldórsson (Reykjavík: Hið íslenzka fornritafélag, 1959), p. 283; *Fljótsdæla saga*, in *Austfirðinga saga*, ÍF XI, ed. Jón Jóhannesson (Reykjavík: Hið íslenzka fornritafélag, 1950), pp. 227-30; *Fóstbræðra saga*, p. 161. In all these cases the emphasis is on a regular person fighting a relatively undefined paranormal entity in human shape, in one case a "blámaðr" (blue man), but the accusation seems to be that the antagonist is powered by magic.

329 Rainer Maria Rilke, *The Duino Elegies & The Sonnets to Orpheus*, ed. and trans. Stephen Mitchell (New York: Vintage Books, 2009), p. 141.

Index

Z

Printed in Great Britain
by Amazon

53110362R00136